The Armies of Ptolemaic Egypt

Cleruchs, Mercenaries and *Machimoï* 323–30 BCE

Stéphane Thion

Helion & Company Limited
Unit 8 Amherst Business Centre
Budbrooke Road
Warwick
CV34 5WE
England
Tel. 01926 499 619
Email: info@helion.co.uk
Website: www.helion.co.uk
X, formerly Twitter: @helionbooks
Facebook: @HelionBooks
Visit our blog https://helionbooks.wordpress.com/

Published by Helion & Company 2026
Designed and typeset by Mary Woolley, Battlefield Design (www.battlefield-design.co.uk)
Cover designed by Paul Hewitt, Battlefield Design (www.battlefield-design.co.uk)

Text © Stéphane Thion 2025
Photographs and illustrations © as individually credited
Cover drawing by Marco Capparoni © Helion & Company 2025

Every reasonable effort has been made to trace copyright holders and to obtain their permission for the use of copyright material. The author and publisher apologise for any errors or omissions in this work and would be grateful if notified of any corrections that should be incorporated in future reprints or editions of this book.

ISBN 978-1-804518-25-0

British Library Cataloguing-in-Publication Data.
A catalogue record for this book is available from the British Library.

All rights reserved. No part of this publication may be reproduced, stored in a retrieval system, or transmitted, in any form, or by any means, electronic, mechanical, photocopying, recording or otherwise, without the express written consent of Helion & Company Limited.

For details of other military history titles published by Helion & Company Limited contact the above address or visit our website: http://www.helion.co.uk.

We always welcome receiving book proposals from prospective authors.

Dedication

In memory of Angus McBride, who sparked my passion for the Ptolemaic army

Acknowledgements

The author would like to extend a special thank you to Stephen Ede-Borrett for his contribution and Simon Miller for the infectious passion he has for this era.

Contents

Dedication		iii
Acknowledgements		iv
Introduction		vii
Sources		ix
Chronology		xii
1	The Ptolemaic Dynasty	15
2	Main Components of the Ptolemaic Army	20
3	Organisation of the Ptolemaic Army in the Third Century BCE	48
4	The Ptolemaic Army in Battle: Gaza, Raphia, and Panion	79
5	The Transformation of the Ptolemaic Army in the Second Century BCE	87
6	The Fall: the First Century BCE	106
7	Military and Civilian Dress	113
8	An Opponent of Ptolemaic Dynasty: The Jewish Army of the Second and First Centuries BCE	117
Conclusion		124
Colour Plate Commentaries		126
Appendix: Numbered and ethnic evidence of hipparchies, compiled from the work of Launey, Lesquier, and Van't Dack.		135
Bibliography		147

Introduction

Hellenistic Egypt, with its many papyri preserved by a dry climate, is the natural starting point for anyone wishing to study the institutions of Alexander the Great's successors. No other Hellenistic kingdom has so many sources, including in the military field. Of course, there are still many grey areas, as most of the surviving papyri are accounting or legal documents, such as loan contracts. But through all these documents, we discover many characters, with their origin and function. Officers, and in some cases the military unit they commanded, parade before our eyes. Finally, a few rare, well-preserved stelae provide us with lists of soldiers and officers. Even the literary sources are exceptional. Polybius was inspired to detail the raising of the Ptolemaic Army that faced its Seleucid counterpart at Raphia in 217 BCE.

One striking aspect of the Ptolemaic Army is the modernity of its organisation. It was a far cry from the pyramidal structures revealed by contemporary tacticians, notably Asclepiodotus in his *Tactica*. The situation is surprisingly reminiscent of seventeenth-century Europe: regimental commanders, company commanders and an intermediate unit, equivalent to a battalion, make up the Ptolemaic infantry. The cavalry had a similarly simple organisation, with a regiment-sized unit broken down into the equivalent of companies. But as with modern armies, in times of war, when large numbers of troops had to be mobilised, these regiments, called *chiliarchies* and *hipparchies* depending on their original arm, were brought together in larger corps. This is when the phalanx appeared for the infantry. Polybius also mentions the *merê*, which appear to be small corps of varying size. We find no trace of these large units in papyri or other inscriptions. This is probably because, in the Ptolemaic Kingdom, the usual service was limited to garrison duties and guarding the frontiers. It is hard to imagine these soldiers being equipped with pikes, as they were when they had to fight shoulder to shoulder in the phalanx. So, it seems that the Hellenistic infantryman was not as specialised as one might think.

This decisive point brings us to the last characteristic that the Ptolemaic military institution shared with its Seleucid neighbour: it was an army of mercenaries and cleruchs and not an army of citizens like that of the Greek cities or Macedonia. Every year, the Greek cities called young men of military age to arms. The *ephebes*, aged between 18 and 20, were trained daily in the gymnasium. This conscription system gave the Greeks well-trained contingents. This was not the case with the Ptolemies, who refused to call on the Egyptian population. The Ptolemies therefore did everything in their power to attract Macedonian, Greek, Thessalian and even Thracian settlers, thanks to the cleruchy system. But once settled, these colonists tended to lose their effectiveness through lack of training, and their successors, known as *epigones*, had no experience of combat. The Ptolemies' best troops were mercenaries.

Once the organisation of the army had been deciphered, all that remained was to imagine the Ptolemaic soldier. This is the purpose of the many plates scattered throughout the book. For the most part, these computer graphics have been produced from the many stelae, painted or unpainted, and the few mosaics that have survived.

This new edition is an expanded version of the work published in 2012. It includes numerous additions and references are now systematically detailed.

Sources

The sources used to produce this work are of several kinds:

 - The works of Greek and Roman historians: the main historians used here are Polybius, Diodorus Siculus and Plutarch. Of these three authors, Polybius is of the greatest value, as he is also the author of a military treatise that has now disappeared (see below). Polybius was born in Megalopolis, an Arcadian city, around 198 BCE. His father, Lycortas, was *strategos* of the Achaean league. Consequently, Polybius had a front-row seat to observe the development of political and military affairs of Arcadia. He later became a politician and a cavalry officer (*hipparchês*). In 167 BCE, he was one of the 1,000 Achaean nobles who were hostages of Rome. He then became counsellor to Fabius and Scipio Aemilianus. Polybius is mainly known as an historian. His main work is *The Histories*, originally written in 40 volumes. Only the first 5 books have come down to us complete. Polybius's *Histories* begin in the year 264 BCE and end in 146 BCE, the year of the destruction of Carthage and Corinth. The five first books cover the affairs of different states, including Ptolemaic Egypt. Objectivity, critical reasoning and rigour are qualities now associated with Polybius's work. Book V of *The Histories* is of the greatest interest for this work because, as well as detailing the order of battle of the Ptolemaic Army, it describes the recruitment of the army prior to operations.

 - Tactical treatises from the same period or from several centuries later. Such sources have been criticised in the past for not necessarily describing the reality of the time. 'This tactical literature of antiquity has been relegated to the dustbin of history,' wrote E. Van 't Dack.[1] Although several questions remain, this author has shown that many of the ranks and subdivisions of the army presented by such theorists can be found in the epigraphy of the Ptolemaic period.[2] The main source here is Asclepiodotus's *Tactica*. Arrian's *Ars Tactica* was used to supplement this text. Asclepiodotus the philosopher

---

1   E. Van't Dack, *Ptolemaica Selecta, Etudes sur l'armée et l'administration Ptolemaic* (Leuven: Studia Hellenistica, 1988), vol. 29.
2   Van't Dack, *Ptolemaica Selecta*, pp.47–64.

lived in the first century BCE. His treaty is really a service manual, with no historical references, and was probably copied from the work of his master, Poseidonios. A few clues suggest that the original work was written before 168 BCE.[3] Arrian (L. Flavius Arrianus) was born in Nicomedia, Bithynia, between 85 and 90 CE. Arrian is said to have been a military tribune during the winter of 114–115, and *legatus augusti pro praetore* (imperial legate propraeter) of the province of Cappadocia from 131 to at least 137, two positions that gave him solid military experience.[4] The *Ars Tactica* was written in 137 CE. Like his works on the history of Greece and Macedonia (*Anabasis, History of the Succession of Alexander*), this text reveals the author's strong interest in Hellenistic military history. This treatise is well worth consulting, as a complement to that of Asclepiodotus, because Arrian was a military man. Additionally, according to Pierre-Olivier Leroy:

> Arrian's *Ars Tactica* belongs to the same tradition as Asclepiodotus' treatise and, more obviously, Aelianus *Tacticus*. The subject matter and the plan adopted are the same in Asclepiodotus and Arrian, but the former is more concise, and Arrian follows Aelianus' text, often to the word. Finally, this tradition can be traced back to two lost treatises, one by Polybius and the other by Poseidonius, which both Arrian and Aelianus cite among their predecessors. Neither author quotes Asclepiodotus, but it is possible that his treatise is one with that attributed by our two authors to Poseidonios, whose pupil Asclepiodotus may have been.[5]

> Asclepiodotus' *Tactica*, Arrian' *Ars Tactica* and Aelian's military treatise were all handbooks of drill and tactics proposed or even potentially practised by the successors of Alexander the Great.

- Archaeological finds, in particular military equipment and soldiers' stelae. Among the epigraphic documents consulted, special mention should be made of the work published by Etienne Bernand on the Greek inscriptions of Hermoupolis Magna.[6]

- Among these archaeological documents are the papyri, which are unique to ancient Egypt. These papyri are an unrivalled treasure trove. To help us identify documents relating to the Ptolemaic military institutions,

---

3   Asclepiodotus (text compiled and translated by Lucien Poznanski), *Traité de Tactique*, (Paris: Les Belles Lettres, 1992), p. XIII.
4   Arrian, *L'Art Tactique & Histoire de la succession d'Alexandre*, texts introduced, translated and commented by Pierre-Olivier Leroy (Paris: Les Belles Lettres, 2017), pp.14–15 and 20–21.
5   Arrian, *L'Art Tactique*, p.42.
6   Etienne Bernand, *Inscriptions grecques d'Hermoupolis Magna et de sa nécropole* (Le Caire: Institut français d'Archéologie Orientale, 1999).

we have drawn on Jean Lesquier's invaluable work.[7] The appendices to Lesquier's book contain papyri references for lists of cleruchs, *katoikoi*, *epigones*, officers, junior officers and soldiers of the Ptolemaic Army. We have also consulted primary sources directly, such as the Flinders Petrie Papyri[8] or the Hibeh Papyri.[9]

- Finally, secondary sources, work carried out by researchers, have of course also been used. These include the work of G. T. Griffith,[10] M. Launey[11] and N. Sekunda,[12] in addition to those of J. Lesquier and E. Van 't Dack already mentioned.

Since ancient historians and theorists have been translated into many languages, and to facilitate access to footnoted references, these will be indicated in book/chapter/section form without page numbers. However, the pagination will be indicated when reference is made to the introduction or comments in the French edition.

---

7 Jean Lesquier, *Les institutions militaires de l'Egypte sous les Lagides* (Paris: Ernest Leroux Editeur, 1911), p.11.
8 John P. Mahaffy & J. Gilbart Smyly, *On the Flinders Petrie Papyri* (Dublin: Royal Irish Academy, 1905).
9 Bernard P. Grenfell & Arthur S. Hunt, *The Hibeh Papyri Part I* (London: Egypt Exploration Fund, Kegan Paul, and Bernard Quaritch, 1906).
10 Guy Thompson Griffith, *The Mercenaries of the Hellenistic world* (Chicago: Ares Publisher, 1935).
11 Marcel Launey, *Recherches sur les armées hellénistiques* (Paris: De Boccard, 1987).
12 Nick Sekunda, *Seleucid and Ptolemaic Reformed Armies, 168–145 BC, volume 2: The Ptolemaic Army* (Dewsbury: Montvert Publications, 1995).

Chronology

324 – Death of Alexander.

323 – Ptolemy Soter, Satrap of Egypt.

312 – Battle of Gaza: Ptolemy defeats Demetrios I Poliorcete, son of Antigonus the One-Eyed.

305 – Ptolemy I Soter Sovereign of Egypt.

301 – Battle of Ipsos.

285 – Ptolemy Soter associates his son Ptolemy Philadelphus with the throne.

283 – Reign of Ptolemy II Philadelphus.

274–271 – First Syrian War against Antiochus I. Philadelphus annexes Phoenicia and Eastern Cilicia.

259–253 – Second Syrian War against Antiochus II and Antigonus Gonatas. Naval defeat at Cos and loss of territory in Cilicia, Pamphylia and Ionia.

246 – Reign of Ptolemy III Euergetes.

246–241 – Third Syrian War or War of Laodicea (repudiated wife of Antiochus II) against Seleucus II. Ptolemy defeats Seleucus in Syria and Anatolia. He reaches Babylon. Gains territory in northern Syria but loses Cyclades following naval defeat at Andros.

222 – Reign of Ptolemy IV Philopator.

222–217 – Fourth Syrian War against Antiochus III. Ptolemy IV managed to hold onto Coele-Syria thanks to his victory at Raphia (22 June 217).

208 – Ptolemy Epiphanes joins the throne.

204 – Reign of Ptolemy V Epiphanes.

202–195 – Fifth Syrian War against Antiochus III and Philip V. Loss of Coele-Syria following the defeat at Panion in 200 BCE.

181 – Reign of Ptolemy VI Philometor.

170–168 – Sixth Syrian War against Antiochus IV. Rout of the Egyptian army in 169 near Mount Cassius. Under pressure from Rome, Antiochus evacuates Egypt.

170 – Reign of Ptolemy VII Euergetes II.

150 – Ptolemy VI helps Alexander Balas usurp Demetrios I Soter, thanks to the victory of a coalition of the Kings of Egypt, Pergamon and Judea over the Syrian King (Battle of the river Oinoparas).

147–145 – Campaign of Ptolemy VI against Alexander Balas, who had become sovereign of the Seleucid kingdom.

CHRONOLOGY

145 – Reign of Ptolemy VIII Euergetes II Physcon (rival of Ptolemy VII Neos Philopator).
116 – Reign of Ptolemy IX Soter II and his mother Cleopatra.
107 – Reign of Ptolemy X Alexander I.
103 – Battle of Asophon on the banks of the Jordan, where Ptolemy IX, then known as Lathyros, defeats Alexander Jannaeus, King of Judea.
88 – Reestablishment of Ptolemy Soter II.
80 – Reign of Berenice (daughter of Soter II), then Alexander II (Ptolemy XI Alexander II), Reign of Ptolemy XII Auletes (or Philopator II).
58 – Ptolemy Auletes expelled from Egypt. Reign of Cleopatra-Tryphena and Berenice IV, daughters of Auletes.
56 – Berenice IV reigned alone, with Seleucos Cybiosactus and then with Archelaus, supposed son of Mithridates Eupator.
55 – Ptolemy Aulete restored to the throne of Egypt.
51 – Reign of Cleopatra and her elder brother, Ptolemy XIII Dionysos or Philopator. Battle of Pharsalus.
47 – Capture of Alexandria by Caesar, death of Ptolemy. Reign of Cleopatra and her brother, Ptolemy XIV Philopator II.
44 – Cleopatra reigns with her son, Ptolemy XV Philopator Philometor Caesar.
31 – Battle of Actium.
30 – Capture of Alexandria by Augustus and end of the Ptolemaic monarchy.

THE ARMIES OF PTOLEMAIC EGYPT

Ptolemaic Egypt around 310 BCE. (Map drawn by the author)

1

The Ptolemaic Dynasty

The fragmentation of Alexander's Empire began with the assassination of his regent Perdiccas in 321 BCE. The division of Triparadeisos then awarded Macedonia to Antipater, Thrace to Lysimachus, Asia Minor to Antigonus, Babylonia to Seleucus and Egypt to Ptolemy, son of Lagos.

Ptolemy, often referred to as Ptolemy I Soter, was born around 367 BCE in the city of Pella, which was the capital of the ancient Kingdom of Macedon. According to Arrian, Ptolemy was one of Alexander's relatives who were forced to flee when Alexander became suspicious of his father.[1] After Philip's death, Alexander appointed Ptolemy to his guard. During Alexander's campaign to conquer the Persian Empire, Ptolemy played a significant role as one of his most trusted commanders. He was present at many of the major battles, including the famous Battle of Gaugamela in 331 BCE, where Alexander decisively defeated the Persian King Darius III. When the Macedonians had just entered India, Ptolemy killed an Indian chief with his own hands. Then, at the head of an army corps, he repulsed the enemy.[2] He was one of the trusted companions and generals of Alexander the Great, sharing in his conquests and ambitions.

According to Arrian, after Alexander's death,

> Perdiccas, on the pretext of purifying the army, seized those who had most clearly distinguished themselves in the mutiny that had occurred, pretending to do so by order of Arrhidaeus (Alexander's half-brother), and executed them in his presence, frightening the rest of the army. Shortly afterwards, he also executed Meleager. As a result, Perdiccas was suspected by everyone. However, he decided to proclaim those he suspected as satraps, claiming they were acting

---

1 Arrian, *The Anabasis of Alexander*, book III, 3.
2 Arrian, *The Anabasis of Alexander*, book IV, 8.

THE ARMIES OF PTOLEMAIC EGYPT

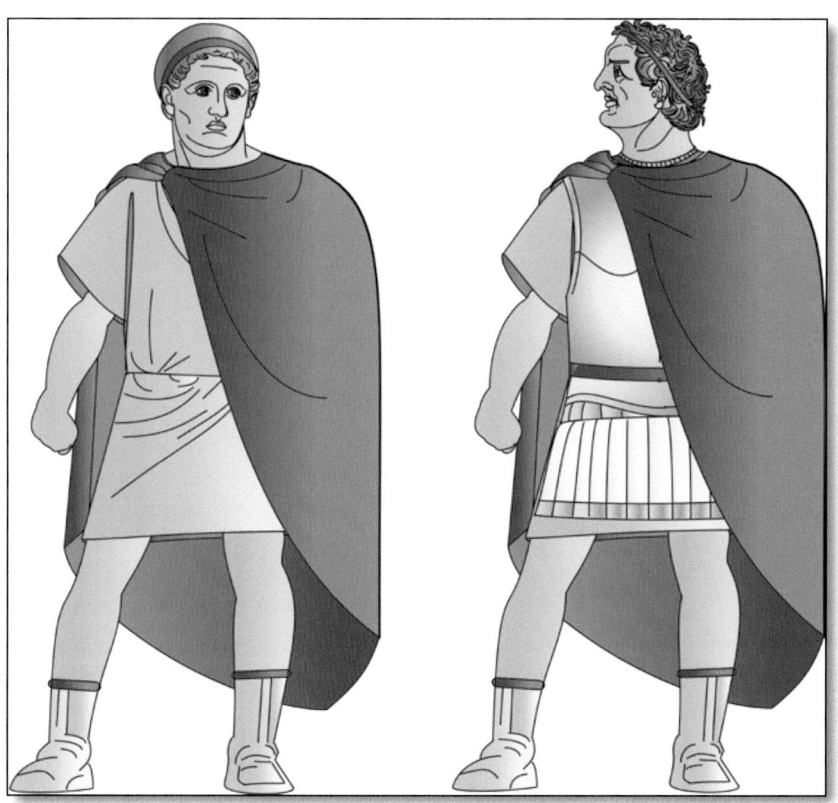

Ptolemy I Soter, based on a bust and a coin depicting him. (Artwork by the author)

on orders from Arrhidaeus. So, Ptolemy son of Lagos was given command of Egypt, Libya and the Arabian regions bordering Egypt.[3]

Later, on the pretext that Ptolemy had refused to appear before the army assembly, Perdiccas invaded Egypt but was defeated. He then behaved arrogantly towards his own soldiers, who murdered him. After the death of Perdiccas, Ptolemy conciliated the other Diadochi, acquiring a reputation for benevolence.[4]

Ptolemy's rise to power in Egypt was not without challenges. After Alexander's death in 323 BCE, there was a struggle among his generals, subsequently known as the Wars of the Diadochi, to determine the division of the empire. These were to clash constantly, and after some 40 years only three great Kingdoms remained: Macedonia under Antigonus Gonatas, son of Antigonus the One-Eyed, Asia under Antiochus I, son of Seleucus, and Egypt under Ptolemy II Philadelphus, son of Ptolemy I Soter.

Ptolemy's rule in Egypt was marked by stability and prosperity. One of Ptolemy's most enduring legacies is the city of Alexandria, which was founded in 331 BCE. Situated on the Mediterranean coast, Alexandria quickly became one of the most important cities in the ancient world.

---

3   Arrian, *History of the Diadochi or Events after Alexander*, books IV-V, 4–5.
4   Arrian, *History of the Diadochi or Events after Alexander*, books VI-IX, 28–29.

Ptolemy invested heavily in the city, attracting scholars, scientists, and philosophers from across the Mediterranean. The Library of Alexandria, which he established, became the largest repository of knowledge in the ancient world, housing works from various cultures and disciplines. Under Ptolemy's rule, Egypt flourished economically, thanks in part to its strategic location for trade between Europe, Africa, and Asia. The Ptolemies were skilled administrators, managing the fertile lands of the Nile Delta and implementing policies that promoted agriculture, trade, and industry. In terms of religion, Ptolemy adopted the traditional Egyptian cults and deities, presenting himself as a Pharaoh in the Egyptian tradition. This blend of Greek and Egyptian religious practices helped to legitimise his rule among the native Egyptian population.

Ptolemy himself was known for his military prowess and diplomatic acumen. He expanded Egypt's territory into parts of modern-day Libya, Palestine, and Cyprus, while also forging alliances with neighbouring states to ensure Egypt's security.

His reign laid the foundation for the prosperity and stability of the Ptolemaic dynasty, which would continue to rule Egypt for nearly three centuries, until the kingdom was eventually conquered by the Roman Empire in 30 BCE. Strabo sums up the sequence of different rulers at the head of the Ptolemaic Kingdom as follows:

> From the hands of Ptolemy, son of Lagos, Alexander's immediate successor, the sceptre of Egypt passed into the hands of Philadelphus, then Evergetes, Philopator the lover of Agathocles, Epiphanes and Philometor, the son gradually taking his father's place. Only Philometor was succeeded by his brother Evergetes II, known as Physcon, followed by Ptolemy Lathyros and, after him, Auletes, Cleopatra VII's father. After the third of the Ptolemies, all these, lost to vices and debauchery, were very bad Kings, but the worst of all were the fourth, seventh and last, Auletes, who added to the shame of his other deportments that of professing a real passion for the flute, even showing himself so proud of his talent as a virtuoso that he was not ashamed to set up music competitions in his palace and to mingle with the competitors to compete for the prize.[5]

By the first century BCE, the Ptolemaic dynasty had begun to decline due to internal strife, economic challenges, and external pressures. Rivalry among Ptolemaic siblings and the interference of foreign powers weakened the kingdom. In 48 BCE, Cleopatra VII, the last active ruler of the dynasty, became embroiled in the Roman civil war between Julius Caesar and Pompey. After Caesar's victory, Cleopatra aligned herself with him, but Egypt eventually fell under Roman control after the defeat of Cleopatra and

---

5   Strabo, *Geographika*, book XVII, 11.

THE ARMIES OF PTOLEMAIC EGYPT

Mark Antony at the Battle of Actium in 31 BCE. In 30 BCE, Egypt was annexed by the Roman Empire, marking the end of the Ptolemaic period.

The last rulers of the dynasty were Ptolemy XV Caesarion, son of Caesar and Cleopatra, born in 47 BCE and assassinated in 30 BC; then Ptolemy XVI Philadelphus, son of Antony and Cleopatra; and finally, Ptolemy XVII, who was assassinated by Caligula. The throne of Egypt finally passed to Tiberius in 14 CE.

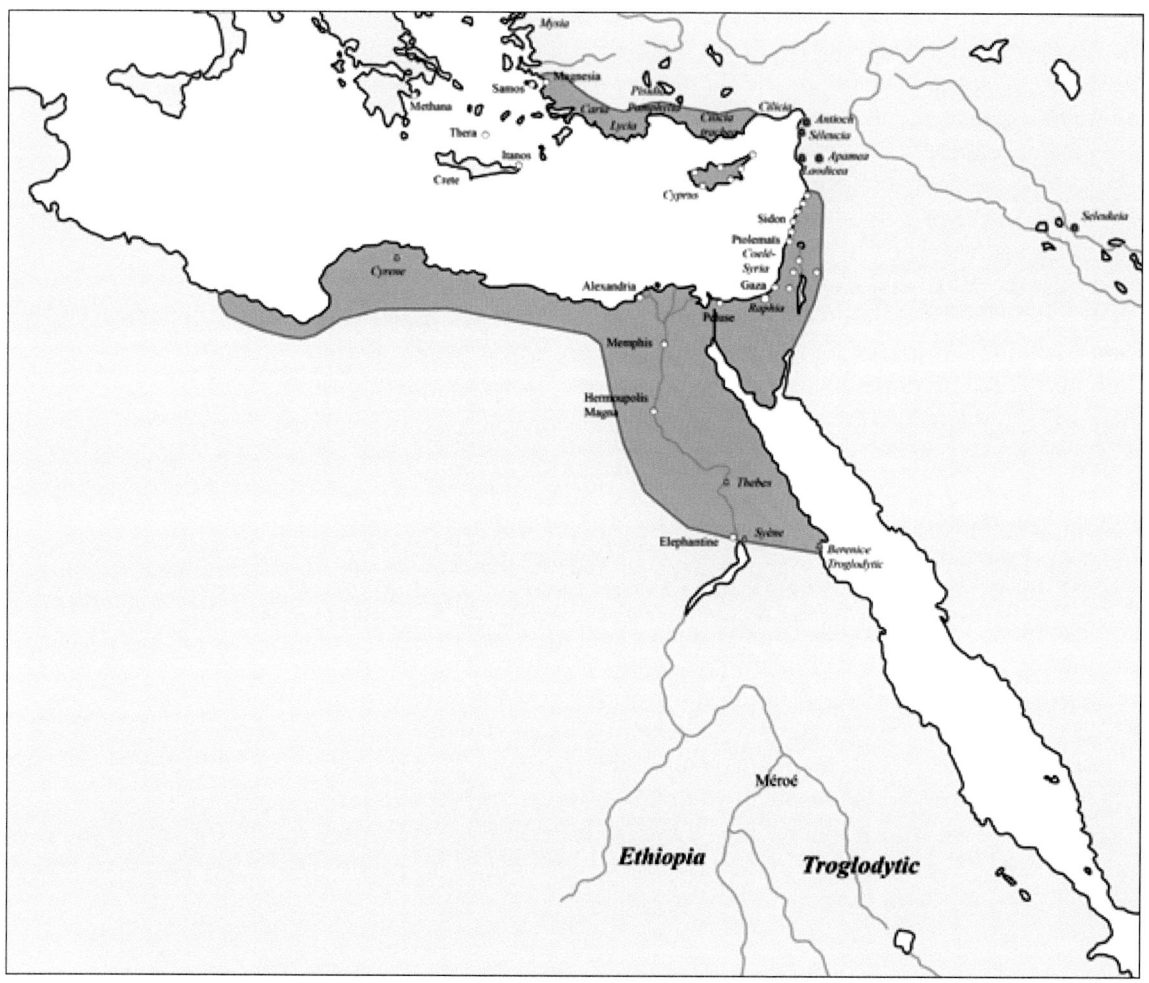

Ptolemaic Egypt around 275 BC. Dots represent Ptolemaic garrisons (Map drawn by the author)

THE PTOLEMAIC DYNASTY

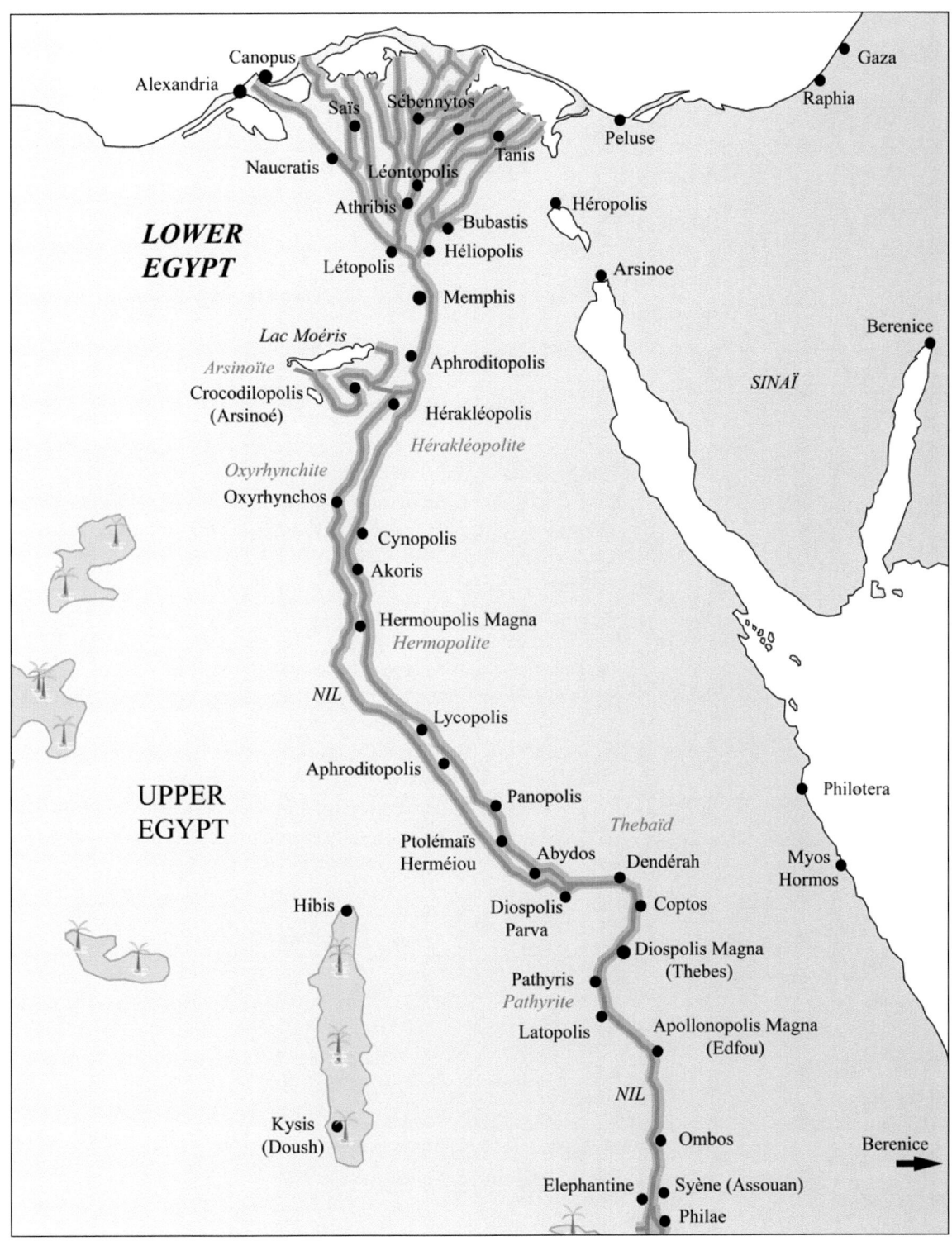

Map of the Egyptian Nomes in the Ptolemaic era (Map drawn by the author)

2

Main Components of the Ptolemaic Army

The Ptolemaic Army was made up of three categories of troops in terms of recruitment: the 'regulars', so called by Lesquier,[1] the mercenaries, and the natives. At Raphia, for example, Polybius distinguishes between the phalanx, the mercenaries and the indigenous Egyptians or Lybians 'armed in Macedonian style.'[2] From another point of view, there were two branches to this army: the permanent corps, made up of the guard and some of the mercenaries, and the corps of cleruchs, mobilised only in times of conflict. Indeed, Hellenistic Egypt, like many other contemporary states, could not rely on a standing army. Accordingly, the Ptolemaic State maintained a militia of soldiers ready to answer the King's call. These militiamen received the benefit of *arouras* of lands rather than pay.[3] In times of peace, the Ptolemaic rulers kept only the guard troops and mercenaries to man the garrisons.

Cleruchs

Ptolemy Soter, wishing to stimulate Greek immigration to establish a reserve of soldiers, offered them plots of land, the cleruchy, in exchange for a military service obligation. Later, Ptolemy Philadelphus established

Ptolemy I Soter and officers (Artwork by the author)

1 Lesquier, *Les institutions militaires de l'Egypte sous les Lagides*, p.11.
2 Polybius, *Histories*, book V, 2, 84.
3 Auguste Bouché-Leclercq, *Histoire des Lagides* (Paris: Ernest Leroux Editeur, 1907), tome 4, Chapitre XXVII, pp.2–3.

MAIN COMPONENTS OF THE PTOLEMAIC ARMY

a number of veterans in the *Nome* of Arsinoe.[4] The Greek colonist, then called a cleruch, received his cleruchy for life, even though it remained the property of the King. As Jean Lesquier points out, military service was intermittent but real.[5]

The *cleruchy* was originally an Egyptian institution. The army of the last pharaohs consisted of a territorial militia, the *machimoi*, in addition to mercenaries.[6] In the time of Herodotus, the *machimoi* allegedly owned half of the land in Egypt, with an average tenure of 12 *arouras*. Ptolemy Soter reinstated this institution to provide for the recruitment of the regular army. Then the system was extended, at least in part, to mercenaries and finally, by the end of the third century, to Egyptian *machimoi*. As the meaning of the term cleruch expanded to include natives, mercenaries, and the police, a new designation, that of *katoikos*, appeared under Ptolemy Epiphanes to refer to non-native cleruchic soldiers. The *katoikoi* were, like the cleruchs, permanently established settlers, and they formed the main component of garrisons and military colonies. The sons of cleruchs are called *epigones* (*epigonoi*). They apparently had the same military duties as their fathers, replacing them in the army when the latter could no longer serve.

The cleruchs were part of the *nomes* and placed under the authority of the *strategos* who commanded them. A *nome* or district (νομός in Greek) was the territorial division in ancient Egypt. The Ptolemies created some new *nomes*, such as the Antinoopolite, and renamed some ancient *nomes* – thus, the Crocodilopolite became the Arsinoïte. Analysis of a sample of 305 entries, of which 197 (65 percent) are cavalrymen shows that two-thirds of the settlers were cleruchs or *katoikoi* in Arsinoïte, 11 percent in Oxyrhynchite, 8 percent in Heracleopolite and 6 percent in Hermopolite.

There were four categories of cleruchs in the third century BCE: the *hekatontarouros* who own 100 *arouras*, the *hebdomochontarouros* who own 70 arouras, the *triachontarouros* who own 30 *arouras*, and the *pentarouros* who own five. A *hekatontarouros* is a cavalryman of the numbered *hipparchies* or a soldier of the *agema*, the *hebdomochontarouros* is a cavalryman of the ethnic *hipparchies*, the *triachontarouros* is the regular infantry, and the *pentarouros* the indigenous soldiers.

In the second century BCE, this classification evolves and goes to eight classes: holders of 100, 80, 30, 25, 20, 10, 7, and 5 *arourai*, with one *aroura* being 27.62 ares. The cavalrymen of the numbered *hipparchies* are endowed with 100 or 80 *arouras*,[7] and the regular infantry remains at 30 *arourai*.[8]

---

4   John P. Mahaffy & J. Gilbart Smyly, On the Flinders Petrie Papyri (Dublin: Royal Irish Academy, 1905), LIV, p.19.
5   J. Lesquier, *Les institutions militaires de l'Egypte sous les Lagides,* p.42.
6   J. Lesquier, *Les institutions militaires de l'Egypte sous les Lagides,* p.43.
7   J. Lesquier, *Les institutions militaires de l'Egypte sous les Lagides,* p.13.
8   J. Lesquier, *Les institutions militaires de l'Egypte sous les Lagides,* p.14.

THE ARMIES OF PTOLEMAIC EGYPT

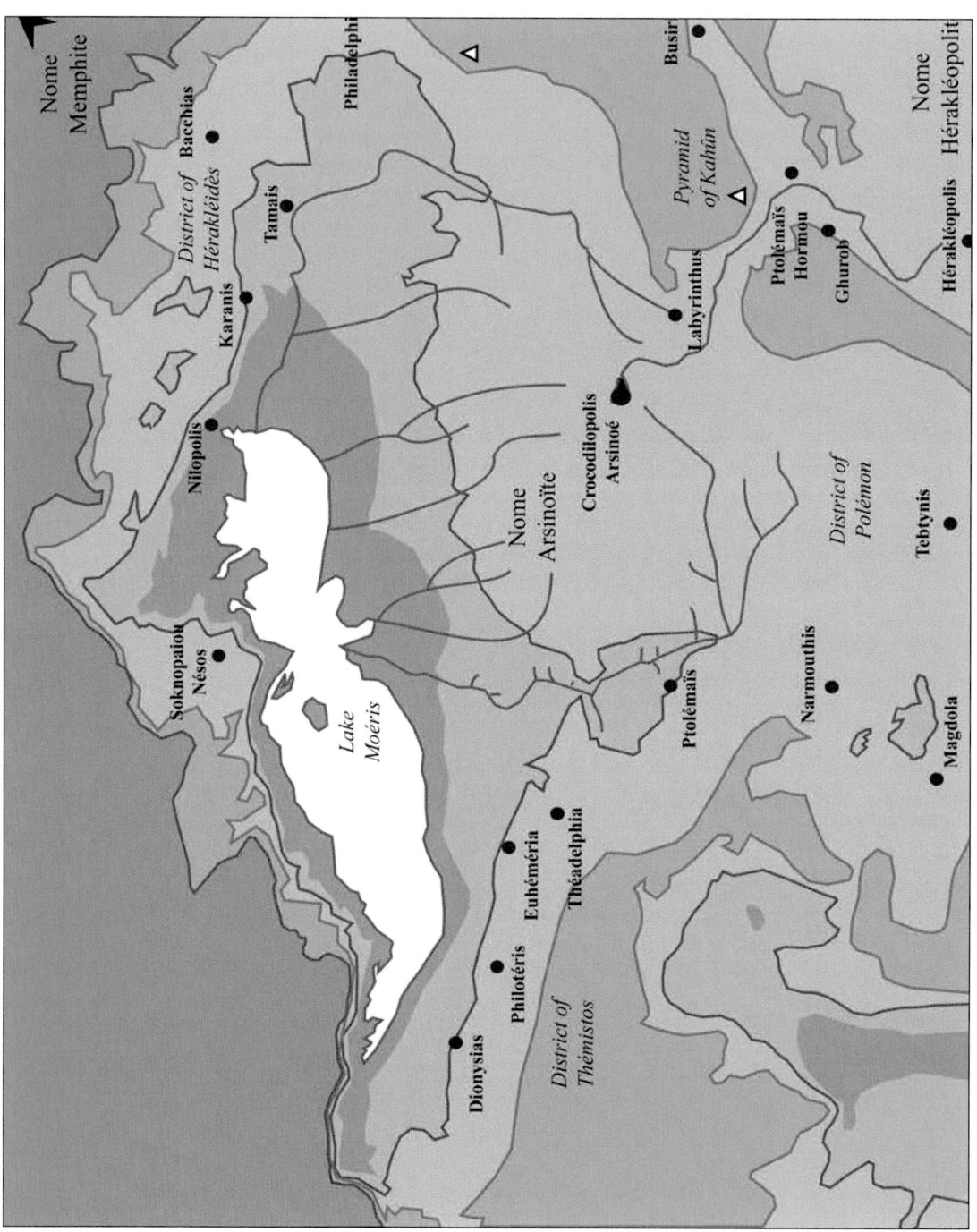

Map of Arsinoïte, a *nome* counting numerous cleruchies. (Map drawn by the author)

MAIN COMPONENTS OF THE PTOLEMAIC ARMY

Indigenous cavalrymen are endowed with 30 *arourai*, and infantrymen from 5[9] to 25.

The origin of the cleruchs varied greatly. In Arsinoïte, from 250 BCE onwards the majority were Macedonians, Greeks and Thracians, followed by Cyreneans and settlers from Asia Minor. Between 200 and 150 BCE, Macedonians and Semites are more numerous, followed by Thracians and Greeks. From 150 to 100 BCE Macedonians remain by far the most numerous other ethnic origins becoming marginal.[10] At the same time, the number of settlers fell sharply between 250 and 50 BCE: minus 67 percent between 250–200 and 200–150 BCE, minus 45 percent between 200–150 and 150–100 BCE and again down 66 percent between 150–100 and 100–50 BCE in Launey's prosopography.[11]

Officers' equipment, late period. Dish from the Fouquet collection (Perdrizet, *Les terres cuites grecques d'Egypte de la collection Fouquet*, 1921, plate LXXXIX)

The Guard

In Macedonia, the *agema* formed an elite corps, the guard. The Ptolemaic rulers strove to maintain this corps, which was made up mainly of Macedonians. This term does not necessarily refer to their origin or ethnicity, but rather to the citizens of Egypt's two poles, Alexandria and Ptolemais, and the volunteers of Hellenic origin who had settled in Egypt thanks to the cleruchy system. Boeotians and Euboeans, for example, rubbed shoulders with true Macedonians. This royal guard formed the garrison of Alexandria.

Different units of guard may have appeared in the third century BCE, more likely in the second century BCE: the *logchophoroï* (spear carriers) and the *machairophoroï* (*machaira* bearers, the *machaira* is a sword) both being recorded until the first century BCE. These two units seem to have evolved into a police force.

---

9   J. Lesquier, *Les institutions militaires de l'Egypte sous les Lagides*, p.48.
10 M. Launey, *Recherches sur les armées hellénistiques*, tome I, p.89
11 M. Launey, *Recherches sur les armées hellénistiques*, tome I, p.89

THE ARMIES OF PTOLEMAIC EGYPT

The term *aulên*[12] was used by Polybius for the cavalry of the guard. In 218 BCE, the royal guard counted 700 horsemen, and the agema 3,000 men. At least three inscriptions confirm the existence of mounted guards of the *aulên*, one from 252–251 BCE[13] and two from 205–193 BCE.[14] According to Bouché-Leclerq, this was a corps of royal pages, recruited from the sons of civil servants and the most prominent families.[15] However, it should be noted that a papyrus from 228 BCE seems to refer to a cavalryman from the *agema*.[16]

The cleruchs of the *agema* generally had a tenure of 100 *arouras*[17], while the cavalrymen of the guard probably had a larger tenure, although we do not know the size.

Machairai in the collection of the Metropolitan Museum of Art, New York. Iron, they are missing their handles which would have been wood or bone. The upper sword is 56.5cm (22¼ inches) long and weighs 0.7kg (1.5lb). The lower is slightly longer and heavier but exact details were not available. (Public Domain)

Cavalry

The regular cavalry (*hippeïs*) was organised into numbered *hipparchies* or *hipparchies* with ethnic names. In inscriptions referring to numbered *hipparchies*, the riders had names proving they were not of indigenous origin. In the third century, when they were established as cleruchs, they

---

12   Theodor Mommsen, *Polybii Historiae* (Berlin: F. Hultsch, 1897), Book V, 65, line 6 (p.488).
13   M. Launey, *Recherches sur les armées hellénistiques*, tome II, p.1246.
14   W. Peremans & E. Van 't Dack, *Prosopographia Ptolemaica*, (Louvain: Studia Hellenistica, 1952), vol. 8, p.34. Peremans & Van 't Dack, *Prosopographia Ptolemaica*, pp.225–226 & 268.
15   Bouché-Leclercq, *Histoire des Lagides*, tome 3, Chapitre XXI, II.
16   M. Launey, *Recherches sur les armées hellénistiques*, tome II, p.1128.
17   J. Lesquier, *Les institutions militaires de l'Égypte sous les Lagides,* p.3.

were granted tenures of 100 arouras. These *hekatontarouroï* were the most important of the cleruchs. Less well-endowed horsemen received tenures of 70 or 80 *arourai*.[18]

According to Lesquier, the ethnically named *hipparchies* formed part of the regular cavalry.[19] Papyri have left us traces of four of these units: the Thessalians, the Thracians, the Mysians and the Persians. When they were cleruchs, these cavalrymen received only 70 or, from the second century onwards, 80 arouras. The Mysians, Thracians and Persians only appear in inscriptions from the time of Raphia (220–219 BCE), with two or three names found for each. The Mysians may appear in a Geneva papyrus dated 29 May 146 BCE: a unit of this ethnic group was ordered with other soldiers to take a boat in Heracleopolite for Peluse (the north-eastern branch of the Nile delta) and then Ptolemais in Coele-Syria.[20] These Mysians were probably going to take part in Ptolemy VI's campaign against Alexander Balas in 145 BCE, but nothing confirms that they were still cavalrymen. The *hipparchia* of the Thessalians appeared at the same time and continued until the middle of the second century. We know at least 10 names of riders who belonged to this *hipparchia*. From 180 to 170 BCE, this *hipparchia* was known as the '*hipparchia* of the Thessalians and other Greeks.'[21]

While the nation, whether Thessalian, Thracian, Mysian or Persian, may indicate the origin of these new settlers, new postings, such as a change of regiment, complicates the picture. For example, a Persian, a *katoikos* cavalryman, might be assigned to a numbered *hipparchia* or to another ethnic regiment. There was even probably a Persian *epigone* who was considered a Mysian within the fourth *hipparchia*.[22]

In practice, these ethnic groups may distinguish between the way they fought and the equipment used by the horsemen of these *hipparchies*: Thessalians, Thracians, Greeks and Persians adopted a different formation for fighting. According to Asclepiodotus, Thessalians adopted a rhombus formation, Thracians and Scythians invented the wedge formation and Greeks invented the square formation.[23] Similarly, the equipment of a Macedonian or Thessalian cavalryman differed from that of a Thracian, Greek or Persian. Indeed, Polybius noted that the Thessalians were 'invincibles' when massed in *ilai* (squadrons), whereas the Aetolians excelled in dispersed combat.[24]

---

18   J. Lesquier, *Les institutions militaires de l'Egypte sous les Lagides,* p.13.
19   J. Lesquier, *Les institutions militaires de l'Egypte sous les Lagides,* p.13.
20   Paul Schubert, *Les papyrus de Genève* (Genève: Bibliothèque Publique et Universitaire, 1996), vol. 3, p.107.
21   Marcel Launey, *Recherches sur les armées hellénistiques* (Paris: De Boccard, 1987), tome I, p.220.
22   M. Launey, *Recherches sur les armées hellénistiques*, tome I, pp.445–446.
23   Asclepiodotus, *Tactica*, VII, 1–4.
24   Polybius, *Histories*, book IV, 1, 8.

THE ARMIES OF PTOLEMAIC EGYPT

Terracotta depicting a soldier with a weapon, possibly a cleruch (Perdrizet, *Les terres cuites grecques d'Egypte de la collection Fouquet*, 1921, plate LXIII)

Arrian distinguished between well-protected cavalrymen using long spears (*xystophoroi*), those using short spears (*doratophoroi*) and shields (they would then be called *thureophoroi*, if they wore long shields), and light cavalrymen.[25] Among foreign cavalry, a distinction is made between the horse archers, or Scythians, and the Tarentines, who only fight from a distance, in skirmishes, the former with the bow and the latter with the javelin, and the other horsemen who go into contact combat after they used up their javelins.[26]

The numbered *hipparchies* were therefore probably made up of *xystophoroi*, the Thessalian *hipparchia* of *doratophoroi*, the Thracian *hipparchia* of *thureophoroi* or, more probably, horsemen fighting with javelins and in melee, while the Mysian *hipparchia* must have represented javelinists fighting like the Tarentines or Aetolians. As for the Persian *hipparchia*, they are more likely horsemen with equipment and combat tactics similar to those of the Thracians than mounted archers.

Diodorus Siculus tells us that, probably in 275 BCE, Ptolemy II Philadelphus launched an expedition against the Ethiopians:

> From ancient times until Ptolemy, nicknamed Philadelphus, no Greek had penetrated Ethiopia and had not even advanced as far as the borders of Egypt. All these places were too inhospitable and dangerous to travel through. We have a more accurate knowledge of them since the expedition this King made to Ethiopia at the head of a Greek army.[27]

On this occasion, according to Agatharchides of Cnidus, Philadelphus equipped an *hipparchia* of 500 horsemen that he had enlisted in Greece to protect them from the poisoned darts used by the Ethiopians:

> He gave special armour to those who were to be the first to expose themselves and lead the rest of the corps; there were 100 of them. He clothed them and their horses in tightly woven woollen blankets (*stolas piletas*), known in the country as '*kasas*', so that the body was entirely covered in them, apart from the eyes.[28]

---

25 Arrian, *Ars Tactica*, 4,4.
26 Asclepiodotus, *Tactica*, VII, 1–4.
27 Diodorus Siculus, *Library of History*, vol.1, book I,37.
28 S. Micunco, *La géographie dans la Bibliothèque de Photios: Le cas d'Agatharchide*

MAIN COMPONENTS OF THE PTOLEMAIC ARMY

'*Stolas*' is a generic term for equipment or clothing. It can refer to military equipment or a piece of armour. '*Piletos*' means 'made of treaded wool', '*pilos*' being used for the wool or carded wool felt that lines the inside of the helmet. By extension, '*pilos*' is used to describe a felt blanket, a horse rug or a felt breastplate. Finally, '*kasas*' is the accusative of '*kases*', a term used by Xenophon to designate Persian saddlecloths. It can also be translated as thick garment.

The creation of the Thessalian *hipparchia* may therefore date back to this expedition and, a noteworthy innovation, it would have been temporarily equipped in the manner of the Sassanian or Byzantine *clibanarii* of the early Middle Ages.

A bronze Boeotian helmet found in the bed of the Tigris River in today's Turkey. This type was probably the most commonly worn cavalry helmet under Ptolemy Soter (Ashmolean Museum, Oxford)

Regular Infantry

The regular infantry was made up of what Polybius called the 'Macedonians'. They form the phalanx and perhaps the peltasts. The papyri refer to these men only as *pezoi*. As cleruchs, they are granted a tenure of generally 30 *arourai*.[29] In 218–217 BCE, at the Battle of Raphia, the phalanx numbered 5,000 or 25,000 men – depending on interpretation of Polybius.[30] The papyri show these footmen grouped into corps that were sometimes numbered: the *chiliarchies*.

Polybius identifies peltasts separately. There were 2,000 of them at Raphia. They form a more lightly armed infantry than the men of the phalanx but should not be equated with the peltasts of the fifth and fourth centuries BCE. The *pelte* refers to a smaller shield than the *aspis*, with a diameter of 60–65cm rather than 85–90cm, making this infantry a more versatile troop type. It originates with the reforms of Iphicrates in 374 BCE – an Athenian and an experienced warrior who 'was said to have a profound knowledge of strategy and to be gifted with remarkable natural sagacity.'[31] He did away with the cumbersome shield of the Greek hoplites and introduced *peltes*, 'which had the double advantage of covering the body sufficiently

---

(Reims / San Marino: Ecole Doctorale de Sciences de l'Homme et de la Société / Scuola Superiore di Studi Storici), p.434.
29 J. Lesquier, *Les institutions militaires de l'Egypte sous les Lagides*, p.3.
30 Griffith, *The Mercenaries of the Hellenistic world*, pp.122–123.
31 Diodorus Siculus, *Library of History*, vol.1, book XV,64.

THE ARMIES OF PTOLEMAIC EGYPT

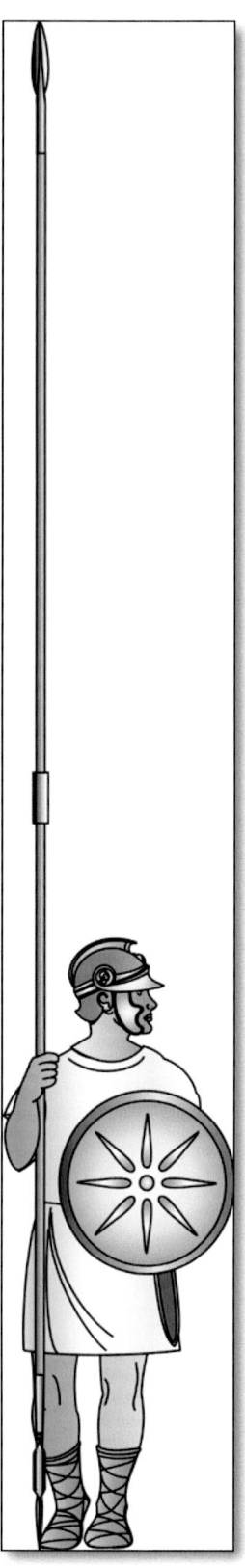

Illustration of the possible appearance of a *Peltastos*. (Artwork by the author)

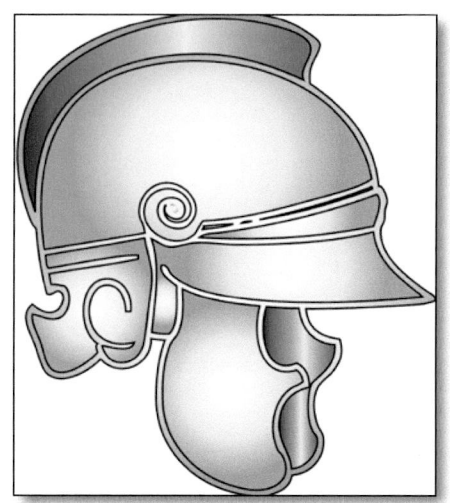

Hellenistic helmet based on a model found at Melos in Greece (now Milo), now in the collection of the Musée du Louvre, Paris. (Artwork by the author)

and leaving the soldier free to move.'[32] Diodorus of Sicily adds that, 'this useful reform having been adopted, the men with the old shields, formerly called hoplites because of the shields, received the name of peltasts from the light shield they carried.'[33] But what distinguishes the peltast of Iphicrates from his lighter Thracian predecessor is his offensive armament, which was lengthened: 'As for the spear and sword, he made them undergo an entirely opposite change; for he made the spear one and a half times longer than it was and lengthened the sword almost twice as much.'[34] As for the armour, Cornelius Nepos tells us that he 'changed the character of their breastplates, giving them linen ones in place of bronze cuirasses or mail armour. In that way he made the soldiers more active; for while he diminished the weight of their armour, he contrived to protect their bodies equally well without overloading them.'[35] The peltast of Iphicrates is therefore the precursor of Alexander the Great's hypaspist and of Antigonus Doson's or Philip V's peltast.

Peltasts appears in the Ptolemaic army at the Battle of Raphia. But they are not a permanent formation. Socrates of Boeotia was responsible for raising these 2,000 men in Greece and for training them.[36] Most of them may well have come from Boeotia, because by 220 BCE at the latest, the Boeotian infantry was equipped as *peltaphoros* (bearer of the *pelte*).[37]

It is possible that the raising of these peltasts was inspired by Philip V's elite troops. During the War of the Allies of 220–217 BCE, the King of Macedonia constantly surrounded himself with his peltasts, which at the

---

32   Diodorus Siculus, *Library of History*, vol.1, book XV,64.
33   Diodorus Siculus, *Library of History*, vol.1, book XV,64.
34   Diodorus Siculus, *Library of History*, vol.1, book XV,64.
35   Cornelius Nepos, *Lives of the Great Captains*, XI, 1.
36   Polybius, *Histories*, book V, 2, 65.
37   Yannis Kalliontzis and Christel Müller, *Nouveaux catalogues militaires de Chorsiai en Béotie* (Bulletin de Correspondance Hellénique, 2020), 144.1, https://doi.org/10.4000/bch.1064

MAIN COMPONENTS OF THE PTOLEMAIC ARMY

time numbered 2,000 men.³⁸ There were 3,000 at Sellasia in 222 BCE.³⁹ They often operated alongside light infantry, Illyrians and mercenaries, making them relatively mobile troops.⁴⁰ But they were capable of fighting shoulder to shoulder: 'Philip decided that the peltasts would be the first to enter the river bed and that they would take up position on the other bank in compact order, company by company (*tágma synêspikotas*)'.⁴¹ The Etolian cavalry fell back against the infantry, who 'stood firm behind a wall of shields.'⁴² And later, against the town of Palé in 218 BCE, 'Philip first sent his peltasts forward, company by company, with orders to force their way through the breach.'⁴³

Peltasts were probably distinguished from *agema* and the rest of the phalanx by the absence of *cnemides* (leg protection), a lighter cuirass, or even the absence of this type of protection, and a shorter pike measuring between eight cubits (3.55m for a cubit of 44.4cm, the estimated size of Iphicrates' peltast pike) and 12 cubits (5.33m, the size of the smallest *sarissa*).

The phalanx itself had heavier equipment. By analogy, based on the Macedonian regulations of Amphipolis, it included a pike (*sarissa*), a sword (*machairas*), a helmet, *cnemides* to protect the shins and *cotthybos*, which referred to body protection, possibly a linen cuirass. Officers replaced this with a metal cuirass or half-cuirass (*thorakos* or *emithorakos*).⁴⁴ Asclepiodotus also lists, for this type of soldier, the large shield (he uses the term *aspis* whereas Polyen uses the term *peltas*), the cuirass (*thoraxos*), the *cnemids* (*cnêmisi*) and the *sarissa*. According to Asclepiodotus, '"the best shield in use in the phalanx is the Macedonian, made of bronze, eight palms high (59-60 cm) and not too concave.'⁴⁵ The size of the shield, as indicated by Asclepiodotus is confirmed by several examples discovered in Macedonia. However, many monuments, such as that of Paul Emile at Delphi, depict shields that are more likely to have a diameter of around 70cm.

Terracotta of a woman with a round shield (Perdrizet, *Les terres cuites grecques d'Egypte de la collection Fouquet*, 1921, plate LVIII)

---

38 Polybius, *Histories*, book IV, 3, 67.
39 Polybius, *Histories*, book II, 3, 65.
40 See Polybius, *Histories*, book V, 1, 22 for an example.
41 Polybius, *Histories*, book IV, 3, 64.
42 Polybius, *Histories*, book IV, 3, 64.
43 Polybius, *Histories*, book V, 1, 5.
44 Miltiade B. Hatzopoulos, *L'organisation de l'armée macédoniennes sous les Antigonides: Problèmes anciens et documents nouveaux* (Athènes: Centre de recherche de l'antiquité grecque et romaine, Fondation Nationale de la Recherche Scientifique, 2001), 30, pp.80–81.
45 Asclepiodotus, *Tactica*, V, 1.

THE ARMIES OF PTOLEMAIC EGYPT

Terracotta of the Goddess Athena with a round shield (Perdrizet, *Les terres cuites grecques d'Egypte de la collection Fouquet*, 1921, plate LVIII)

The *pezos* defensive armament includes the helmet. Hellenistic helmets, such as those depicted on the small monuments at Delos, on the balustrade of the Propylon of Athena Nikephoros, on the frieze of the high altar at Pergamon or on the walls of the tomb of Lyson and Kallikles, have a domed helmet with elongated visor, a small neck guard, *paragnathides* (cheek protectors) and a crest. One of the two helmets depicted on the walls of the tomb of Lyson and Kallikles has its skull painted red. The Musée du Louvre has a specimen of a Hellenistic bronze helmet from Melos (see illustration page 28). The various monuments mentioned above, as well as the paintings in the tomb of Lyson and Kallikles, also depict *cnemides*.

The distinctive weapon of the man of the phalanx is the pike, known as the *sarissa*. In 1970, archaeologist Manolis Andronicos found remains of weapons dating from around 330–320 BCE near the Macedonian tomb of Vergina. These consist of an iron spear point (27.3cm long), an iron *sarissa* point (51cm long), an iron *sarissa* heel (18cm long) and an iron socket (17cm long). The size of the *sarissa* seems to have varied from one era to another. Asclepiodotus gives a length from 10 to 12 cubits (4.44m to 5.33m) but he used the word '*doru*', spear.[46] Arrian mentions a length of up to 5.3m (16ft),[47] while Polybius puts it at 14 cubits (6.22m). According to him, 'the *sarissa* was 16 cubits long. Since then, it has been shortened by 2 cubits to make it more convenient, and after this retrenchment there remains, from the place where the soldier holds it to the end that passes behind him and serves as a counterweight to the other end, 4 cubits.'[48] The remains found at Vergina allow us to estimate the length of the *sarissa* at the time of Philip II at 6 metres 20, in line with the figure given by Polybius.

For close combat, the Macedonian soldier was also armed with a sword possibly of a machaira style. The Amphipolis regulations list the short, single-edged sword (*machaira*), but the classical Greek double-edged sword (*xiphos*) continued to be used, as evidenced by those depicted in the tomb of Lyson and Kallikles or on the tombs of Sidon. The swords depicted on the base of the monument at Delos are short, fairly broad swords of the type mentioned in a Macedonian regulation found at Amphipolis. The balustrade of the Propylon of Athena, in Pergamon, and the statue of Demetrios Poliorcetes, in Athens, show models of swords comparable to these.

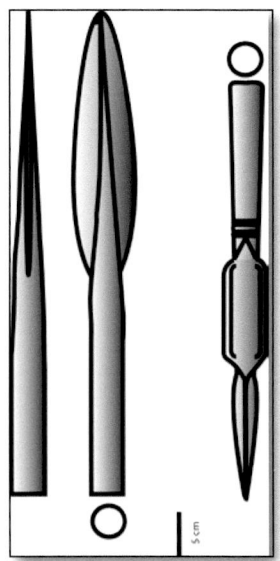

Illustration of the tip and butt of a sarissa (Artwork by the author)

---

46   Asclepiodotus, *Tactica*, V, 1.
47   Arrian, *Ars Tactica*, 12,7.
48   Polybius, *Histories*, book XVIII, 1, 29.

MAIN COMPONENTS OF THE PTOLEMAIC ARMY

The phalanx was made up of ranks, the rank being called *lochous*, *stixous* or *dekania* depending on the period, which could be arranged in several ways: the order used for marches, which Asclepiodotus does not designate by any particular term and where the men are placed at intervals of 4 cubits (1.8 metres); the compact order (*pykôsis*), shield against shield, used to attack the enemy and where the intervals are 2 cubits (0.9 metre); and the close order (*synaspismos*) used to defend, when the enemy attacks, and where the intervals are 1 cubit. To switch from one order of battle to the other, the phalanx reduces its depth and doubles its ranks, for example from 32 to 16 and then 8. The various formations thus obtained will adopt particular names according to their depth. Asclepiodotus lists them: square phalanx (*tetragômos*), parallel phalanx (*plagia*) when it is wider, perpendicular phalanx (*orthê*) when it is deeper than it is wide.[49]

According to Polybius, the Hellenistic phalanx fought in close order 16 ranks deep. If a man in the phalanx occupies a square of one metre on a side and the length of the *sarissa* is 6.20 metres, a phalanx has a density of 5 pikes per metre. An infantryman in loose order, such as the Roman legionary, who occupies a space of one to two square metres, will therefore be faced with 5 to 10 pikes. Asclepiodotus notices that when the Macedonian phalanx used a compact order, with the *sarissa* projecting 10 cubits (4.44 metres), 'it seemed irresistible to the enemy.' And he added:

Clay model of a sword, if not a dagger (Perdrizet, *Les terres cuites grecques d'Egypte de la collection Fouquet*, 1921, plate XCI)

> It is obvious that even the spears of the fifth rank protrude from the front, for the soldiers of the second rank, set back two cubits, brandish the points of their spears eight cubits from the front, those of the third rank six, those of the fourth four, and finally those of the fifth rank two cubits, so that there are five spears protruding in front of the first rank. It is said that it is thanks to these lines of spears that the Macedonians not only terrify their enemies by their appearance, but also exalt the courage of each squad leader, who sees himself protected by five defenders.[50]

Interestingly, Polybius relates the same effect:

> When the phalanx is in its proper state, and the soldier who is alongside or behind joins his neighbour as much as he should, the pikes of the second, third and fourth ranks go further beyond

---

49 Asclepiodotus, *Tactica*, X, 21.
50 Asclepiodotus, *Tactica*, V, 1.

the first than those of the fifth, which are only two cubits [90cm] beyond the first rank. From this it follows that before the first row there are five pikes, each two cubits shorter than the others, as they move away from the first row to the fifth. Now, as the phalanx is 16 rows deep, it is easy to imagine the impact, weight and strength of this order. It is true, however, that beyond the fifth rank the pikes are of no use in combat. This is why they are not extended forward but leaned on the shoulders of the preceding rank with the point upwards, so that when pressed they break the impetuosity of the lines, which pass beyond the first ranks and could fall on those who follow them. These back rows do have their uses, however. For, as they march towards the enemy, they push and press those in front of them and deprive those in front of them of any means of turning back.[51]

Illustration of a shield, modelled on a limestone possibly of a Ptolemaic manufacture. Collection of the AllardPierson Museum, Amsterdam. (Artwork by the author)

Plutarch also mentions the impressive effect that the sight of a phalanx in compact order can have. Thus, at the Battle of Pydna in 168 BCE, when the Macedonians, 'took in hand the shields they were carrying suspended from their shoulders, lowered their pikes all at once and presented them to the enemy,' the consul Paul Emile, 'at the sight of this impenetrable hedge of shields, pressed against each other, and of this forehead bristling with pikes, confessed that he had never seen a more terrible sight, and he has often spoken since of the impression this sight had made on him.'[52]

The Natives

In the third century BCE, Egyptians appeared under the term *machimoi*, but they were mainly assigned to public services and routine tasks. According to some papyri, there were also elite *machimoi*, known as *epilektoi*, and others assigned to guarding ships. In 312 BCE, at Gaza, some of the Egyptians were used to transport ammunition and other baggage, while others appeared to be 'armed and serviceable for battle,'[53] perhaps as light infantry. It was not until the Battle of Raphia that the natives were armed in Macedonian style. Polybius lists 20,000 Egyptian infantrymen and 3,000 Libyans as forming the phalanx[54]. The leader of the latter was Ammonios of Barca, a town in Cyrenaica. In the second century BCE, the *machimoi* became part of the cleruchy system, which involved military obligations. Then, during the first

---

51 Polybius, *Histories*, book XVIII, 1, 29.
52 Plutarch, *The Parallel Lives, Life of Aemilius*, XXXI.
53 Diodorus Siculus, *Library of History*, book XIX, 80, 4.
54 Polybius, *Histories*, book V, 2, 65.

MAIN COMPONENTS OF THE PTOLEMAIC ARMY

century BCE, the term *machimoi* evolved as they begin to include Greek and Arabic names.

The Egyptians and Libyans also provided cavalry units, about which little is known, other than the name of these units: *ilaarkies*.

Mercenaries

Greeks, Cretans and Thracians made up most of the mercenaries employed by the Ptolemies. They are called *mistophoroi* or *xenoi* in Greek. At the very beginning of his reign (221 BCE), Ptolemy IV Philopator lined up 3,000 Greek mercenaries from the Peloponnese, mainly Lacedaemonians, and 1,000 Cretans. Three years later, for the Battle of Raphia, he assembled 2,000 mercenary horsemen, 8,000 Greek infantrymen under the Achaean Phoxidas, 2,000 Cretans and 1,000 Neo-Cretans under Cnopias of Allaria. There were also 2,000 Thracian and Galatian mercenaries, in addition to the 4,000 men from these two nations.[55] The 2,000 peltasts are also probably Greek mercenaries, mainly Boeotians. In 200 BCE, 6,000 Aetolians were enlisted as mercenaries in the Ptolemaic army. In the years 163–162 BCE, Ptolemy the Younger, known as Physcon, raised a 'powerful corps of mercenaries' in Greece,[56] but had to dismiss them under pressure from the Roman Senate. He would later recruit a corps of 1,000 Cretans. Later, in the first century, Semites would form the main source of recruitment, alongside Cilicians and Syrians, who are to be found in large numbers in the army that faced Caesar.

In the third century BCE, Cilicia, Lycia and parts of Pamphylia and Caria were included in the Ptolemaic Kingdom. The same is true of part of Thrace in the second half of that century, under Ptolemy III Euergetes. These nations provided many mercenaries for the Ptolemaic rulers. The Celts of Thrace, whose lands bordered those of the Ptolemies, and the Galatians of central Anatolia also provided mercenaries until the end of the third century BCE. Several stelae from the necropolis of Ibramieh, dating from the end of that century, prove that a Galatian unit was stationed in Alexandria at the time. However, if we exclude the Battle of Raphia, Celts seems to form a small proportion of the mercenaries, and the Greeks are the main source of mercenaries in the third century BCE. The Cretans were renowned as excellent archers

Terracotta from the Fayoum depicting an Amazon bearing a shield with a distinctive *pelte* of Amazonian type. (Perdrizet, *Les terres cuites grecques d'Egypte de la collection Fouquet*, 1921, plate LXXIV)

---

55 Polybius, *Histories*, book V, 2, 65.
56 Polybius, *Histories*, book XXXI, 2, 17.

THE ARMIES OF PTOLEMAIC EGYPT

Terracotta of a Nubian warrior bearing a double-headed axe (Perdrizet, *Les terres cuites grecques d'Egypte de la collection Fouquet*, 1921, plate CI)

throughout the Hellenistic world, and they provided mercenaries to all armies at the time. Polybius says that no one could match them for ambushes, raids, pillaging, night attacks and *coups de main* requiring cunning. On the other hand, 'faced with an enemy advancing in close ranks, they show themselves to be cowardly and without any firmness.'[57]

Newly raised mercenaries could later become cleruchs. Polybius identifies 4,000 Thracians and Galatians at Raphia, whom he describes as colonists and *epigones*.[58] This term referred to the sons of colonists who were subject to military service in exchange for tenure.

The Emergence of the Thureophoros

Greek historians distinguish two types of infantries: heavy infantry, represented first by the hoplite and later by the *sarissaphoros* (pikeman), and light infantry, comprising peltasts, slingers, and archers. Thucydides and Xenophon only mention these two types of troops. Polybius mainly describes these two categories, although he distinguishes more or less mobile troops within heavy infantry. And he attributes to Philip V of Macedonia the words: 'It is generally the lightest and most mobile units that are exposed first and suffer the first losses, while it is to the phalanx and heavy infantry that the merit of the final success is attributed.'[59]

The hoplite, a term meaning 'armed man', was the Greek heavy infantryman fighting in a tight formation. To become a hoplite, a young citizen entered the gymnasium at the age of 18 for a two-year training. During this training, they were called *ephebes*. Then, at the age of 20 and after completing the training, he was enrolled in a lists as a conscript. Hoplite training was comprehensive, not limited to heavy infantry combat. Thus, in the years 335–322 BCE, the training of Athenian *ephebes* included javelin throwing, archery, and combat with the hoplite's heavy weapons. As early as the end of the sixth century BCE, it already included the *hoplitodromos*, a 400m race performed by the *ephebe* equipped with his shield and helmet. This distance corresponds to the extreme range of the bow, which the hoplite had to cover as quickly as possible.

---

57 Polybius, *Histories*, book IV, 1, 8.
58 Polybius, *Histories*, book V, 2, 65.
59 Polybius, *Histories*, book X, 3, 25.

MAIN COMPONENTS OF THE PTOLEMAIC ARMY

Although the hoplite had comprehensive training, the problem of the heaviness of the phalanx arose as early as the fifth century BCE. Faced with armies composed of light infantry, heavy infantry often proved to be useless. According to Xenophon, 'The Greek rearguard received blows and could not return them; .... So Xenophon decided to attack, and he did so with the hoplites and peltasts who were with him in the rearguard; but they pursued in vain, they did not take any enemy.'[60] This disadvantage becomes a significant handicap when it can turn a battle into defeat. This was the case in a fight recounted by Xenophon and taking place at the end of the beginning of fourth century BC: 'There all the peltasts and hoplites of Piraeus armed themselves; immediately their runners advanced, launched missiles, arrows, stones, hit with the sling. The Lacedaemonians, closely packed, and seeing several of their own wounded, began to retreat.'[61]

Initially, around 440 BCE, the response was to create lighter hoplites, without cuirass or greaves: the *ekdromoi*. Then, in the fourth century BCE, Iphicrates further evolved the armament.

Iphicrates was one of the greatest captains of peltasts, going so far as to inflict a defeat on a Spartan *mora* with his light troops at Lechaion in 390 BCE.[62] Around 374 BCE, knowing perfectly the qualities and weaknesses of these troops, he managed to make his hoplite formations more mobile. Diodorus Siculus mentions this reform, as does Cornelius Nepos:

> It was he who changed the infantryman's armour: until then they had carried huge shields, spears, and small swords. Iphicrates, to facilitate the impact and manoeuvres, replaced the round shield with the *pelta*, and that is why infantrymen have been called peltasts ever since. He doubled the dimensions of the pike and gave more length to the swords; finally, adopting another material for making cuirasses, he substituted linen for bronze and iron. Henceforth, freer in his movements and relieved of the weight of his armour, the soldier had one that protected him equally without overwhelming him.[63]

Thus, Iphicrates' reforms allowed the emergence of two new types of troops: on the one hand, the hoplite equipped with a smaller shield, a longer spear, and linen armour, a type of soldier that can be equated to Alexander's hypaspist and then to Philip V's peltast; on the other hand, the Macedonian pikeman equipped similarly but with an oversized pike: the *sarissa*. The first type seems to have persisted until the third century BCE, as several indications show:

---

60 Xenophon, *Anabasis*, book III, 4.
61 Xenophon, *Hellenica*, book II, 3.
62 Xenophon, *Hellenica*, book II, 3.
63 Cornelius Nepos, *Lives of the Great Captains, Iphicrates*.

- Diodorus Siculus's conclusion on Iphicrates' experiment, stating that the experience was a success.[64]
- A passage from Diodorus stating that in 355 BCE, the Phocidian general Philomelus 'received from the King 15 talents, added to this sum about as much from his own fortune, hired foreign mercenaries, and raised among the Phocians 1,000 elite men whom he named peltasts.'[65]
- A treaty between the Aetolians and Acarnanians, dating from 263–262 BCE, showing three pay scales corresponding to three types of soldiers (two Corinthian drachmas per day for a hoplite, nine Corinthian obols for a soldier equipped with a half-cuirass, and seven Corinthian obols for the lightly armed soldier).[66]
- The reappearance of a comparable type of peltast under the reign of Philip V of Macedonia (221–179 BCE).

Egyptian terracotta depicting the God Bes. The size of the shield and the fact that the miniature is armed with a sword make it more likely to be a *peltaphoros* or *sarissophoros*'s shield. (Perdrizet, *Les terres cuites grecques d'Egypte de la collection Fouquet*, 1921, plate XLI)

However, a century after the reform, new influences would lead to the evolution of the equipment of the citizen and the mercenary: the predominance of the phalanx would create a need for flexibility and mobility. Thus appeared the Hellenistic *thureophoros*.

In 279 BCE, the Celts crossed into Greece. After several defeats at Thermopylae, they bypassed the Greek army and sacked Delphi. These warriors, apparently appearing out of nowhere, were equipped with a shield previously unknown in Greece and Asia: the *thureos*.

However, according to Pausanias, if the Battle of Thermopylae was the Greek soldier's first contact with this new type of shield, there is hardly a reason for him to have been impressed by Gallic weaponry:

The Greeks marched into battle in good order and in great silence. At the moment of the melee, their heavy infantry advanced, but only as much as was necessary, always holding their phalanx tightly packed; while the light infantry also kept its ranks, raining a hail of missiles on the barbarians and killing many of them with arrows and slingshots.[67]

---

64 Diodorus Siculus, *Library of History*, vol.1, book XV, 64.
65 Diodorus Siculus, *Library of History*, vol.1, book XVI, 24.
66 Hatto H. Schmitt, *Die Staatsverträge des Albertums* (Munich: Verlag C.H. Beck, 1969), vol. 3, p.142.
67 Pausanias, *Description of Greece, X – Phocis*, XXI, 1.

MAIN COMPONENTS OF THE PTOLEMAIC ARMY

Throughout these battles, the Greeks resisted well, and their battle lines were effective. It seems nevertheless obvious that the Gallic warrior, who was widely employed as a mercenary in the third and second centuries BCE, greatly contributed to the spread of this new equipment.

The first recorded mention of soldiers equipped with the *thureos* in a Hellenistic Army by a historian dates to 220 BCE. This was the army of the Seleucid Satrap Molon rebelling against the young Antiochus III:

> Given the enemy's disposition in front, the cavalry [of Molon] was divided between the two wings, the intermediate space being occupied by the *thureophoros* and the Gauls as well as all the rest of the heavy infantry. As for the archers, slingers, and other troops of this kind, they were deployed on both wings, alongside the horsemen, towards the outside. In front of the front line, at intervals, there were scythed chariots.[68]

What this passage tells us is that the *thureophoros* was considered close to a heavy infantryman who took his place in the centre of the battle line, like his predecessor the hoplite. But this passage from Polybius gives us no indication of the origin of these men.

We also know that Philopoemen equipped the Achaean infantry with *thureoi* thanks to this passage from Plutarch, which takes place around 208 BC:

> He [Philopoemen] began by changing their battle order and their armour: they carried *thureoi*, indeed, but so narrow and thin that they did not cover their whole bodies. Their spears (*dorasi*) were much shorter than the Macedonians' *sarissai*; and while their lightness made them suitable for long-range strikes, it gave them a significant disadvantage in melee combat. They were not accustomed to the battle order known as the spiral. Their square phalanx, which had no front, and which they did not know how to fortify, like the Macedonians, by pressing their shields against each other, exposed them to being easily pierced and broken through. Philopoemen changed this defective way of arming them: instead of these short spears and *thureoi*, he gave them large shields and *sarissai*, covered them with helmets, breastplates, and greaves; and instead of letting them run and flit like light troops, he trained them to stand and fight.[69]

---

68   Polybius, *Histories*, book V, 2, 54.
69   Plutarch, *The Parallel Lives, Life of Philopoemen*, 13.

This passage is generally interpreted by commentators as the transformation of the Achaean soldier from *thureophoros* to *peltaphoros* (light pikeman) or *sarissaphoros* (pikeman). But Plutarch, trying to explain why and how Philopoemen transformed his infantry by equipping them in the Macedonian style, confuses the issue. His words imply that the infantryman equipped with the *thureos* fought like light infantry, whereas this thesis seems excessive: the *thureos* is a shield at least as large as the Macedonian pikeman's one, even if it is smaller than the *aspis* of the hoplite and the *scutum* of the Roman legionary. Plutarch does not possess Polybius's military culture. Perhaps he misinterpreted a passage from Polybius in his *Life of Philopoemen*, which we no longer possess. Polybius describes the heavy Achaean infantry in 222 BCE, during the Battle of Sellasia: 'Behind them were positioned the Acarnanians and Epirotes. Behind the latter, 2,000 Achaeans were placed in reserve. As for the cavalry, Antigonus arranged them in the valley of Oenus under the command of Alexander, supported by 1,000 Achaean infantry and an equal number of Megalopolitans.'[70] The Achaeans here are considered as elite infantry having a role comparable to the Megalopolitan pikemen. A little later, in 221 BCE, Polybius describes the Battle of Caphyae as follows:

Terracotta from Egypt depicting the God Hapocration. He carries a trumpet and a *thureos* shield. (Perdrizet, *Les terres cuites grecques d'Egypte de la collection Fouquet*, 1921, plate XCIII)

Aratus [the Achaean strategist], ... thought, seeing the enemy cavalry withdraw, that they were fleeing, and then sent the armoured units (*thorakitai*) from his wings to join the light troops and engage in combat with them. Himself, pivoting the rest of his men to form them into a column, led them at a run towards the enemy.... Just as their comrades were giving way and fleeing, the Achaeans from the armoured units, sent to the rescue, arrived disorderly and in small groups on the battlefield.... The Achaeans, who were falling back on Aratus' heavy infantry, believed that it had remained in position on the strong positions it originally occupied.[71]

Then Polybius later specified that, following this defeat, the assembly of the Achaean people reproached Aratus for 'not having thought of engaging in action on the plain by deploying his hoplites.'[72] He clearly distinguishes two infantry corps in Aratus' army: heavy infantry and light infantry, but there would be three types of heavy infantry: hoplites, the armoured (*thorakitai*), and the *epilektoi* (i.e. chosen men), the latter

---

70 Polybius, *Histories*, book II, 3, 65.
71 Polybius, *Histories*, book IV, 1, 12.
72 Polybius, *Histories*, book IV, 1, 14.

being the only permanent troops of the federal government, numbering 3,000 under Aratus. If we believe Plutarch, the Achaean hoplite, the *thorakitai* who wears the mail coat, and the *epilektoi* were supposed to carry the *thureos*. Consequently, it seems that the Achaean soldier was a heavy infantryman, at least some units of which were equipped with the *thureos*, before its transformation into a *peltaphoros* (lighter pikeman).

Further on, Polybius, recounting Antiochus's passage through the mountains of Hyrcania during his offensive against the Parthians in 210 BCE, also lists *thureophoros*: 'Following these people [archers, slingers, and javelin thrower]), Antiochus advanced some 2,000 Cretans armed with round shields and placed under the command of Polyxenidas of Rhodes, and, to bring up the rear, *thorakitai* and *thureophoroi*, commanded by Nicomedes of Cos and the Aetolian Nicolaos.'[73] A little later, Polybius distinguishes this mobile infantry, which presumably includes *thorakitai* and *thureophoroi*, from the phalanx, just as he distinguishes elsewhere between the peltasts or hypaspists of Philip V of Macedonia and light infantry. But he does so to distinguish them from the latter within the heavy infantry. Pikemen, *thureophoroi*, and *thorakitai* together constitute the line infantry. Polybius makes this distinction here because, unlike the phalanx, 'light troops and mobile infantry, on the other hand, could very well climb up bare rock.'[74] But when it comes to fighting in mountainous terrain, it is the light troops that take action: 'Thus, slingers, archers, and javelin throwers, sometimes advancing in small groups, sometimes concentrating their attacks to seize the best positions, while the Cretan infantry, ready to intervene, advanced parallel to them in good order and at a slow pace, along the slopes just above the ravine, forced the barbarians to withdraw to regroup around the pass.'[75]

It seems that there is no real difference between this 'mobile infantry' and the Roman legion. Moreover, Polybius opposes the pikeman to the legionary as he could oppose him to the mobile infantry:

> The Roman soldier, with his equipment, also occupies (like the man of the phalanx) a space of three feet. But in combat, each man performs his movements independently of the others, because he must cover his body with an oblong shield, which he turns each time from the side from which the blow comes, and because he wields a sword with which he strikes both thrust and cut.... Everyone knows that the phalanx requires a flat and bare terrain, a terrain that is not cut by any space such as ditches, ravines, hills, slopes, or watercourses, because any of these accidents is enough to paralyse or dislocate a troop thus formed.... Now, in cases of this kind, an army formed in the Macedonian fashion is an instrument that is not very manoeuvrable

---

73 Polybius, *Histories*, book X, 4, 29.
74 Polybius, *Histories*, book X, 4, 30.
75 Polybius, *Histories*, book X, 4, 30.

THE ARMIES OF PTOLEMAIC EGYPT

Terracotta from Egypt depicting a soldier with a *thureos* shield. (Perdrizet, *Les terres cuites grecques d'Egypte de la collection Fouquet*, 1921, plate XCIV)

or even completely ineffective, because, in the phalanx, men cannot be used either in small units or individually, whereas, on the contrary, the Roman formation renders the best services. Every Roman soldier, indeed, as soon as, equipped with his weapons, he has entered operation, can adapt to any place, any circumstance, and of facing all sides.[76]

These descriptions of infantry equipped with the *thureos* do not allow us to grasp the chronology of its spread well. It is through epigraphy and the study of the Boeotian foot soldier that we can better understand this process. Feyel believes that, thanks to the numerous inscriptions referring to conscripts as *peltaphoros*, the Boeotian foot soldier was equipped in the Macedonian fashion with the *sarissa* and the *pelta*, around 250–245 BCE.[77] But it seems that before transforming their hoplites into *peltaphoros*, the Boeotians had first transformed them into *thureophoroi* (*thureos* Thureos holders). A military catalogue, or roll, found at Acraephia lists the conscripts by introducing the document with the mention 'is registered as *thurephoros*',[78] later catalogues dated after 225 BCE registering them as *peltaphoros*.[79] More recent research done at Chorsiai in Boeotia suggests that military catalogues referring to *thureophoroi* dated from 223 to 205 BCE,[80] while the *peltaphoros* appears from 197 BCE. We can deduce from this that the *thureophoros* did not spread uniformly across Boeotia, with some cities raising conscripts as *thureophoroi* and others as *peltaphoroi* at the same time. Therefore, the Boeotian league seems to have equipped its hoplites as *thureophoroi* between 250 and 225 BCE, perhaps even earlier.

Chronologically, the *thureos* may have spread in Greece through Thrace or Asia Minor, then Boeotia and finally Achaia. It is then possible that the Argolis, Arcadia, Elis, and Attica adopted it subsequently. It is known that later, at the Battle of Sellasia, the Megapolitans (a city in Arcadia) were equipped in the Macedonian fashion by Antigonus Doson, and the Lacedaemonians did the same under the impetus of Cleomenes.

---

76 Polybius, *Histories*, book XVIII, 1, 32.
77 Michel Feyel, *Polybe et l'histoire de la Béotie au IIIe siècle avant notre ère* (Paris: De Boccard, 1942), p.197.
78 Paul Perdrizet, *Inscriptions d'Acraephiae* (Bulletin de Correspondance Hellénique, 1899), 23, p.204.
79 Paul Perdrizet, *Inscriptions d'Acraephiae* (Bulletin de Correspondance Hellénique, 1899), 23, pp.193–205.
80 Yannis Kalliontzis and Christel Müller, *Nouveaux catalogues militaires de Chorsiai en Béotie* (Bulletin de Correspondance Hellénique, 2020), 144.1, https://doi.org/10.4000/bch.1064

MAIN COMPONENTS OF THE PTOLEMAIC ARMY

It is also possible that the *thureos* spread in Greece from the north, that is from Illyria. The Illyrians, who equipped themselves with the *thureos* like their Celtic and Roman adversaries, were frequently used as mercenaries in the Macedonian armies. They are found in Antigonus's army at the Battle of Sellasia in 222 BCE, and then in a brigade with the *thorakitai* at Mantinea in 207 BCE:

> Meanwhile, Philopoemen, who had divided his army into three corps, had them leave Mantinea, one composed of Illyrians and *thorakitai*, as well as all the mercenaries and light troops, by the road leading from the sanctuary of Poseidon; the other, namely the phalanx, by the road immediately west of the first; and the third, finally, namely the cavalry of the Confederation, by the following road.... On the left wing, Philopoemen himself commanded the entire body of mercenaries, in compact formation.[81]

The spread of the *thureos* across the Seleucid Asia is clearer: it could only have occurred through the Galatians who travelled to Asia Minor via Thrace and Bithynia towards the end of 278 BCE:

> They [the Gauls] fought anyone who resisted, imposed tribute on those who sought peace, reached Byzantium, and held sway for a long time over the coast of the Propontis, exacting tribute from the cities in the region. Then the desire to cross into Asia seized them, for they heard the immense wealth of that land praised around them; they took Lysimachia by deceit, conquered the entire Chersonese by force of arms, and reached the edge of the Hellespont.... Then the Gauls gathered again and lent contingents to Nicomedes [King of Bithynia], who was at war with Ziboetas, who occupied part of Bithynia.... Leaving Bithynia, the Gauls advanced into Asia.[82]

Terracotta from Egypt depicting an angel with a *thureos* shield (Perdrizet, *Les terres cuites grecques d'Egypte de la collection Fouquet*, 1921, plate XXXVIII)

These Gallic warriors, who will be called Galatians (*koinon galaton*) from 275–250 BCE onwards, may have succeeded in impressing the Hellenistic soldier. This is at least what the Roman consul Cnaeus Manlius Vulso thought when he addressed his troops in 189 BCE, before the Battle of Mount Olympus:

---

81   Polybius, *Histories*, book XI, 3, 11.
82   Titus Livius, *The History of Rome*, XXXVIII, 16.

THE ARMIES OF PTOLEMAIC EGYPT

I am not unaware, soldiers, that among all the peoples of Asia, the Gauls are reputed to be the most warlike. This fierce nation has settled in the midst of the most peaceful peoples after traversing the entire world. Gigantic stature, long red hair, large shields, oversized swords, war songs at the moment of charging the enemy, terrifying shouts, trampling, clinking of weapons and shields clashed together according to a national custom, everything seems combined in them to inspire terror. But let those who are not familiar with these barbaric customs, the Greeks, the Carians, the Phrygians, be frightened by them: the Romans, accustomed to all this noise, see it only as a vain scarecrow.[83]

Terracotta from Egypt depicting a Galatian warrior with a *thureos*. (Perdrizet, *Les terres cuites grecques d'Egypte de la collection Fouquet*, 1921, plate XCIII)

Terracotta from Egypt depicting a Galatian warrior with a *thureos*. (Perdrizet, *Les terres cuites grecques d'Egypte de la collection Fouquet*, 1921, plate XCIII)

---

83 Titus Livius, *The History of Rome*, XXXVIII, 17.

MAIN COMPONENTS OF THE PTOLEMAIC ARMY

Later, not before 250 BCE and likely *c.* 220 BCE under the influence of its Seleucid neighbour, Ptolemaic Egypt seems to have gradually adopted this equipment. Indeed, in that year, in Cappadocia, Mithridates I of Pontus and his Galatian allies inflicted a defeat on Ptolemy.

The armament of the *thureophoros* does not appear in the descriptions of historians, apart from that of Plutarch mentioning a short spear (*dorasi*) rather than a spear (*doru* or *doratos*). But this description, as we have seen, is questionable. We must therefore examine the representations provided by frescoes, stelae, and statuettes.

The Stelae of Hellenistic Soldiers Found in Sidon (Lebanon)

The stelae of Sidon represent, according to Nicolas Sekunda, mercenaries in the service of the Ptolemaic dynasty in the second century BCE.[84] These stelae were found in a necropolis in the Sidonian countryside in 1897. They are now in the collection of the İstanbul Arkeoloji Müzeleri. Five of these stelae depict *thureophoroi*.

According to Launey, Hekataios of Thyateira, a Lydian, is:

> …wearing sturdy military boots laced above the ankle, he wears a tunic (brown) and the large uniform *chlamys* (yellow), falling to the calf. The oval shield (ridge, central umbo in the shape of lightning), held by the left arm, covers him from the shoulder to the middle of the thigh: this is the classic *thureos* of Hellenistic light infantry.… The helmet is that of most soldiers of Sidon: round crown, prominent visor, neck guard, crest, and long floating plume. The offensive armament includes a short sword attached to the left hip, and a long spear.[85]

Nick Sekunda refers to this helmet as a 'Sidon type A' model.[86]

Salmas of Adada is a Pisidian in, 'short tunic; no *chlamys*; military boots; helmet with dome, brims, adorned with a mane; spear, oval shield with a central ridge and umbo; leather or metal cuirass covering the torso and ending over or on a mail shirt covering the abdomen, over the tunic.'[87] This is a *thorakites*, meaning 'armoured soldier' in Greek. Polybius describes them as 'soldier armed in the Roman fashion.'[88]

---

84   M. Sekunda, *The Ptolemaic Army*, p.19.
85   M. Launey, *Recherches sur les armées hellénistiques*, Tome I, p.450.
86   N. Sekunda, *The Ptolemaic Army*, pp.21 & 23.
87   M. Launey, *Recherches sur les armées hellénistiques*, tome I, p.476.
88   Polybius, *Histories*, book XXX, 3, 25.

THE ARMIES OF PTOLEMAIC EGYPT

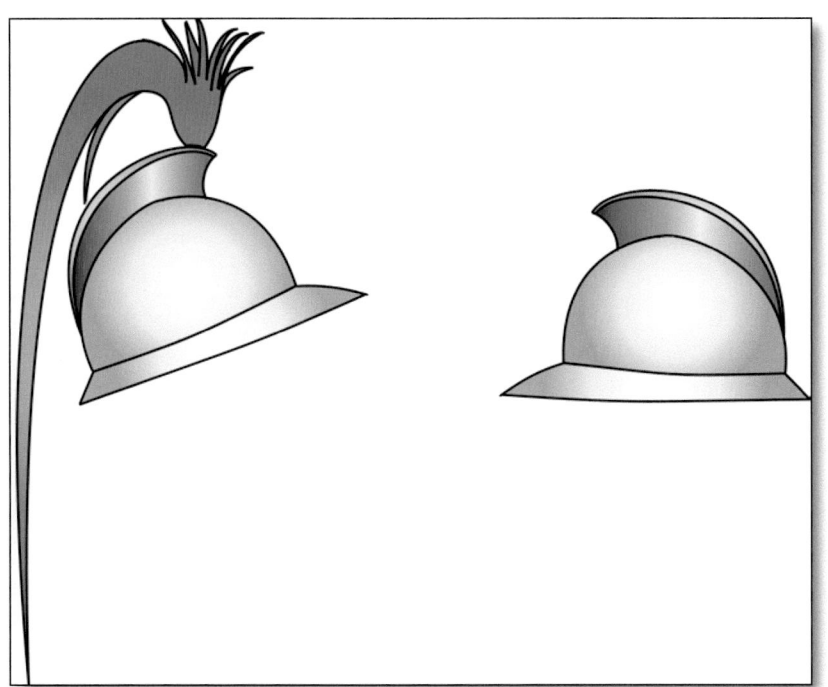

Helmets of the 'Sidon A' type (Artwork by the author)

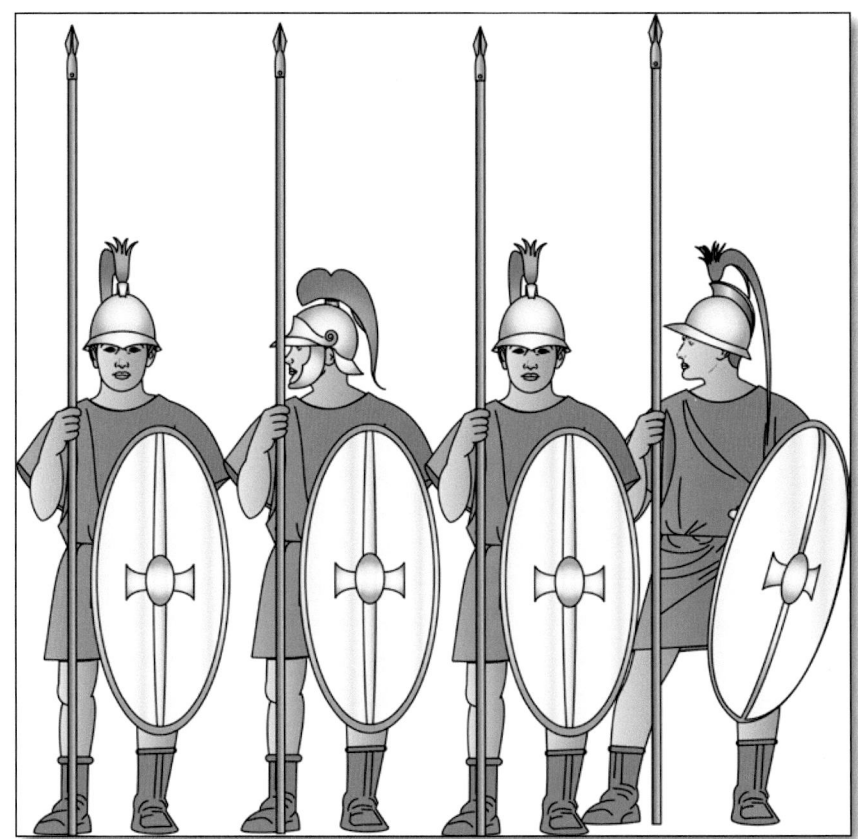

Representations of *thureophoroi* inspired by stelae from Sidon depicting Hekataios, Kartadis and Dioskourides. (Artwork by the author)

MAIN COMPONENTS OF THE PTOLEMAIC ARMY

Dioskourides of Balboura is a Pisidian in, 'short tunic, no *chlamys*, military boots; helmet with a round crown, adorned with a scroll on the side, equipped with a neck guard, a visor, cheek-pieces, a plume; oval shield, with a central ridge and umbo decorated with a dovetail plate; triangular sword, scabbard suspended on the left on a baldric.'[89]

Another stele depicts a Lycian from Rhodiapolis armed with a spear, a white *thureos*, a helmet of the same type as the previous ones, a red chiton, a white or yellow chlamys, and military boots. The stele of a Carian whose name is not identifiable depicts a similar soldier. Kartadis, a Lycian, also carries a white *thureos*, a 'Sidon type A' helmet adorned with a crest, a chiton, and military boots. Other stelae show Cretan, Pisidian, or Thessalian soldiers equipped differently, especially with regard to the shape of the shields.

Unfortunately, there are few other stelae elsewhere, but Marcel Launey mentions the pediment of the stele of the Boeotian Eubôlos, in the collection of the Tanagra Museum, which depicts a Boeotian helmet with a neck guard and a *thureos*-type shield, confirming that the Boeotian soldier was equipped as a *thureophoros* before being transformed into a *peltaphoros*.[90]

Artwork representing *thureophoroi*, based on Sidon's stelae. The man on the left is an officer or a *thorakites*. (Artwork by the author)

---

89 M. Launey, *Recherches sur les armées hellénistiques*, tome I, p.476.
90 M. Launey, *Recherches sur les armées hellénistiques*, tome I, p.160.

Defensive equipment of the *thureophoros* consists of a helmet and their distinctive shield, smaller than the Roman scutum, at approximately 90 to 100cm long by 40 to 50cm wide according to my estimations, whereas the scutum measured around 140cm tall by 75cm wide. The *thorakitai* additionally benefit from the protection of a mail shirt.

The offensive armament consists of a sword and a spear, measuring 1.80 to 2 metres based on their depictions. On the tomb of Dioscurides of Balboura, the sword is clearly distinguished, triangular in shape, and could measure 60 to 65cm.

The Stelae of Galatians Warriors

The Metropolitan Museum of Art in New York possesses three Ptolemaic stelae from the necropolis of Ibramieh, dating from the second half of the third century BCE. The three painted stelae depict Galatian warriors (Bitos, son of Lostoielcos, Isidoros, and ?attos – the first letter is illegible), naked and covered with a blue cloak. These stelae and some other ones from other museums are described in Launey[91] and in a thesis written by Virginie Kraus:[92]

> Bitos, son of Lostoielcos, is dressed in a large blue *chlamys* cloak, beneath which he is naked. He holds a spear and a large white *thureos* shield (extending from his chin to his feet).

> ?attos (the first letter is illegible) is dressed in a large blue *chlamys* cloak, beneath which he is naked. A servant carries his spear and *thureos* shield. The shield is white and blue-green on the edges (possibly representing an iron rim), with bright red crescents at the top and bottom of the shield and a large yellow and black motif in the centre. This may be a Gorgon's head.

> Isidoros is dressed in a large blue *chlamys* cloak beneath which he is naked. He has no weapons.

> Sisono, a Galatian son of Anaximos, is dressed in a white *chlamys* cloak and possibly a tunic. He is armed with a spear and a large shield. It is impossible to reconstruct the colours of the shield and *chlamys*.

---

91 M. Launey, *Recherches sur les armées hellénistiques*, Tome I, p.530.
92 Virginie Kraus, *Recherches sur les productions figurées faites pour les personnes privées vivant en Egypte à l'époque Ptolémaïque* (Metz: Université de Lorraine, 2018), pp.102–103.

MAIN COMPONENTS OF THE PTOLEMAIC ARMY

Stelae number 246 from the Musée de Saint-Germain-en-Laye: Aideratos, son of Aidosotis is dressed in a large *chlamys* cloak beneath which he may be naked. He wears a helmet, a large shield, and a spear. It is impossible to reconstruct the colours of the shield and *chlamys*.

Stelae number 247 from the Musée de Saint-Germain-en-Laye: a Galatian soldier dressed in a large white *chlamys* cloak beneath which he may be naked. He carries a large white shield and a spear.

Stelae number 248 from the Musée de Saint-Germain-en-Laye: Pyrrhos, a Galatian, is dressed in a large *chlamys* cloak. He carries a spear and a large shield. It is impossible to reconstruct the colours of the shield and *chlamys*.

Stelae number 244 from the Musée de Louvre: a naked Galatian soldier with a long spear and a large shield. He likely wore a helmet. Stelae number 252 from the Musée du Louvre: Ketositos, a Galatian soldier and his servant, is dressed in a large red brown *chlamys* cloak and a short white-yellow tunic, black boots (*crepides*) on his feet, and possibly a cuirass. He carries a spear and a large shield.

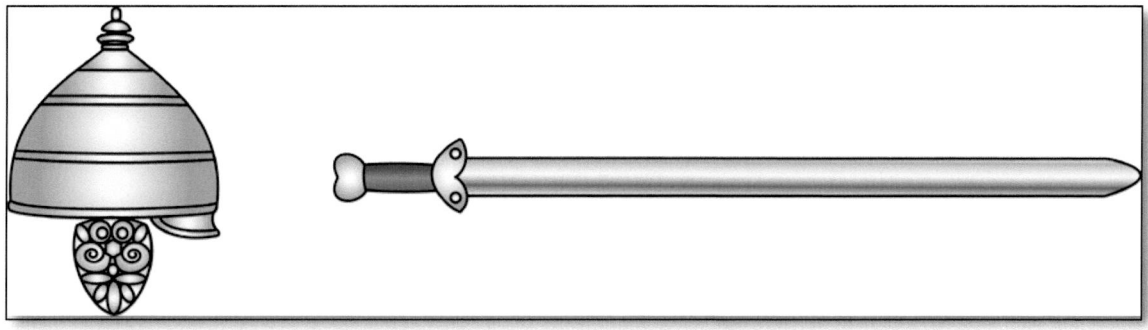

Helmet and sword of the types worn by Galatian warriors. (Artwork by the author)

3

Organisation of the Ptolemaic Army in the Third Century BCE

Under Ptolemy Soter, 23,200 magnificently armed cavalrymen and 57,000 infantrymen marched in a parade in Alexandria.[1] Under Ptolemy Philadelphus, a roll of the Ptolemaic Army included 20,000 cavalrymen, 200,000 infantrymen, 400 Ethiopian elephants and 2,000 war chariots.[2] Appian reports even more impressive figures: 'The Kings of my own country [Egypt] alone had an army consisting of 200,000 foot, 40,000 horse, 300 war elephants, and 2,000 armed chariots, and arms in reserve for 300,000 soldiers more.'[3] This is probably what this sovereign was able to muster in wartime with guards, cleruchs, mercenaries and *machimoi* combined. On the eve of Raphia, just over 50 years later, Ptolemy Philopator managed to bring together 12,700 cleruchs, including 4,000 Gauls and Thracians, 17,000 mercenaries and 25,300 Lybians and Egyptians.[4]

Strategoi were general officers, but the term *strategos* refers to both a rank and a function. *Strategoi* were in charge of external possessions, such as Cyprus and Coele-Syria, as well as elephant hunting grounds. Below them in the military hierarchy were the senior officers, some of whom were eponymous, meaning that they gave their name to their detachment or unit. In principle, these units changed their name after the death of their officer, and a son might succeed him. The highest ranks with an eponymous function in the military hierarchy are *ilarcheis* for the cavalry and *chiliarchoi* for the infantry. There are few eponymous *hipparcheis*, as most *hipparchies* have ethnic names or are numbered.

---

[1] Athenaeus, *Callixenes*, 5, 34.
[2] Giacomo Lumbroso, *Recherches sur l'économie politique de l'Egypte sous les Lagides* (Turin: Bocca Frères, 1870), p.232.
[3] Appian, *Roman History,* Preface, 10.
[4] Polybius, *Histories*, book V, 2, 65.

ORGANISATION OF THE PTOLEMAIC ARMY IN THE THIRD CENTURY BCE

Ptolemaic Cavalry in the Third Century BCE

Hipparcheis and *hêgemônes* are the senior officers in the Ptolemaic hierarchy. The *hiparchês* is at the head of a cavalry unit comparable to a regiment and called a *hipparchia*. This unit is generally numbered or had an ethnic name. Its size is unknown, but it probably numbered around 500 men, or 512 men according to theorists who favour multiples of 8.[5]

Ptolemaic epigraphy provides a wealth of information on the *hipparchies*. Thus, five *hipparchies* numbered one to five are known with certainty in the third century. Up to 10 numbered *hipparchies* appeared in the following century, with all but numbers 6 and 9 attested at least once in second-century BCE papyri. As we have seen, there were also four *hipparchies* with ethnic names: Thessalians, Thracians, Mysians and Persians. These names must have quickly come to represent the weaponry or fighting style rather than the geographical origin of these horsemen, and they are sometimes referred as 'pseudo-ethnic' units.[6]

Coming back to the five numbered *hipparchies* in the third century, we have more than 10 known cavalrymen's names as references for nearly all of these *hipparchies*. At the same time, we have almost 120 names for which the *hipparchia* number is unclear or missing. A few names of cavalrymen belonging to a 7th and 8th *hipparchia* appear in the second century and potentially a 10th *hipparchia* in the first century. This is probably the result of the transformation of ethnic *hipparchies* into numbered *hipparchies* if not a more formal designation of these same units.

We will now look at the empirical data for each of the common *hipparchies*, and a full list of these inscriptions is provided in the appendix.

A study of the 14 inscriptions that can be used, spanning the period from 246 to 173 BCE, shows that the recruitment area of the 1st *hipparchia* is the Arsinoïte *nome*. It was not until 174 BCE that the name of a sub-unit commander, probably an *ilarchês*, appeared: Dositheos. In 173, we have a second name for another probable *ilarchia*, Diodôros. And a third one at

Hellenistic cavalry helmet. This type of helmet is commonly depicted on Hellenistic gems and would be typical of the third and second centuries BCE. A very stylised version is depicted on a coin from Ptolemy VI Philometor, in the collection of the British Museum. This one is based on a relief from the temple of the Goddess Athena Polias Nikephoros in Pergamon. (Artwork by the author)

---

5 Asclepiodotus, *Tactica*, VII, 4; Arrian, *Ars Tactica*, 18,3.
6 For example: Nick Sekunda, *Seleucid and Ptolemaic Reformed Armies 168–145 BC, volume 1: The Seleucid Army* (Dewsbury: Montvert Publications, 1994), p.21.

the same time but without a precise date, Kritônos. Among the riders of the first *hipparchia*, we can cite this example, from 218 BCE:[7]

'βασιλεῖ Πτολεμαίωι χαίρειν Πίστος Λεοντομένους, Πέρσης τῆς ἐπιγονῆς. ἀδικοῦμαι ὑπὸ Ἀριστοκράτου, Θραικὸς, (ἑκατονταρούρου) τῆς α ἱπ(παρχίας), τῶν κατοικούντων ἐν Αὐτοδί[κηι.]', meaning 'King Ptolemy rejoices that Pistos Leontomenous, Persian of the epigones, is wronged about Aristokrates, Thracian, owner of 100 *arouraï*, of the first *hipparchia*, of the *katoikoï* from Autodikē'. In this inscription, 'α' designate the number 'one'

There are 20 inscriptions clearly designating the 2nd *hipparchia*, to which we can add three by deduction. These inscriptions cover the period from 268 to 137 BC. The recruitment area of this *hipparchia* is also Arsinoïte. The name of a sub-commander, probably an *ilarchês* appeared in 238–237 and in 222 BCE, Ptolemaios. A second name, Hippokrates, appeared between 226 and 208. A third name, Eteôneôs, appeared between 243 and 220–219. But Eteôneôs, whether he or his father, seems to have been the *hipparchês* of this *hipparchia* from 228 or 222 BCE (*tôn Ptolemaiou tou Eteôneôs*). Another inscription names Lika, in 238, with Hiera Nesos in Arsinoïte as the recruiting area but without the *hipparchia* number. Hiera Nesos was part of the recruitment area of the second *hipparchia* and could therefore have been one of its subcommands – i.e. *ilarchês* – at that time. We also have the name of the *epilarchês* of the unit of Ptolemaios and Pythaggelos within the second *hipparchia*, Polemaïos. This is an example of an inscription quoting a rider from the second *hipparchia* from a Flinders Petrie papyrus, a contract for a loan:[8]

'Απολλώνιος Ηρακεωτης οι τρεις τ(ων) …κρατους της δεμτερας ιππαρχιας', meaning 'Apollônios of Herakleia of Hippokrates' men of the second *hipparchia*.'

There are 12 inscriptions referring to the 3rd *hipparchia*, covering the period from 268 to 145 BCE, with one other possible name. This *hipparchia*'s recruitment area was once again Arsinoïte, at least from 171 BCE onwards. We know part of the name of a *hipparchês* from this unit, ?limnaios, a Cyrenian living in Herakleopolitis, but there is no mention of a date. Here is an example of an inscription quoting a rider from the third *hipparchia* from a Flinders Petrie papyrus, a fragment of the will of Aphrodisios of Heraclea of 225 BCE:[9]

---

7   P. Enteux 48 II 1–2 https://papyri.info/ddbdp/p.enteux;;48

8   John P. Mahaffy, *The Flinders Petrie Papyri with transcriptions, commentaries and index, Part II* (Dublin: Royal Irish Academy, 1893), XLVII, lines 31–32.

9   John P. Mahaffy, *The Flinders Petrie Papyri with Transcriptions, Commentaries and*

'Φιλαδελφειος των Ιπποκρατο(υς της) τριτες ιππαρχιας εκατονταρουρος', meaning '(unreadable name) of Philadelphia, of Hippocrates, of the third *hipparchia*, owner of 100 *arouraï*.'

There are 15 proven inscriptions designating the 4th *hipparchia*, to which we can add a possible 16th and add another six names by cross-referencing the officer's name. This *hipparchia* seems to have been recruited in Memphis in 273 BCE, then in Arsinoïte and Hermopolite between 228 and 139. Lykophronos commanded a unit, probably an *ilarchia*, from 273 BCE, Lysanoros commanded another one around 233–232, Menelaos headed the first one around 228–221 BCE. Here is an example of an inscription quoting a rider from the fourth *hipparchia* from the same Flinders Petrie papyrus (225 BCE):[10]

'Ιασω(ν) Ιασωνος των εκτ.... υρω ιων της τεταρτες ιππαρχιας εκατονταρουρος', meaning 'Iason, son of Iason .... of the fourth *hipparchia*, owner of 100 *arouraï*.'

There are 10 inscriptions, to which five others could be added by analogy, designating the 5th *hipparchia*. These inscriptions cover the period from 290 to 115 BCE. The area of recruitment for this *hipparchia* remains mostly Arsinoïte. The only sub-unit commander name to appear was Andriskos, between 236 and 226 BCE. Ptolemaios of Nauta could have been the *hipparchês* of this unit at the same time (*tôn Andriskou tôn Ptolemaiou tou Nauta*). Here is an example of an inscription quoting a rider from the fifth *hipparchia* from a Flinders Petrie papyrus, a legal dispute about a loan in the third century BCE:[11]

'Σωρωι Κωιωι της ε τIτ ρ Ă', meaning 'Sôsôs Kôiôs of the fifth *hipparchia*, owner of 100 *arouraï*.' In this inscription, 'ε' designate the number 'five', 'τIτ' an '*hipparchia*' and 'ρ Ă', '*hekatontarouros*' meaning 'owner of 100 *arouraï*'.

There is no inscription designating a 6th *hipparchia* in the third century BCE, nor for the 7th or 8th *hipparchies*. However, one name of a cavalryman of a 9th *hipparchia* is recorded, without any officer name.

Other names of sub-commanders appear in the inscriptions, although it is not possible to assign them with certainty to a numbered *hipparchia*.

Index, Part I (Dublin: Royal Irish Academy, 1891), XIX, line 10.

10   Mahaffy J., *The Flinders Petrie Papyri with Transcriptions, Commentaries and Index, Part I*, XIX, lines 2–3.

11   Mahaffy J., *The Flinders Petrie Papyri with Transcriptions, Commentaries and Index, Part II* XXI, (c) line 9.

We can thus identify eight cleruchs and perhaps a ninth belonging to the unit of Zoilos between 259 and 229 BCE, whose recruitment area was Oxyrhynchite and Herakleopolite. Oxyrhynchite seems to become a recruitment area for the 5th *hipparchia* at the beginning of the second century BCE. We have seen that in the third century the recruitment area for this unit was Arsinoïte. It is therefore possible that Zoilos was commander of a unit within the 5th *hipparchia*, in the years 259–229, but this remains a hypothesis. Finally, the unit of Philonos had Tholthis and Takona in Oxyrhynchite as its recruitment area between 222 and 202 BCE. Among the three known horsemen belonging to this Philonos' unit are two *Dekanikes*: Diodoros in 222–221 BCE and Philonades in 203–202 BCE. Because of his area of recruitment, Oxyrhynchite, Philonades could also be a commander of a unit in the 5th *hipparchia*.

Two inscriptions reveal horsemen belonging to the unit of Toubios in 259–25 BCE, two of whom were cleruchs from Birta in Ammanitis. This area of recruitment is new and does not suggest a *hipparchia*'s recruitment area. The 6th *hipparchia*, about which we know nothing, was perhaps recruited in this region, but this remains highly conjectural.

As far as the ethnic *hipparchies* are concerned, they all have their recruitment area in common, once again Arsinoïte. Ten inscriptions identify cavalrymen belonging to the *hipparchia* of the 'Thessalians and other Hellenes', from 222 to 173 BCE. In 220–219 BCE, Herakleitos, seems to be an *ilarchês*. Three inscriptions identify horsemen belonging to the Mysian *hipparchia*, four to the Thracian *hipparchia* and two to the Persian *hipparchia* over the period 220–219, without any *ilarchês*' name being identified. Below are some examples of riders belonging to ethnic *hipparchies*, all taken from the same papyrus dealing with military taxes:

'Πρόταρχος Ιασονος (της) των Μυσων τΙτ ο Ᾰ γης της περι Σαμαρειαν', meaning 'Protarchos son of Iason, of the Mysian *hipparchia*, owner of 70 *arouraï*, of the land of Samaria'.[12] In this inscription, 'τΙτ' means '*hipparchia*' and 'o Ᾰ', 'owner of 70 *arouraï*'.

'Πτολεμαιος Νικ...ρευς της των Θραικων τΙτ ο Ᾰ', meaning 'Ptolemaios, son of Nikanor (?), of the Thracian *hipparchia*, owner of 70 *arouraï*'.[13]

'Ἡρακλεωτου της των Θεσσαλος τΙτ ο Ᾰ', meaning 'Herakleôs of the Thessalian *hipparchia*, owner of 70 *arouraï*'.[14]

---

12 Mahaffy & Smyly, *On the Flinders Petrie Papyri*, CXII (e) lines 4–5, p.284.
13 Mahaffy & Smyly, *On the Flinders Petrie Papyri*, CXII (e) lines 13–14, p.285.
14 Mahaffy & Smyly, *On the Flinders Petrie Papyri*, CXII (f) lines 8–9, p.286.

'(Πτολ)εμαιος Ερμογ(ενους) (της τ)ων Περσων τIτ ο Ă', meaning 'Ptolemaios, son of Ermogenos, of the Persian *hipparchia*, owner of 70 *arouraï*'.[15]

If the number of numbered *hipparchies* was really 10, which is doubtful from empirical evidence, plus the four pseudo-ethnic *hipparchies* and the *aulên* (the guard) were added, the cavalry as a whole was likely grouped into two wings of at least five *hipparchies*. Since Ptolemy Soter could field 23,200 cavalrymen and Philadelphus 20,000, these two rulers could have formed around 20 *hipparchies*, including at least 10 numbered, four pseudo-ethnic and one for the guard. On this assumption, the *hipparchia* would have numbered around 1,000 horsemen at the time.

At the end of the century, at the Battle of Raphia, Ptolemy's cavalry numbered roughly 5,000 men, including 700 guard cavalrymen, around 2,300 from Egypt and Libya and 2,000 Greek cavalry and mercenaries.[16] The 2,300 cavalry from Egypt and Libya therefore probably comprised five numbered *hipparchies* of cleruchs, each with 450 to 500 men, while the 2,000 Greek and mercenary cavalry were probably made up of four pseudo-ethnic *hipparchies*, each with around 500 men. These figures suggest that, by this time, the average number of men in a *hipparchia* had fallen to about 500.

There does not seem to be any organisation, at least a permanent one, above the *hipparchia*. According to Asclepiodotus and Arrian, two *hipparchies* together form an *ephipparchia* of 1024 men and two *ephipparchies* form a *telos* of 2048 men, each corresponding to a wing of the phalanx. The entire cavalry then forms an *epitagma* of 4096 men.[17] If there is no evidence of the existence of *ephipparchia* and *telos* in the epigraphy, the rank of *epitagmatos* appears three times, but rather for the second century BCE.[18] For example, Mnasis who is *epitagmatos* and *phrourarchos* or Drytôn who is *epitagmatos hipparchês*:[19]

'Μνασισ Αργειος των διαδοχων και ιππαρχης επ ανδρων και των του επιταγματος και φρουραρχος Φιλων', meaning 'Mnasis of Argos, *diadochos* and *hipparchês* of men and in the *epitagmatos* and *phrourarchos* Philôn's unit'.[20]

---

15   Mahaffy & Smyly, *On the Flinders Petrie Papyri*, CXII (e) lines 22–23, p.285.
16   Polybius, *Histories*, book V, 2I, 65.
17   Asclepiodotus, *Tactica*, VII, 11.
18   Van't Dack, *Ptolemaica Selecta*, p.52.
19   Van't Dack, *Ptolemaica Selecta*, p.52.
20   Peremans & Van 't Dack, *Prosopographia Ptolemaica*, p.36 (2062).

'Δρυτων, Κρης,... των διαδοχων και (των) του επιταγματος ιππαρχων επ ανδρων (other possibility: ιππαρχης)', meaning 'Drytôn, Cretan..., *diadochos* and *epitagmatos* of men of the *hipparchia*'.[21]

Additionally, there is some evidence of *hipparcheis* answering to eponymous senior officers. Examples include the *hipparchês* Tryphôn, who was part of the command of Antandros in 282–281 BCE,[22] and Philotas, a *hipparchês* who was part of the command of Andronikos in 239 BCE.[23] These eponymous officers probably commanded one of the intermediate formations between the *hipparchia* and the *epitagma*, if not an *epitagma*.

The *hipparchia* was divided into several *ilai* or *eilai*, a term that also referred to Alexander's squadrons. In his time, the *hipparchia* seems to count two to four *ilai* of 200 horses, with the *ilê* itself counting four *tetrarchies* of possibly 50 horsemen.[24] This figure is credible because it allows a wedge of 49 horses to be formed, the training adopted by Philip of Macedonia cavalry.[25] Two centuries later, the tactician Arrian counted eight *ilai* within a *hipparchia*, but the *ilê* is now of 64 men.[26] In Hellenistic Boeotia, an agreement dated after 288 or 287 BCE between horsemen from Orchomena and Chaeronea reveals four *ilarchies* within one *hipparchia*: those of Saukléas, Pouthodôros, Eumeilos and Aristion.[27] The *ilê*'s officer was naturally the *ilarchês*. As far as Ptolemaic epigraphy is concerned, it is possible to identify two sub-unit commanders, probably *ilarcheis*, within the second *hipparchia* between 226 and 222 BCE, Hippokrates and Ptolemaios, probably a third one, Etôneôs, and an *epilarchês*, Pythaggelos. We know a dozen *ilarcheis*' names for the period 250–200 BCE, from the epigraphy (cf. Appendix). Below is an example of an inscription mentioning an *ilarchês*, possibly Etôneôs, from the Flinders Petrie papyri, number XI informing on the will of Ammonios (234 BCE):[28]

'Αμμωνιος Ανδρομα(χου) ...αχειος των ετε(ω)νεως ε... ιλαρχης', meaning 'Ammônios son of Andromachos from (place name), of Etôneôs .... *ilarchês*'.

In addition to *ilarcheis*, the papyri give us the names of *epilarcheis*. For Asclepiodotus, the *epilarchia*, commanded by an *epilarchês*, was an

---

21 Peremans & Van 't Dack, *Prosopographia Ptolemaica*, p.49 (2206).
22 Peremans & Van 't Dack, *Prosopographia Ptolemaica*, pp.52 (2239) and 5 (1836).
23 Peremans & Van 't Dack, *Prosopographia Ptolemaica*, pp.52 (2240) and 6 (1839).
24 Arrian, *Ars Tactica*, 16,11.
25 Arrian, *Ars Tactica*, 16.6; Asclepiodotus, *Tactica*, pp.14 and 19.
26 Arrian, *Ars Tactica*, 18,2.
27 Paul Roesch, Roland Etienne, *Convention militaire entre les cavaliers d'Orchomène et ceux de Chéronée* (1978), Bulletin de Correspondance Hellénique, 102-1, pp.359–374, p.360.
28 Mahaffy & Smyly, *On the Flinders Petrie Papyri*, XI line 15, p.21.

intermediate formation between the *ilê* and the *hipparchia*.²⁹ The *epilarchia* would have brought together two *ilai* for a total of 128 men. However, Jean Lesquier believes that it was more likely to be a lieutenant to the *ilarchês*.³⁰ We know six *epilarcheis*' names, all from between 243 and 222 BCE: Ammônios, Ergodatês, Herakleidês, Kephalôn, Polemaïos and Theodoros.³¹ This is the inscription referring to Polemaïos:³²

'βασιλεῖ Π[το]λεμαίωι χαίρειν Πολεμαῖος, Μακεδών, τῶν Πυθαγγέλου καὶ Πτολεμαίου τοῦ υἱοῦ αὐτ[ο]ῦ ἐπιλάρχης, κληροῦχος' meaning 'King Ptolemy greets Polemaïos, Macedonian, of Pythaggelos and son of Ptolemaios, *epilarchês* and cleruch'.

Under Alexander of Macedon and probably under the first two Ptolemies, the *ilê* was made up of four *tetrarchies* of about 50 cavalrymen. According to Plutarch, Philostephanos of Cyrene, a historian who lived in the middle of the third century, attributes to Lycurgus of Lacedemonia the initiative to divide the horsemen into *oulamos* of 50 men formed into a square.³³ Subsequently, the *tetrarchia* seemed to disappear: the *ilê* was divided into several *lochoi* commanded by *lochagoi*. However, this process had already been initiated under Alexander of Macedon: according to Arrian, he divided each *ilê* in two *lochoï* in 331 BCE.³⁴ This year, the *lochos* became an intermediate formation between the *ilë* and the *tetrarchia*. The rank of *epilochagos* appears in two inscriptions from the middle of the third century. Here is one of them from 225–224 BCE:³⁵

'Πολεμων Δοκρος των Πυθαγγελου επιλοχαλος' meaning 'Polemôn of Dokros, *epilochagos* of Pythaggelos'.

The *epilochagos* was possibly a lieutenant, an 'assistant', for the *epilarchês* as suggested by Lesquier.

Finally, there was one last rank below the *lochos*: the *dekanikos*. The *lochos* was probably divided into two *dekanies*, a unit reminiscent of Xenophon's *dekas*. The *dekas* could then have had 6 or 8 men. There are

---

29 Asclepiodotus, *Tactica*, VII, 11.
30 J. Lesquier, *Les institutions militaires de l'Egypte sous les Lagides*, p.91.
31 Peremans & Van 't Dack, *Prosopographia Ptolemaica*, pp.53–54; Launey, *Recherches sur les armées hellénistiques*, Tome II, see Appendix for page references.
32 Peremans & Van 't Dack, *Prosopographia Ptolemaica*, p.54 (2264); P. Enteux. 55; https://papyri.info/ddbdp/p.enteux;p.55.
33 Plutarch, *The Parallel Lives, Life of Lycurgus*, L.
34 Arrian, *Anabasis of Alexander*, 3, 16, 11.
35 Peremans & Van 't Dack, *Prosopographia Ptolemaica*, p.55 (2271);

around 16 inscriptions referring to the *dekanikos* in Ptolemaic epigraphy, for example:[36]

'Πτολεμαιος Δ .... των Φιλωνος δεκανικός', meaning 'Ptolemaios .... of Philonos men, *dekanikos*'.

The Hibeh papyrus from 238–237 BCE, an official correspondence concerning cleruchs, states that a number of cleruch cavalrymen have died so their cleruchy can be taken back. This papyrus refers to one *lochagos*, Damônos, and three *dekanikoi*, Leagros, Philonos and Lika out of two *lochagoi* and five *dekanikoi*.[37]

To conclude this subject, it is worth mentioning an interesting, but enigmatic, papyrus: document no. 54 of the Flinders Petrie papyrii, entitled 'Cavalry Horses'.[38] This papyrus, probably dating between 252 and 248 BCE regulates the maintenance of cavalry horses. The last fragment lists names preceded by signs that might indicate a command rank.

Two names, Dêmeas and Antipatros, are preceded by the sign ✝. In the Coptic alphabet, this sign represents a t. The Coptic alphabet was not created until the end of the first century CE but is derived from Greek. It may therefore be a distortion of the Greek letter *tau*.

One name, Euklês, is preceded by the sign î (with a much larger arrowhead).

One name, Apollônios, is preceded by the letters **Δε** underscore with two dots (..).

One name, Diodôros, is preceded by the sign *.

One name, Arnakos, preceded by a **Y** with an ° on top followed by the sign ⁻**ε**.

One name, Drakôn, is preceded by a **Y** with an ° on top followed by a small **ε** on a top of a **Π** and with a dot (.) below the **Π**.

Five names, (Hera)kleidês, Persên, Andrôn, Diôn and Strâton are preceded by the sign **Γέ**.

Four names, Thormiôn, ... todamos and Prôtômachos are preceded by the **Y** with an ° on top followed by a **Γέ**.

At least three names of the two last categories are missing.

---

36 Peremans & Van 't Dack, *Prosopographia Ptolemaica*, p.56 (2283).
37 Grenfell & Hunt, *The Hibeh Papyri Part I*, p.238, lines 15–16.
38 Mahaffy & Smyly, *On the Flinders Petrie Papyri*, LIV, pp.156–159.

ORGANISATION OF THE PTOLEMAIC ARMY IN THE THIRD CENTURY BCE

```
                    COLUMN II.

τωι ....[
ιπποσκοποις οι δε αιρ.....[
κατ ενιαυτον

     †  Δημεας              Y͂ ε̄  Αρνακος
     Δε  Απολλωνιος          ∧  Ευκλης           5
    (†  Αντιπατρος)         Y͂ π̇  Δρακων
 Y͂  Γε̇  Φορμιων              ✱  Διοδωρο[ς
    Γε̇  [Ηρα]κλειδης        Γε̇ (Περσην)
 Y͂  Γε̇  [...]ͅοδαμος         Γε̇ (Ανδρων)
             ]....           Γε̇  Διων
                         Y͂  Γε̇  Πρωτομαχος    10
                             Γε̇  Στρατων
```

Copy of the papyrus named 'cavalry horses'. From Mahaffy & Smyly, *On the Flinders Petrie Papyri*, LIV, p.158. (Public Domain)

Three names are in a frame: Antipatros (the frame also containing the sign), Persên and Andrôn (the frame not containing the sign).

Mahaffy and Smyly suggest that Dêmeas and Antipatros can be *hipparcheis*, Euklês an *ilarchês* and Diodôros a *chiliarchos*. They additionally suggest that (Hera)kleidês, Persên, Andrôn, Diôn and Strâton are *pentakosiarchoi* and that an *omicron* ('o') over a *gamma* ('g') refers to *ouragos* (file closer).

It seems that the sign before Euklês is an *iota* ('i') thus referring to an *ilarchês*. Consequently, the sign before Dêmeas and Antipatros can refer to *hipparcheis*. Indeed, Dêmeas appeared earlier in the text and is possibly the most senior officer. Accordingly, the sign before Dêmeas and Antipatros can be a *phi*, if we refer to Mahaffy's alphabet table in 'The Flinders Petrie Papyri'.[39] But the fact that there is only one revealed *ilarchês* for two *hipparcheis* in this list is puzzling.

Concerning Diodôros; he is unlikely to be a *chiliarchos* because this rank does not exist in the cavalry. However, the sign ✱ has already been used in a Flinders Petrie papyrus to designate an infantry unit,[40] probably a *chiliarchia*. It is therefore possible that Diodôros is a *chiliarchos* and listed here because he owns a horse as an officer.

Drakôn, because the sign preceding the name represents an epsilon ('e') above a pi ('p'), can be an *epilarchês*. And because the first sign represents an 'o' over a 'g', he would be an *ouragos epilarchês* (an *epilachês* who is also file closer), which make sense in a rhombus formation.

---

[39] John P. Mahaffy, *The Flinders Petrie Papyri with transcriptions, commentaries and index* (Dublin: Royal Irish Academy, 1891), p.65 (columns IV and IX).

[40] Mahaffy & Smyly, *On the Flinders Petrie Papyri*, LIV, p.287 (CXII, h l.2).

The sign preceding the name Arnakos is not clear: it designates an *ouragos* but this sign is followed by another letter and then an *epsilon* ('ε'). One hypothesis is that the long horizontal line before the 'ε' could be an incomplete letter, for example the top bar of a *gamma* or less likely *pi*. Column three of Mahaffy's table of alphabet suggest such a possibility.[41] Not having had access to the original manuscript, I am unable to confirm this hypothesis, but if it were the case, it could be an additional *hêgemôn* (see below). However, if the sign is only the upper bar of the *gamma*, the accent of the 'έ' will still be missing.

Terracotta from Achmounein depicting a cavalryman, possibly a cleruch. (Perdrizet, Les terres cuites grecques d'Egypte de la collection Fouquet, 1921, plate XCI)

Finally, we have at least 8 ranks, probably 11–12 if the missing lines refer to this grade, where the first letter can be a *gamma* ('g') and the second an *epsilon* ('έ'), resulting in 'Gέ' either as file leaders or file closer (i.e. with the *ouragos* sign). However, it is unclear whether the sign represents a Γέ or a Γε with another sign on it. This sign can refer to the *hêgemôn*, which would designate the Aslcepiodotus' rank of *tetrarchos*.[42] A *hêgemôn* could represent all kind of officer who act as intermediary between the *strategos* and the soldiers.[43]

If, according to Asclepiodotus and Arrian, an *hipparchia* is made of four *ilai*, this papyrus potentially lists one *hipparchia* (with two commander's names, the second one being possibly the previous *hipparchês*), two *ilarchies* and four to six *tetrarchies*, each with one *tetrarchos* and one *ouragos*.

To summarise Ptolemaic cavalry organisation, table 1 below compares the theoretical organisation of Hellenistic cavalry according to Alsclepiodotus with the epigraphic data.

---

41 Mahaffy, *The Flinders Petrie Papyri with transcriptions, commentaries and index*, p.65 (column III).
42 Pierre Ducrey, *Nouvelles remarques sur deux traités attalides avec des cités crétoises* (Bulletin de Correspondance Hellénique, 1970), 94-2, p.650.
43 Michel Feyel, *Un nouveau fragment du règlement militaire trouvé à Amphipolis* (Revue Archéologique, 1935), vol. 2, p.48.

ORGANISATION OF THE PTOLEMAIC ARMY IN THE THIRD CENTURY BCE

Table 1: Asclepiodotus's Cavalry Organisation and Empirical Evidence

Asclepiodotus's cavalry organisation (theory)	Epigraphy and other references (empirical evidence)
Epitagma	At least three examples[44]
Telos	No evidence
Ephipparchia	No evidence
Hipparchia	Almost 200 examples
Epilarchia	Seven examples
Ilarchia	Twelve examples
Lochos	At least nine *lochagoi* and *epilochagoi* (Lesquier considers *lochoi* to be part of the cavalry)[45]
Dekania	At least 16 *dekanikoi*

Mercenaries were organised along the same lines. For example, the Eteôneôs cavalry corps, based in Arsinoïte under Ptolemy Euergetes, included among its officers a *hipparchês*, Philotas, an *ilarchês* and two *epilarcheis*.[46]

Cavalry Formations

According to Asclepiodotus and Arrian, there were three cavalry formations: the square (perfect or oblong), the rhombus, and the wedge. The rhombus is a Thessalian formation that allows you to 'make it easier for horses to retreat and convert'.[47] The rhombus looks like a diamond: the *ilarchês* is at the corner of the head. It can be formed in rows or lines. In a third way of forming the rhombus, the two men who follow on both sides of the *ilarchês* must have the heads of their horse level with the rump of the *ilarchês*' horse. The following ranks are multiplied in this way until they reach halfway up the rhombus, from where they gradually diminish to complete the figure of this order.[48] According to Asclepiodotus, the longest rank is placed in the middle with an odd number of riders, for example 11, then, before and after, two ranks with two fewer riders, and so on. In this example, an *ilê* of 61 horses is arranged in 11 rows with one, three, five, seven, nine, eleven, nine, seven, five, three and one riders.[49] The Flinders Petrie papyrus

---

44   Van't Dack, *Ptolemaica Selecta*, p.52.
45   J. Lesquier, *Les institutions militaires de l'Egypte sous les Lagides*, p.91.
46   J. Lesquier, *Les institutions militaires de l'Egypte sous les Lagides*, p.300.
47   Asclepiodotus, *Tactica*, VII, 2.
48   Arrian, *Ars Tactica*, 17.1–17,2.
49   Asclepiodotus, *Tactica*, VII, 6–10.

number 54 discussed above suggests strongly that the rhombus formation was used in the third century: the ranks of *ouragos hêgemôn* and *ouragos epilarchês* seems to designate the last man of the diamond, a specific file closer. Asclepiodotus confirms this by naming the last of the *ilê*'s horseman as an *ouragos*.[50]

A rhombus formation, formed in rows, from Asclepiodotus, *Tactica*, VII, 6 (Artwork by the author)

Third type of rhombus formation, from Asclepiodotus, *Tactica*, VII, 9 (Artwork by the author)

The wedge is said to have been used by the Scythians, followed by the Thracians and then, at Philip's instigation, the Macedonians.[51] 'This formation also seemed to be useful because the leaders were positioned on the perimeter and the front, which ended in a point, made it easy to break up any enemy formation and gave the opportunity to carry out rapid quarter and counter-quarter conversions'.[52] The corner therefore corresponds to half of a rhombus. An *ilê* (or rather a Macedonian *tetrarchia*) of 49 men was thus arranged in seven rows of one, three, five, seven, nine, eleven and thirteen horses. An *ilê* of 64 men would add an eighth row of 15 horses.[53]

Finally, the square is the formation adopted by the Greeks, Persians and Sicilians. 'This formation is easier to arrange than any other, as the men are arranged in line. It makes assaults and retreats simpler and is the

---

50 Asclepiodotus, *Tactica*, VII, 7–8.
51 Arrian, *Ars Tactica*, 16.6.
52 Arrian, *Ars Tactica*, 16,7.
53 Arrian, *Ars Tactica*, 17.1–17.3; Asclepiodotus, *Tactica*, VII, 6–10.

only formation where all the leading men fall en masse on the enemy.'[54] To form a square, *hipparchies* and *ilai* were formed in 5 to 10 ranks. Polybius, referring to the battle of Issos won by Alexander over Darius, states that 'horsemen who are actually going to be engaged in battle cannot be ranged more than eight ranks deep.'[55] Arrian asserts that the correct proportion, in a square formation, is to have half as many horses in depth as in width.[56] For his part, Asclepiodotus explains that the Greeks placed 16 men lengthways and 8 widthways doubling the interval, 'while maintaining the appearance of a square'. He goes on to say that 'others have put three times as many people in the length as in the depth and tripled the interval in the depth so as to reconstitute the shape of a square', adding that this is in his opinion the best solution.[57] A *tetrarchia* or *ilê* of 48–50 men should therefore have 10 men abreast and 5 deep, or 12 men abreast and 4 deep. Asclepiodotus specifies that the Greeks modified the *ilê* in such a way as to place 16 men in front by 8 men in depth, making the *ilé* 128 men.[58]

We know that the square or oblong formation was adopted at least by mercenary Ptolemaic cavalry because of the account of Agatharchides of Cnidus. When Agatharchides describes Ptolemy II Philadelphus' Ethiopian expedition in the first half of the third century BCE, he describes 500 cavalry from Greece, of whom the first to be exposed, 100 men, were equipped with special armour.[59] This account suggests that the *hipparchia*, made up of Greek mercenaries, was in a perfect or oblong square formation, probably comprised 10 *ilai* of 50 men each, arranged 10 abreast and 5 deep. Only the first row of 100 men would have been better protected. This formation is reminiscent of the ancient Spartan *oulamos* mentioned by Philostephanos of Cyrene, 50 men in a square,[60] which the Greeks and Ptolomies would have continued to use until at least the end of the third century BCE.

Consequently, although we have no definitive evidence on the subject, we can assume that the numbered *hipparchies* were possibly made up of well-protected *xystophoroi* fighting in rhombus or wedge. The Thessalian *hipparchia* was probably made up of *doratophoroi* (lancers), fighting in rhombus. The Thracian *hipparchia* was probably made up of medium cavalry, perhaps protected by a *thureos*-type shield, fighting with javelins and swords and probably in a wedge. The Mysian *hipparchia* was probably made up of light horsemen of the Tarentine type, since this name is not found in the Ptolemaic army, occupying the flanks of the army, in square formation harassing the enemy with their javelins. Finally, the Persian *hipparchia*, whose horsemen seem to have a higher social status than the Mysians, were

---

54 Arrian, *Ars Tactica*, 16,10.
55 Polybius, *Histories*, book XII, 10, 18.
56 Arrian, *Ars Tactica*, 16,11.
57 Asclepiodotus, *Tactica*, VII, 4.
58 Asclepiodotus, *Tactica*, VII, 4.
59 S. Micunco, *La géographie dans la Bibliothèque de Photios: Le cas d'Agatharchide*, p.434.
60 Plutarch, *The Parallel Lives, Life of Lycurgus*, L.

probably equipped in a similar way to the Thracians, with round shields, javelins and swords, but fighting in the square or oblong formation attributed to the Persians. There is no indication that this *hipparchia* was equipped with bows. Other potential mercenary *hipparchies* would therefore have been distinguished by the formation adopted and the equipment rather than by the supposed ethnic origin of the riders, but the square would probably dominate.

Ptolemaic Infantry in The Third Century BCE

The organisation of the infantry is also not easy to reconstruct. Several units appear distinctly in the papyri: the *chiliarchia*, the *pentakosiarchia*, the *syntagma*, the *taxis*, the *lochos* and the *dekania*, while others appear later.

The largest Ptolemaic infantry unit was perhaps the phalanx (*phalagx, phalagga* or *phalaggos*), but this term appears in only one papyrus and, a little later in the same document, it is called a *hêgemônia*. Asclepiodotus and Arrian both state that it is not easy to determine the size of a phalanx. For Asclepiodotus, the phalanx was a 16,384-man unit and the *phalangarchia* a 4,096-man unit.[61] Arrian refers to a formation of 16,384 as a *tetraphalangia*, not a phalanx. The *tetraphalangia* breaks down into two *diphalangês* of 8,192 men, itself breaking down into two *phalangarchies* of 4,096 men, commanded by a *phalangarchos*.[62] The phalanx or *tetraphalangia* would therefore be made up of 16 *chiliarchies*. But these are either the visions of theorists or temporary organisations set up to mobilise large numbers of men. Polybius, when describing the composition of the Ptolemaic army at Raphia, tells us only that the phalanx of 25,000 men, even 45,000 men depending on interpretation of Polybius's figures, was commanded by three men, Andromachos of Aspendos, Ptolemaios and Sosibios, the latter at the head of the Egyptian part of the phalanx. Polybius also counts 3,000 Lybians equipped in Macedonian style commanded by Ammonios of Barca, 3,000 men of the *agema* by Eurylochos of Magnesia, the 2,000 peltasts by Socrates of Boeotia and the 8,000 Greek mercenaries by Phoxydas of Melitaia (in Thessaly).[63] Thus, each commander leads 2,000 to 4,000 men, Sosibios and Phoxydas of Melitaia being the exceptions with 20,000 and 8,000 men,

Egyptian terracotta representing what could be a Ptolemaic officer with a *thoraxos* armour (Perdrizet, *Les terres cuites grecques d'Egypte de la collection Fouquet*, 1921, plate XLIX)

---

61 Asclepiodotus, *Tactica*, II, 10.
62 Arrian, *Ars Tactica*, 10,6.
63 Polybius, *Histories*, book V, 2, 65.

respectively. However, Polybius likely did not mention the Egyptian officers who assisted the latter.

The *chiliarchia*, commanded by a *chiliarchos*, 'commander of a thousand', was the most important permanent infantry unit in the Ptolemaic army. Polybius used the term *chiliarchos* to designate the Roman military tribunes, who commanded 10 centuries, or 600 to 1,000 men. The *chiliarchia* certainly had a theoretical strength of 1,024 men, as Asclepiodotus and Arrian testify in their tactical treatises. The *chiliarchies* were perhaps numbered, at least in wartime, as inscriptions reveal a seventh *chiliarchia* in the year of the Battle of Raphia:[64]

'τῶν Εἰκοσιπενταρούρων Ἀρσινοῖτις τῆς ἑβδόμης χιλιαρχίας' meaning '(name) owner of 25 *arouraï*, of Arsinoë, of the seventh *chiliarchia*'.

A Flinders Petrie papyrus also probably refers to the commander of a seventh *chiliarchia*. The inscription reads:[65]

'Πεταλος ⌒ α της ζ *', meaning probably 'Petalos? 7th *chiliarchia*'. The sign '⌒α' is a '⌒' with a little 'α' above and the '*' refers probably to a *chiliarchia*.

Empirically, *chiliarchoi* are attested from 300 to at least 214 BCE, with 14 known names. They are evidence of greater units above the *chiliarchia* because we know them from eponymous names of commanders. Thus, between 300 and 271 BCE, Nikanor, a Macedonian, is *chiliarchos* of Alexandros.[66] Later, in 252–251 BCE, Artemidôros from Ephesus is *chiliarchos* of Philinos.[67] And some years later, in 237–236, Kallimachos is *chiliarchos* of Eurumedontos' unit.[68] There was also at least one *chiliarchia* of the *logchophoroi* (spear carriers) elite unit in the third or second century BCE. Thus, Karadysês, son of Philothêros, is *chiliarchos* of the *logchophoroï* and the second in command of Bithynos.[69] Interestingly, going back to 252–251, Philinos, is at the same time commander of Artemidôros' *chiliarchia*, and of Theophilos' *taxis*.[70] The original inscription, from the 'Papyrus de la societa italiana', reveals the sentence 'of Philinos, Artemidôros Ephesian *chiliarchos*, Theophilos Persês *taxiarchos*, Lysias Mêthymnaios *strategos*; of

---

64 P. Tebt. 1 137; https://papyri.info/apis/berkeley.apis.587
65 Mahaffy & Smyly, *On the Flinders Petrie Papyri*, CXII (h), line 2, p.287.
66 Peremans & Van 't Dack, *Prosopographia Ptolemaica*, p.57 (2295).
67 Peremans & Van 't Dack, *Prosopographia Ptolemaica*, p.57 (2291).
68 Peremans & Van 't Dack, *Prosopographia Ptolemaica*, p.57 (2294).
69 Peremans & Van 't Dack, *Prosopographia Ptolemaica*, p.225 (4336); Launey p.1179.
70 Peremans & Van 't Dack, *Prosopographia Ptolemaica*, pp.56 (2289), 57 (2291) and 29 (2017).

Chrysermos, Artemidôros Selgeus *chiliarchos*.'[71] This intriguing inscription suggests that Philinos has under his command a *chiliarchos*, a *taxiarchos* and a *strategos*.

The *strategos* is a civil rank, a governor. Looking at the rank of *taxiarchos*, it would be surprising that the *taxis* in question will be the sub-unit of the *syntagma*. Mentioning a unit of 128 men alongside a unit of more than 1,000 men and a *strategos* makes little sense. So, I am assuming that this *taxis* is a unit stronger than 1,000 men, maybe the old 1,500-strong *taxis* (Alexander the Great had 9,000 men in six *taxeis* of 1,500). But it would be an exception to give command of a unit between the *chilliarchia* and the above level, which would be the *telos*. In fact, according to Asclepiodotus, the formations superior to the *chiliarchia* would be the *telos* of 2,048 men, the *phalaggarchia* of 4,096 men and the *diphalaggia* or *keras* of 8,192 men. But none of these levels appear in Ptolemaic epigraphy.[72]

The *chiliarchia* is divided into *pentakosiarchies*, commanded by *pentekontarchoi*, 'commanders of five hundred'.[73] The *pentakosiarchia* would therefore theoretically have 512 men or, in practice, around 500 men. These two levels, *chiliarchia* and *pentakosiarchia*, are also attested in Alexander's army and in Arrian's tactical treatise. It thus appears that the Ptolemaic army retained its original organisation, at least until the end of the third century BCE.

There are nine inscriptions referring to *pentakosiarchies* within the Ptolemaic army of the third century BCE. By way of example, Herakleidês is *pentakosiarchos* of Amyntos' unit in 282–281 BCE, Appolôdoros is *pentakosiarchos* of Chrysermos' unit, probably in 231–230[74] and Philôn is *pentakosiarchos* in the agema in 222–221 BCE:[75]

'Φίλων Ἀ[ρκ]ὰ[ς] τοῦ ἀγήματος πεντακοσίαρχος κληροῦχος'
meaning 'Philôn Arkas, cleruch of the *pentakosrachia* of the *agêma*.'

In principle, the *pentakosiarchia* comprised two *syntagmai*, commanded each by a *syntagmarchês*.[76] Through epigraphy, we know of four cases of *syntagmarcheis*, three of whose names clearly stand out: Kleandros in 238–237 BCE, Idaios and Ptolemaios in 236–235 BCE.[77] This is the inscription referring to Antipatros, soldier of Idaios *syntagma*, in a Flinders Petrie papyrus informing on the will of Antipatros of Cyrene, in 235 BCE:[78]

---

71 PSI V 513, https://papyri.info/ddbdp/psi;5;513
72 Asclepiodotus, *Tactica*, II, 10.
73 Asclepiodotus, *Tactica*, II, 10.
74 Peremans & Van 't Dack, *Prosopographia Ptolemaica*, p.58 (2304).
75 Peremans & Van 't Dack, *Prosopographia Ptolemaica*, p.59 (2317); P. Enteux 45: https://papyri.info/ddbdp/p.enteux;;45
76 Asclepiodotus, *Tactica*, II, 8 & 10.
77 J. Lesquier, *Les institutions militaires de l'Egypte sous les Lagides,* p.345.
78 Mahaffy & Smyly, *On the Flinders Petrie Papyri*, XIV, lines 16–17, p.27.

ORGANISATION OF THE PTOLEMAIC ARMY IN THE THIRD CENTURY BCE

'Αντιπατρος κυρηναιος των Ιδαιου συνταγμα κ(λερουχος)', meaning 'Antipatros from Cyrene, of Idaios *syntagma*, cleruch.'

The Flinders Petrie papyrus (XI), narrating the will of Herackleos, a cavalry officer, lists among witnesses a *pentakosiarchos* and a *syntagmarchês* of the *agema*:[79]

Ευμεγεθης Μελιχρως τετανοθριξ μακεδων των Πατρονος συνταγμα του αγηματος κλ(ηρουχος) Μελιχρως κακοπωγων ουλη επ οφρυος αριστεπας Νικα....ος μακεδων ....ειου πεντακοσιαρχος κληρουχος ως Lλ', meaning 'The tall Melichros with long straight hair, Macedonian, cleruch of Patronos *syntagma* of the *agêma*, Melichros with a thin beard and a scar on the left Nika....os Macedonian ....eios *pentakosiarchos* cleruch for the amount of (amount of money)'.

However, the vaguer title of *hêgemôn* is commonly found on Ptolemaic inscriptions. The *syntagma* nevertheless seems to have been the basic unit of the Ptolemaic infantry in the third century. According to Asclepiodotus and Arrian, it comprised 256 men in 16 ranks.

The *syntagma*, if it existed, probably included two *taxis*, commanded by a *taxiarchos*. *Taxiarchoi* appear in some Ptolemaic papyri from this period and Polybius mentions *taxiarchoi* in 202 BC: 'Tlepolemos wanted to win over the general officers, the *taxiarchoi* and the men under

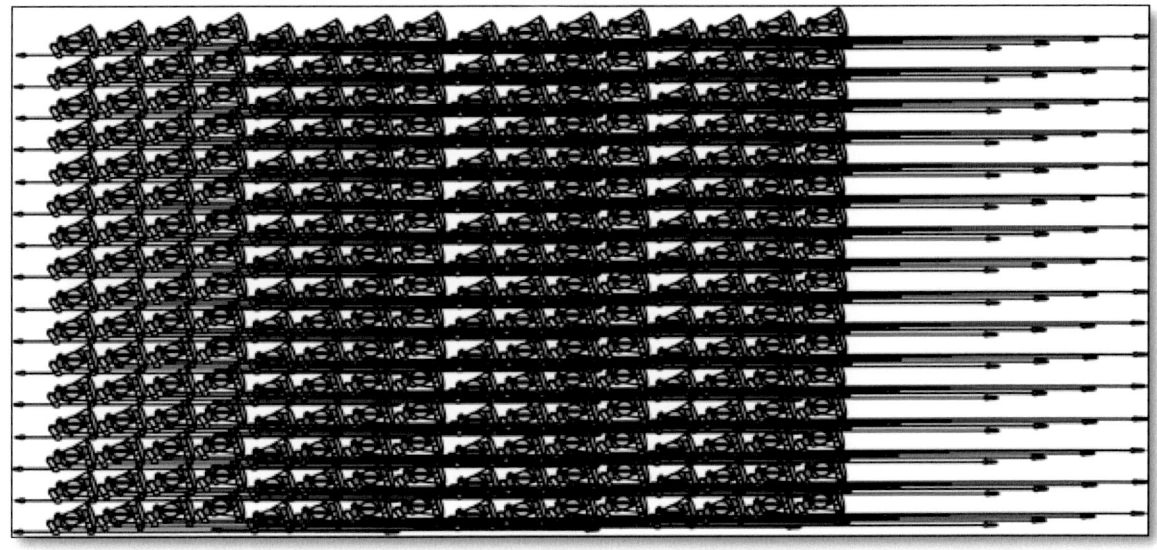

A 16-rank *syntagma*
(Artwork by the author)

---

79   J. Mahaffy, *The Flinders Petrie Papyri with Transcriptions, Commentaries and Index* Part I, XI, p.33

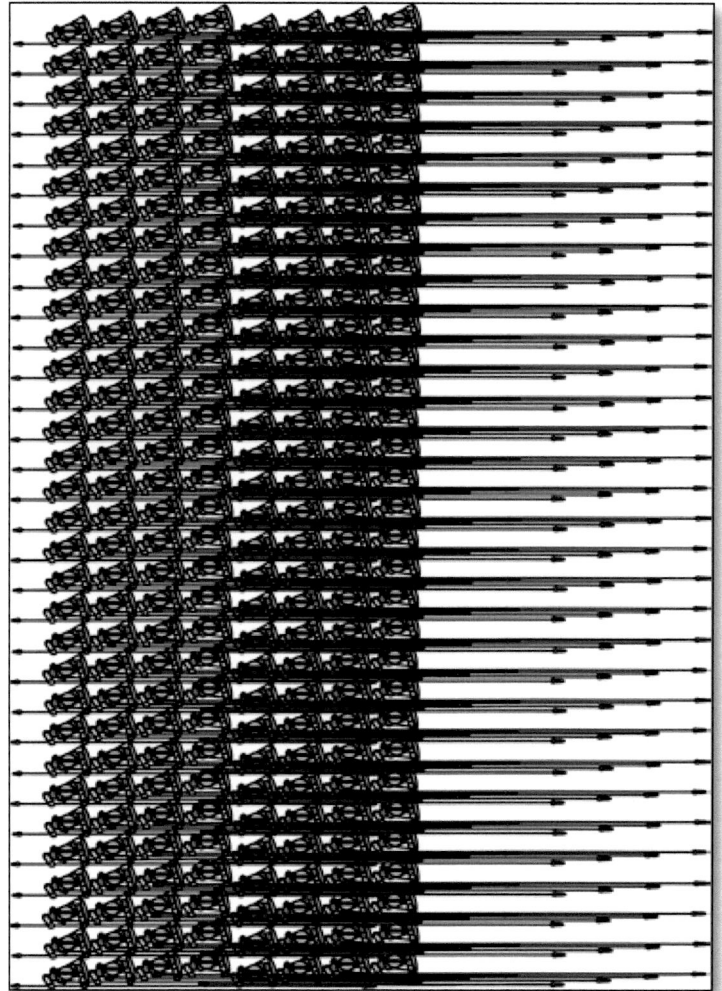

A 8-rank *syntagma*
(Artwork by the author)

their command.'[80] According to Asclepiodotus and Arrian, the *taxis* theoretically numbered 128 men.[81] Later, when Asclepiodotus wrote his treatise, the *taxis* was known as the *hekatontarchia*.[82] They are only two known inscriptions referring to *taxiarchoi* in the Ptolemaic epigraphy: one dating from 237 BCE, where Hnioxos is a *taxiarchos* in Anthippos' unit,[83] and another one dating from 252–251 that has already been mentioned. In this inscription, Theophilos is a Persian *taxiarchos*.[84] However, there is some doubt about the latter type of *taxis* (see my argument above). Consequently, the evidence is weak for the use of *taxis* as *syntagma* sub-unit in the Ptolemaic army.

Two other grades appear in numbers of third century BCE Hibeh and Petrie papyri: *lochagos* and *epilochagos*. For instance, a *lochagos* appears after a *pentakosiarchos* and a *chiliarchos* in a papyrus from 238 or 237.[85] At the beginning of Alexander's reign, the *lochos*, commanded by a *lochagos*, represented a unit of 512 men, but at the end of his reign, the *lochagos* took the name of *pentakosiarchos*. Two or three *lochoi* then formed a *taxis*. Following this logic, the *lochos* would always form part of the *taxis*, logically half of this unit. A *lochos* would command a unit of 64 men. He would then be assisted by the *epilochagos*, unless the latter commands half the unit.

It should be noted here that the Antigonid Macedonian army of Philip V, at the end of this century (according to a regulation probably dating between 218 and 197 BCE), was organised into *chiliarchies* comprising four

---

80 Polybius, *Histories*, book XV, III, 25a.
81 Arrian, *Ars Tactica*, 10,2.
82 Asclepiodotus, *Tactica*, II, 8.
83 Peremans & Van 't Dack, *Prosopographia Ptolemaica*, p.56 (2288).
84 Peremans & Van 't Dack, *Prosopographia Ptolemaica*, pp.56 (2289) and 29 (2017).
85 J. Lesquier, *Les institutions militaires de l'Egypte sous les Lagides*, pp.343–344; Mahaffy & Smyly, *On the Flinders Petrie Papyri*, XIII, (3), lines 2, 10 and 12, p.40.

speirai (equivalent to the *syntagmai*), the *speira* comprising four *tetrarchies* and each *tetrarchia* comprising four *lochoï* of 16 men.[86] We will see later that the *speira* will appear only around 50 BCE in Ptolemaic Egypt.

Finally, in a Hibeh Papyri from 300–271 BCE mentioning a *chiliarchos* named Alexandros, we find one last officer: the *dekanikos*.[87] The *dekanikos*, commander of tens, would therefore be at the head of the smallest unit, the *dekania*. Under Alexander, and therefore probably under the first two Ptolemies, this unit was called *dekas* and was commanded by a *dekadarchos*. It was a rank of 16 men, the probable evolution of an earlier rank of 10 men (hence the reference to the number 10). The rank of *dekanikos* last appears in papyrus around 165 BCE. Asclepiodotus, who wrote after this date, and Arrian used the term *dilochia* commanded by a *dilochitês*[88] to refer to the grouping of two files of 16 soldiers. At this time, the Ptolemaic phalanx probably fought in 16 ranks in compact order, with each file of 16 men commanded by the *dekanikos*. However, this officer most often appeared as the leader of a cavalry unit or in indeterminate cases. The same applies to the rank of *lochagos*, which appears several times in the inscriptions.[89]

At the bottom of the hierarchy is the *dimoirîtês*, which means double pay. Like the *dekanikos*, the *dimoirîtês* originated in Alexander's army, where the *dekadarchos* was the head of the rank and the *dimoirîtês* the head of the half-rank. In the Ptolemaic Army, he would therefore be at the head of the half-rank of eight men, adopted for fighting in close order. There are a few examples of *dimoirîtês* in Ptolemaic epigraphy.[90]

Asclepiodotus says that previously there were five non-ranking staff (*ektaktoi*) in the *taxis*: the *stratokêrux* who is the herald to transmit orders orally, a *sêmeiophoros* who is an ensign to transmit orders visually in the event of noise, the *salpigktês* using a trumpet to transmit orders in poor visibility, the *hypêretês* who is a quartermaster or 'attendant' responsible for distributing pay, rations and allowances,[91] and the *ouragos* meaning the file closer.[92] However, if an *hypêretês* is recorded in two papyri from this

---

86 Militiade B. Hatzopoulos, *L'organisation de l'armée macédoniennes sous les Antigonides: Problèmes anciens et documents nouveaux* (Athènes: Centre de recherche de l'antiquité grecque et romaine, Fondation Nationale de la Recherche Scientifique, 2001), 30, pp.76–77.
87 J. Lesquier, *Les institutions militaires de l'Egypte sous les Lagides*, p.347; Bernard P. Grenfell & Arthur S. Hunt, *The Hibeh Papyri Part I* (London, 1906), document n°30, p.165. See also See Launey, *Recherches sur les armées hellénistiques*, Tome II, pp.1254, 1257 & 1266 for other examples.
88 Arrian, *Ars Tactica*, 10,1.
89 See Launey, *Recherches sur les armées hellénistiques*, Tome II, p.1258 for an example.
90 See Launey, *Recherches sur les armées hellénistiques*, Tome II, p.1224 last line for an example.
91 J. Lesquier, *Les institutions militaires de l'Egypte sous les Lagides*, p.101.
92 Asclepiodotus, *Tactica*, II, 9.

period,[93] and a *kêrux* in 265 BCE,[94] *sêmeiophoros* appear only in papyri dating from the second and first centuries BCE. This suggests that the ensign did not appear as a means of visually transmitting orders until the second century BCE. The evolution of Ptolemaic army organisation suggests that this non-ranking staff was now included at the *syntagma* level (see below).

Table 2 compares the theoretical organisation of Hellenistic infantry according to Alsclepiodotus with the epigraphic data.

Table 2: Asclepiodotus's Infantry Organisation and Empirical Evidence

Asclepiodotus's infantry organisation (theory)	Epigraphy and other references (empirical evidence)
Phalagx (16,384 men)	One example
Diphalaggia or *Keras* (8,192 men)	No evidence
Phalaggarchia (4,096 men)	No evidence
Telos (2,048 men), later *merarchia*	No evidence
Chiliarchia (1,024 men)	Almost 40 examples
Pentakosiarchia (512 men)	19 examples including 10 doubtful
Syntagma (256 men)	Four examples
Taxis (128 men),	Two examples including one doubtful
Hekatontarchia	No evidence before 200 BCE
Tetrarchia (64 men)	No evidence
Dilochia (32 men)	No evidence
Lochos (16 men)	At least nine *lochagoi* and *epilochagoi* but Lesquier & Van 't Dack rank them in cavalry[95]
Dekania (10 men?)	One example of *dekanikos* (see also Table 1)

As with the cavalry, the mercenary infantry was probably organised in the same way as the regular infantry. However, this was not the case for the indigenous troops: a papyrus reveals *machimoi* grouped into several *laarchies*, each commanded by a *laarchês* and identified by eponymous names. At least seven names of *laarchies* are known but only two can be

---

93 See Mahaffy & Smyly, *On the Flinders Petrie Papyri*, CXII, (a) column 1, lines 25 & 34 and Grenfell & Hunt, *The Hibeh Papyri Part I*, p.66 (29 line 22), for some examples.
94 Grenfell & Hunt, *The Hibeh Papyri Part I*, p.66 (29 line 21).
95 J. Lesquier, *Les institutions militaires de l'Egypte sous les Lagides*, p.91; Van't Dack, *Ptolemaica Selecta*, p.54.

ORGANISATION OF THE PTOLEMAIC ARMY IN THE THIRD CENTURY BCE

related to the third century BCE, and actually to the last years of the century (205–193 BCE), Tearoôs and …ôtês.⁹⁶ The inscription referring to them reads:⁹⁷

'…ώτης Ὥρου καὶ Τεαρόως ἀδελφός, (?)λάρχαι', meaning '…ôtês Ôros and his brother Tearoôs, *laarchai*'. But there is a doubt on the name of the unit as it can also be *(ἰ)λάρχαι*.

No inscription allows us to reconstruct the organisation of the Ptolemaic light infantry, whether it was made up of mercenaries or *machimoi*. Asclepiodotus and Arrian describe their possible organisation thus: '… the *systremma* of 1,024 men would be made up of two *xenagia* of 512 men. Continuing in this way, the *psilagia* would have 256 men, the *hekatontarchia* 128 men, the *pentekontarchia* 64 men, the *systasis* 32 men and the *lochos* eight men.'⁹⁸ 'At a higher level, two *systremmai* would form an *epixenagia* (2,048 men) which grouped in pairs will form a *stiphos* (4,096 men), which, grouped in pairs will form an *epitagma* (8,192 men). Eight men outside the ranks (*ektatoi*) complete the *epitagma*, four *epixenagoi* and four *systremmatarchai* whose exact role I do not know.'⁹⁹ The light infantry therefore fought in eight ranks and could be positioned 'according to the requirements of the moment, sometimes in front of the phalanx, sometimes behind it and sometimes on its flanks.'¹⁰⁰ The *hekatontarchia* also includes five additional staff: a herald (*stratokêrux*), an ensign (*sêmeiophoros*), a trumpeter (*salpigktês*), an 'attendant'/quartermaster (*hypêretês*) and a file closer (*ouragos*). Arrian gives the same organisation.¹⁰¹ It is worth noting that, as the organisation of the Ptolemaic heavy infantry differed at some points from that proposed by Asclepiodotus, it is certain that the same applied to the light infantry.

The formations above the *chiliarchia*, or even the *pentakosiarchia*, are probably temporary and consequently only implemented in times of crisis; as they were not suited to garrison duties, they would only be set up in times of war. In the year leading up to the Battle of Raphia, the organisation and training of the soldiers changed under the leadership of Agathocles and Sosibios. These two men struggled to rebuild an army that had been

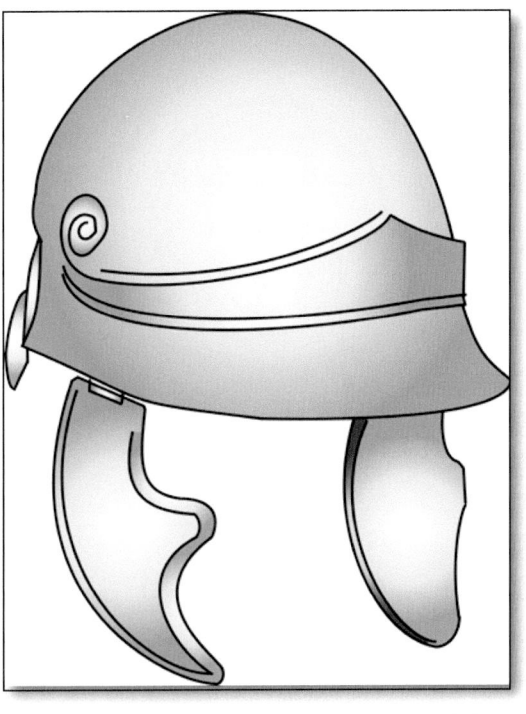

An infantry helmet of the 'Ascalon' type. This bronze helmet, in the collection of the Römisch-Germanisches Museum in Köln, was found in Romania. (Artwork by the author)

---

96 Peremans & Van 't Dack, *Prosopographia Ptolemaica*, pp.32–34, n° 2048 and 2050 for Tearoôs and …. ôtês.
97 OGIS 731; https://epigraphy.packhum.org/text/219143
98 Asclepiodotus, *Tactica*, VI, 3.
99 Asclepiodotus, *Tactica*, VI, 3.
100 Asclepiodotus, *Tactica*, VI, 1.
101 Arrian, *Ars Tactica*, 14.2–14,5.

THE ARMIES OF PTOLEMAIC EGYPT

Terracotta from Achmounein depicting a herald or a trumpeter. He carries a small shield of the *pelte* type, normally carried by light troops. (Perdrizet, *Les terres cuites grecques d'Egypte de la collection Fouquet*, 1921, plate XCIII)

weakened by more than 20 years of peace. After recruiting mercenaries from all over Greece and Crete, who would be grouped together in Alexandria, and organising a levy in Egypt, they had the necessary weapons assembled. The next stage, the most interesting, is described by Polybius:

They began by dividing the men according to age and nationality of origin, then they gave each one the armament that suited him, without considering that with which he had previously served. Then, after disbanding the old formations and abolishing the existing rolls, based on which pay had been paid, they formed new units according to the needs of the moment. They then put the men through training, to accustom them not only to obeying commands, but also to handling their weapons correctly. They also assembled them frequently to review and harangue them. In the course of their work, two men gave them back their weapons. Andromachos of Aspendos (in Pamphylia) and Polycrates of Argos, who had recently arrived from Greece and still retained all the ardour and industry of the Greeks, were of great service to them.[102]

This passage confirms that the old formations were disbanded and that new units were formed 'according to the needs of the moment'. At Raphia, most of the Ptolemaic infantry was integrated into the phalanx. But units of pikemen were useless in peacetime, while light and mixed infantry, such as the *thureophoros*, were well suited to forming garrisons, patrolling borders or ensuring the safety of civilians. The ancient formations mentioned by Polybius were probably mercenary units assigned to garrison duties, and it was therefore necessary to train them, alongside new recruits, in the use of the *sarissa*.

---

102   Polybius, *Histories*, book V, 2, 64.

Elephants

Ptolemy Soter managed to acquire a few Indian elephants from his enemies: in particular, he took 43 from Demetrios after the Battle of Gaza, perhaps adding to those taken from the Regent Perdiccas. But the source of supply, India, was now inaccessible to the Ptolemaic rulers. They then turned towards the country's southern border. According to Agatharchides of Cnidus:

> Ptolemy son of Lagos was the first to establish the hunting of elephants, and even other beasts of the same kind.... Before the Ptolemies, many had used tame elephants in war, such as Porus, King of India, who went to war against Alexander, as did many others.... India produces elephants; the same is true of Ethiopia, which borders Thebes. Libya is also in the same situation.[103]

From the reign of Ptolemy Philadelphus (277–270 BCE), the Ptolemies wanted to secure their recruitment. Having a source of supplies nearby, Meroe, they founded a military station on the shores of the Red Sea, Ptolemais Epitheras, or Ptolemais of the Hunts, commanded by a *strategos* for hunting elephants, the first of whom was Eumedes.[104] Diodorus recounts that Philadelphus, 'who was very fond of hunting elephants, rewarded those who went out to hunt the strongest animals with great gifts. So, having spent a great deal of money on this whim, he assembled a large number of elephants fit for war, and introduced the Greeks to extraordinary animals that had not yet been seen'.[105] Then his son Euergetes personally led an expedition into the heart of Africa with his general Simmias. The Stele of Adulis, which recounts the exploits of Ptolemy Euergetes (246–221 BCE), mentions Ethiopian elephants in his army:

> The Great King Ptolemaios, son of King Ptolemaios and Queen Arsinoē, Gods Adelphoi, children of King Ptolemaios and Queen

Terracotta from Fayoum depicting the God Bes as a herald. He carries a round shield of the type used by *peltaphoroï* or *sarissophoroï*, depending on its size (Perdrizet, *Les terres cuites grecques d'Egypte de la collection Fouquet*, 1921, plate XLI)

---

103 S. Micunco, *La géographie dans la Bibliothèque de Photios: Le cas d'Agatharchide*, p.421.
104 Strabo, *Geographika*, book XVI,3.
105 Diodorus Siculus, *Library of History*, Book III, 36.

Berenike, Saviour Gods, the descendant on the father's side of Herakles, son of Zeus, on the mother's side of Dionysos, son of Zeus, having inherited from his father the kingdom of Egypt and Libya and Syria and Phoenicia and Cyprus and Lycia and Caria and the Cyclades, set out on a campaign into Asia with infantry and cavalry forces and a naval armament and elephants both Troglodyte and Ethiopian, which his father and he himself first captured from these places and, bringing them to Egypt, trained them to military use. But having become master of all the country this side of the Euphrates and of Cilicia and Pamphylia and Ionia and the Hellespont and Thrace, and of all the military forces in these countries and of Indian elephants, and having made the local dynasts in all these regions his vassals, he crossed the river Euphrates, and having brought under him Mesopotamia and Babylonia and Susiana and Persis and Media, and all the rest as far as Bactria, and having sought out whatever sacred things had been carried off by the Persians from Egypt, and having brought them back with the other treasure from these countries, he sent his forces to Egypt through the canals that had been dug.[106]

At the time, the Troglodytic region referred to Eastern Sudan, meaning the territories to the east of the Nile, including ancient Aksum or modern Eritrea. According to Claudius Ptolemy's map, Ethiopia represented Western Sudan, the territories west of the Nile and Meroe. If we are to believe Strabo, the Ptolemies went mainly to hunt elephants in Meroe. But according to Diodorus, there was a place in Libya, near the Nile, 'remarkable for its fertility and where multitudes of elephants, attracted by the richness of the pastures, had made their home. The Libyans and Ethiopians were continually at war for possession of this territory.'[107] It is difficult to locate this Eden today. Pliny reported that, 'Africa produces elephants beyond the deserts of the Syrtes and in Mauritania. There are some in Ethiopia and Troglodytica, but the largest are in India.'[108]

There are two species of elephant in Africa: The African savanna elephant, or *loxodonta Africana Africana*, and the forest elephants, or *loxodonta Africana Cyclotis*, which lives in equatorial Africa. The elephants from Mauritania are of the *loxodonta cyclotis* type, smaller than the other breed, as the region had many forests at the time. These were probably the elephants used by the Carthaginians. As for the others, including those from the Syrtes Desert, it is difficult to know today to which species they belonged.

However, historians agree that, in ancient times, only two breeds of elephant were known: the Indian elephant and the smaller African forest elephant, and consequently, the African savanna elephant appears to be

---

106 OGIS 54.
107 Diodorus Siculus, *Library of History*, Book III, 10.
108 Pliny the Elder, *Natural History*, Book VIII, 11.

ORGANISATION OF THE PTOLEMAIC ARMY IN THE THIRD CENTURY BCE

Terracotta from Egypt depicting an African elephant (Perdrizet, *Les terres cuites grecques d'Egypte de la collection Fouquet*, 1921, plate XCV)

unknown in the ancient Mediterranean world.[109] But recent research into the nuclear and mitochondrial DNA of elephant populations still existing in Eritrea, corresponding to ancient Ethiopia, has shown that these elephants were more likely to be savanna elephants.[110]

Today, African savanna elephants are larger than Indian elephants: up to four metres at the shoulders for the *loxodonta Africana Africana*, three metres for the *loxodonta Africana Cyclotis*, and three and a half metres for the Indian elephant known as *elephas maximus*.

The size, and therefore the origin, of Ptolemy IV Philopator's elephants at the Battle of Raphia is still the subject of much debate. The Ptolemaic Army fielded 73 elephants that day, but only a few of them were willing to fight their Seleucid counterparts. Forty-two were placed in front of the left

---

109 Michael B. Charles, 'Elephant Size in Antiquity: DNA Evidence and the Battle of Raphia', *Historia: Zeitschrift für Alte Geschichte*, 65:1 (2016), pp.53–65.
110 Charles, 'Elephant Size in Antiquity: DNA Evidence and the Battle of Raphia', p.55.

THE ARMIES OF PTOLEMAIC EGYPT

wing and 33 in front of the right wing.[111] Once the two Kings had given the signal for battle, they engaged the elephants first:

> A few only of Ptolemy's elephants ventured to close with those of the enemy, and now the men in the towers on the back of these beasts made a gallant fight of it, striking with their pikes at close quarters and wounding each other, while the elephants themselves fought still better, putting forth their whole strength and meeting forehead to forehead. The way in which these animals fight is as follows: with their tusks firmly interlocked they shove with all their might, each trying to force the other to give ground, until the one who proves the strongest pushes aside the other's trunk. And then, when he has made him turn and has him in the flank, he gores him with his tusks as a bull does with its horns. Most of Ptolemy's elephants, however, declined the combat, as is the habit of African elephants. For unable to stand the sight and smell and the trumpeting of the Indian elephants, and terrified, I suppose, also by their great size and strength, they at once turn tail and take to flight before they get near them.[112]

Terracotta from Egypt depicting an African elephant with a howdah and a mahout. (Perdrizet, *Les terres cuites grecques d'Égypte de la collection Fouquet*, 1921, plate XCV)

This passage from Polybius suggests that only a small number of the Ptolemaic elephants were of sufficient size to challenge the Seleucid elephants. But it also poses two problems for historians. The first concerns the towers referred to at the beginning of the extract, and the fact that the small elephants of the African forests are considered too small to be able to carry them.[113] The second problem concerns the two distinct groups mentioned by Polybius: those who fought and those who fled. As Polybius states that the elephants that ran away were African elephants and that they were smaller than their opponents, we can suppose that

---

111 Polybius, *Histories*, book V, 2, 82.
112 Polybius, *Histories*, book V, 2, 84. Translation: Michael Charles, 'Elephants at Raphia: Reinterpreting Polybius' 5.84–5, *The Classical Quarterly*, 57:1 (2007), p.307.
113 Charles, 'Elephants at Raphia: Reinterpreting Polybius' 5.84–5, p.308.

they were forest elephants, *loxodonta Africana Cyclotis*. The problem is therefore to identify the small group of elephants who remained to fight and who carried a tower. Few historians believe that the Indian elephants captured from Seleucus II in 246[114] were still usable. Even if an elephant can live for over 60 years, this event occurred 26 years earlier. And the possibility that these Indian elephants could have bred on Egyptian soil is unanimously ruled out.[115] Michael Charles therefore proposes two possible scenarios: Ptolemaic elephants were mainly (1) forest elephants with some savanna elephants from ancient Ethiopia (*loxodonta Africana Africana*), only the latter accepting the fight, or (2) only savanna elephants with most of them being too young or poorly trained to match the Indians.[116]

There is still one important factor that does not support either of these scenarios: no ancient author refers to the savanna elephant, as if this race was unknown at the time. Based on this observation, Charles suggests that it is possible that the elephants currently living in Eritrea are a new population that immigrated later.[117] However, there are several factors that could lead us to believe that, in the Hellenistic period, the average size of African elephants was perceived to be smaller, but that certain animals of Ethiopian origin could have reached a size comparable to that of Indian elephants. Firstly, it is possible that in the more arid regions of ancient Ethiopia, most savanna elephants could not have reached standard height. Indeed, Strabo tells us that the cattle and dogs of the Ethiopians were small compared with those found in more temperate zones.[118] Additionally, it is therefore possible that the size of elephants has evolved differently over the ages. For instance, in his *Histoire militaire des éléphants* of 1843, Pier Armandi wrote, 'It has been chiefly observed that the Asian elephant attains a larger size …; the African elephant, on the contrary, is generally smaller.'[119] According to this author, the Asian

Terracotta from Egypt depicting a small African elephant ridden by a soldier (Perdrizet, *Les terres cuites grecques d'Egypte de la collection Fouquet*, 1921, plate XCV)

---

114 OGIS 54, line 16.
115 Charles, 'Elephants at Raphia: Reinterpreting Polybius' 5.84–5, pp.310–311.
116 Charles, 'Elephant Size in Antiquity: DNA Evidence and the Battle of Raphia', p.61.
117 Charles, 'Elephant Size in Antiquity: DNA Evidence and the Battle of Raphia', p.62.
118 Strabo, *Geographika*, book XVII, 2, 1.
119 Pier D. Armandi, *Histoire militaire des éléphants* (Paris: D'Amyot, 1843), p.1.

elephant measures 9 to 10 feet (3 metres) with an average height of 8 to 9 feet (2.40 to 2.70 metres), while its African cousin rarely exceeds 8 feet (2.40 metres), even though travellers make 'mention of elephants of inordinate size'[120] on that Continent. Finally, it is possible that the size selection process was more rigorous among the Seleucids than among the Ptolomies. In fact, Diodorus of Sicily distinguished the two breeds mainly based on their fighting qualities: 'There are [in India] an incredible number of elephants here, far outnumbering those of Libya in courage and strength.'[121]

According to Porphyry of Tyre, Ptolemy Philadelphus had 400 war elephants at his disposal.[122] And Ptolemy IV Philopator seems to have had 500 elephants;[123] at Raphia, he deployed 73 of them.[124] After him, Ptolemy VI Philometor (181–146 BCE) still employed elephants for military purposes, notably in the victory he achieved over Alexander Balas. Agatharchides of Cnidus, who was an adviser to Ptolemy VI, also reports that this ruler 'urged these hunters [of the Ethiopians] to refrain from destroying elephants, wishing to preserve them alive himself: he made them a great many brilliant promises.'[125]

According to Arrian, some elephants bore towers, and their tusks were armed with sharp iron points.[126] This was probably the case with some Ptolemaic elephants, at least with regard to the towers, and statuettes found in Egypt testify to this. Strabo and Aelian mention three fighters in addition to the driver, who was called an Indian at that time. However, several representations show only two fighters in the tower. Pliny speaks of elephants that:

> …when tamed, are used in war; they carry towers full of armed men and largely decide the outcome of wars in the East. They overthrow battalions, they crush soldiers; and yet the slightest cry of a pig frightens them. Wounded and frightened, they always retreat; and then it is for their own party that they are dangerous. African elephants fear those of India and dare not look at them. Indeed, Indian elephants are of a taller stature.[127]

Polybius confirms this when describing the combat of the elephants at Raphia. And Appian, most probably basing himself on the writings of Polybius, reports that, at the Battle of Magnesia between Rome and

---

120 Armandi, *Histoire militaire des éléphants*, p.3.
121 Diodorus Siculus, *Library of History*, Book II, 16.
122 Porphyry of Tyre, *FGrH 260 F42*; Jérôme of Stridon, *Commentary on Daniel XI*, 5.
123 *Third Book of Macchabées*, 5, 1.
124 Polybius, *Histories*, book V, 2, 82.
125 S. Micunco, *La géographie dans la Bibliothèque de Photios: Le cas d'Agatharchide*, p.457.
126 Arrian, *Ars Tactica* 2, 4.
127 Pliny the Elder, *Natural History*, Book VIII, 9.

Antiochus III the Great in 190–189 BCE, Domitius, 'considering that none of the African elephants at his disposal would be of any use to him, given that they were fewer in number and smaller in size, as small ones are afraid of big ones, placed them all in the rear.'[128]

Little is known about the organisation of the elephant corps. Asclepiodotus proposes an organisation of the elephant corps that applied to the Seleucid army: the leader of an elephant is called a *zoarchos*, and that of a pair of beasts, the *therarchia*, is the *therarchos*. Four elephants form an *epitherarchia*, commanded by an *epitherarchos*, and eight elephants are commanded by an *ilarchês*. The *elephantarchês* commands 16 elephants, the *kerarchês* commands 32, and the *phalaggarchês* commands 64.[129] In Egypt, under Ptolemy IV Philopator, the *elephantarchês* was an officer in charge of a depot near Alexandria, which housed 500 elephants.[130] Despite this difference, it is possible that an organisation comparable to that described by Asclepiodotus was adopted by the rulers of Egypt. Additionally, there is no evidence to suggest that the Ptolomies formed specific infantry units, as the Seleucids did, to accompany these animals into battle.

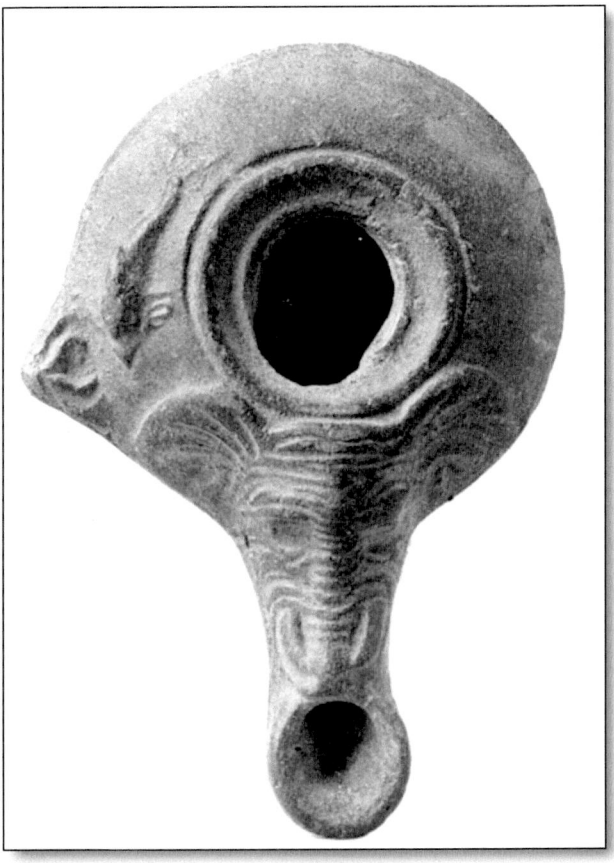

Egyptian terracotta oil lamp depicting an elephant's head (Perdrizet, *Les terres cuites grecques d'Egypte de la collection Fouquet*, 1921, plate XCV)

Recruitment of the Army

The regular army, including the guard, was formed of cleruchs which were summoned when needed in time of war. According to Lesquier, these were soldiers who could be mobilised in times of war.[131] Polybius reports that, before the Battle of Raphia (217), Agathocles and Sosibios were 'entrusted the task of assembling weapons and organising the raising and selection of men' to different officers who 'as competent soldiers, were able to train the troops entrusted to them.'[132]

---

128 Appian, *The Syrian Wars*, 31, 160.
129 Asclepiodotus, *Tactica*, IX.
130 *Third Book of Macchabées*, 5, 1 & 5, 45.
131 J. Lesquier, *Les institutions militaires de l'Egypte sous les Lagides*, pp.32–34.
132 Polybius, *Histories*, book V, 2, 63.

THE ARMIES OF PTOLEMAIC EGYPT

Polybius left us testimonies about the recruitment of mercenaries and the mobilisation of citizens to establish a new army:

(Agathocles and Sosibios) called and gathered in Alexandria the mercenaries they had hired from the cities outside. They also sent officers recruiters outside and gathered the necessary provisions to ensure the subsistence of the troops already available and of the newly enlisted men. (...) They entrusted the task of gathering the armaments and organising the recruitment and selection of men to Echecrates from Thessaly, Phoxidas from Melitaea (in Thessaly), Eurylochus from Magnesia (in Thessaly), Socrates from Boeotia, and Cnopus from Allaria (in Crete).[133]

Terracotta from Egypt depicting a civilian wearing a *pilos* cap and a chiton. (Perdrizet, *Les terres cuites grecques d'Egypte de la collection Fouquet*, 1921, plate XCV)

---

133   Polybius, *Histories*, book V, 2, 64.

Plate 1. Cavalrymen of the Guard, third century BCE
(Artwork by the author)
See Colour Plate Commentaries for further information.

Plate 2. Macedonian cavalrymen of the numbered *hipparchies*, third century BCE
(Artwork by the author)
See Colour Plate Commentaries for further information.

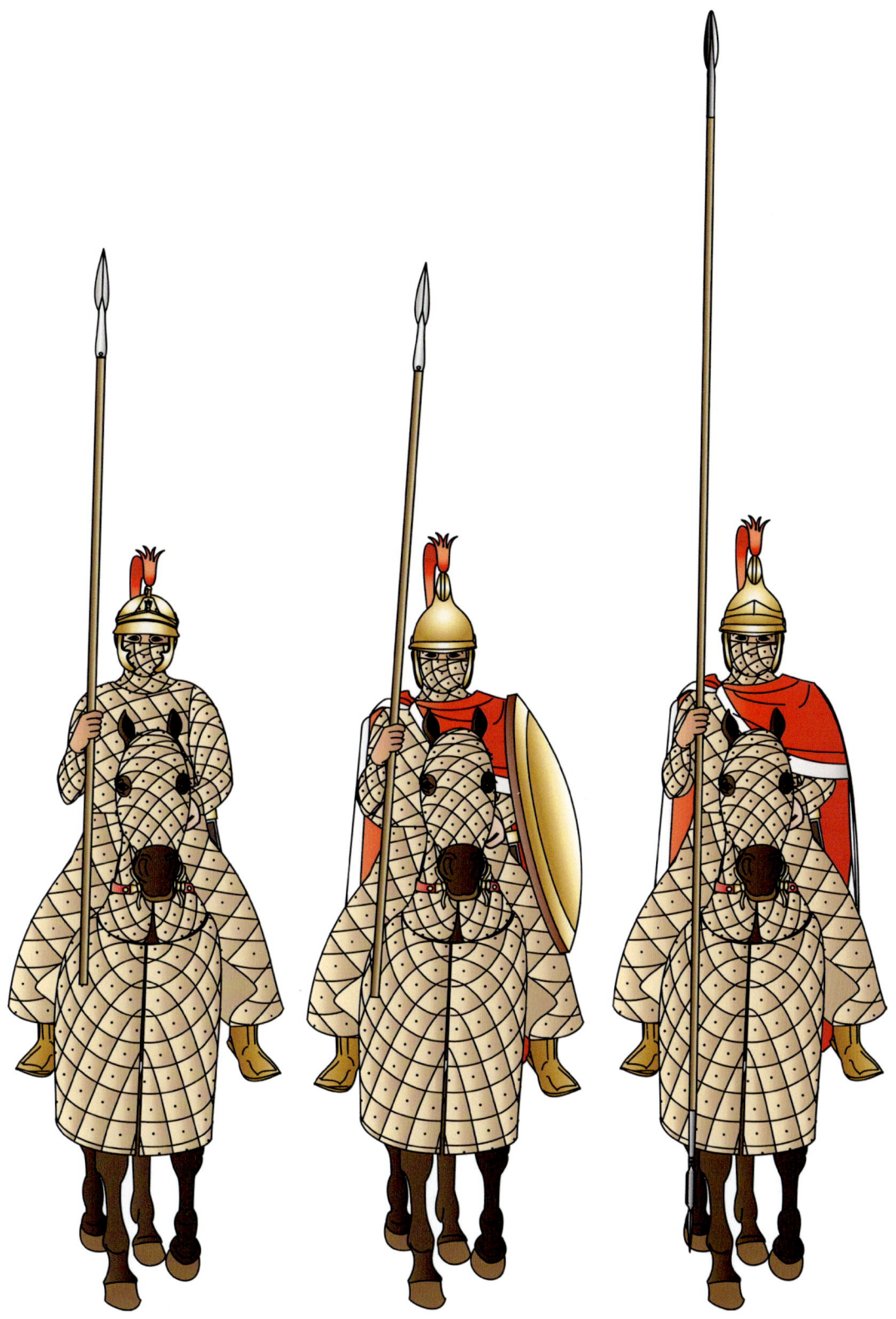

Plate 3. Greek mercenary cavalry, Ethiopian campaign, c. 275 BCE
(Artwork by the author)
See Colour Plate Commentaries for further information.

Plate 4. Cavalrymen of the Thessalian *hipparchy*, third century BCE
(Artwork by the author)
See Colour Plate Commentaries for further information.

Plate 5. Cavalrymen of the Thracian *hipparchy*, third century BCE
(Artwork by the author)
See Colour Plate Commentaries for further information.

Plate 6. Cavalrymen of the Mysian *hipparchy*, third century BCE
(Artwork by the author)
See Colour Plate Commentaries for further information.

Plate 7. Cavalrymen of the Guard, second century BCE
(Artwork by the author)
See Colour Plate Commentaries for further information.

Plate 8. Cavalrymen of the cleruch *hipparchies*, second century BCE
(Artwork by the author)
See Colour Plate Commentaries for further information.

Plate 9. Light cavalrymen, second century BCE
(Artwork by the author)
See Colour Plate Commentaries for further information.

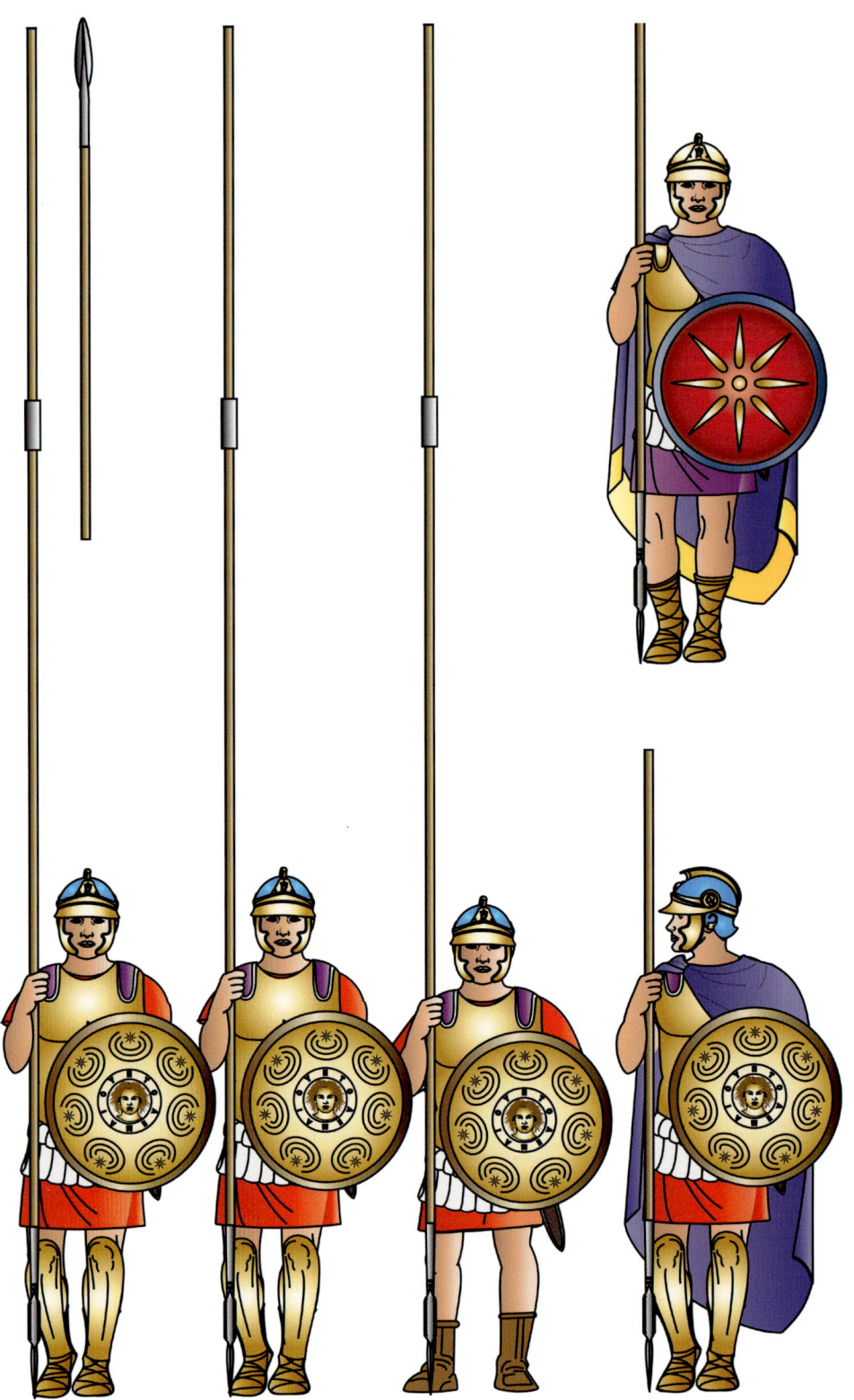

Plate 10. Cleruch pikemen of the Agema, third century BCE
(Artwork by the author)
See Colour Plate Commentaries for further information.

Plate 11. Socrates' Peltasts, end of third century BCE
(Artwork by the author)
See Colour Plate Commentaries for further information.

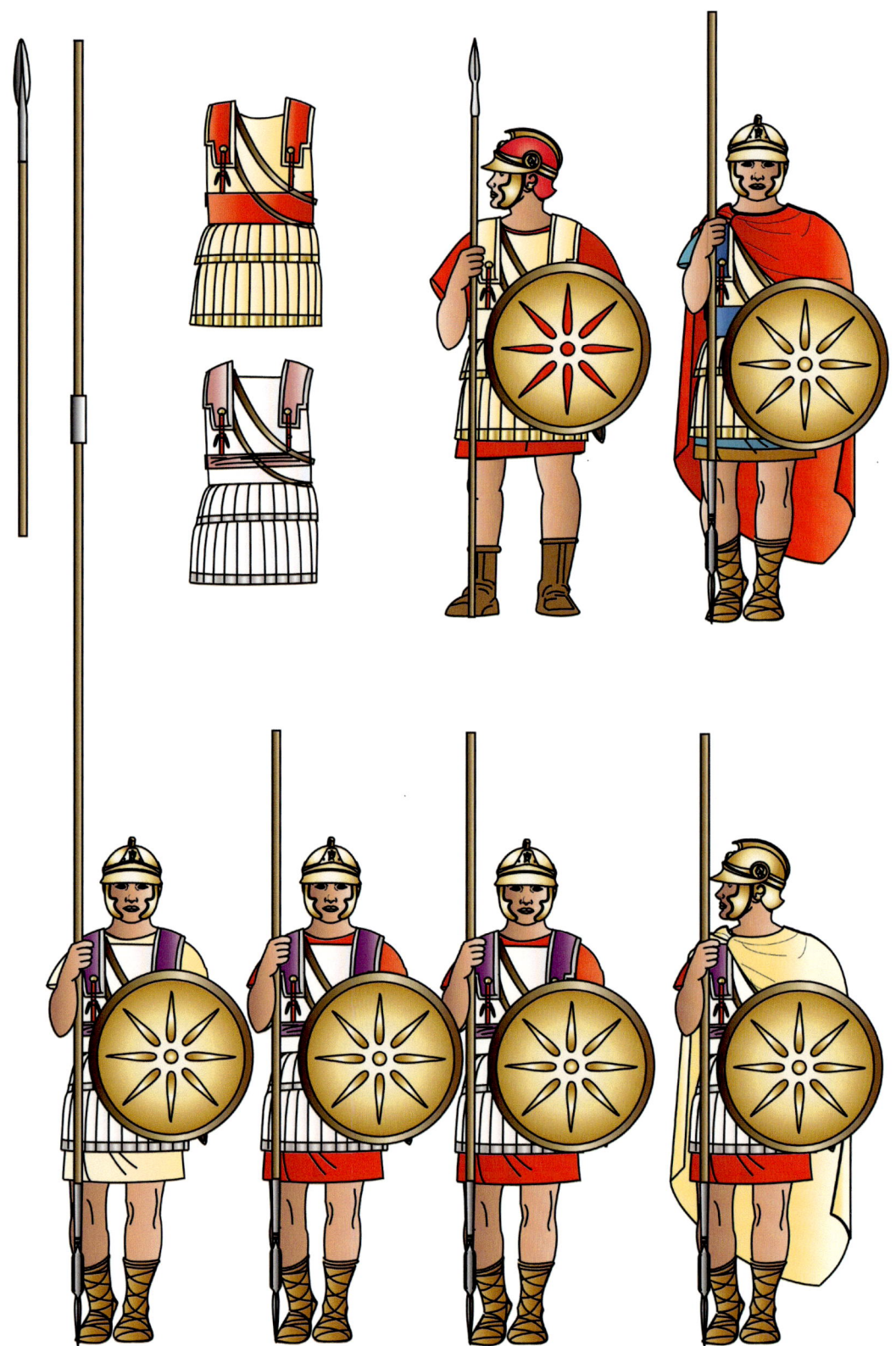

Plate 12. Cleruchs of the phalanx, third century BCE
(Artwork by the author)
See Colour Plate Commentaries for further information.

Plate 13. Cleruchs of the phalanx, third century BCE
(Artwork by the author)
See Colour Plate Commentaries for further information.

Plate 14. Cleruchs of the Agema, second century BCE
(Artwork by the author)
See Colour Plate Commentaries for further information.

Plate 15. Cleruchs of the phalanx, second century BCE
(Artwork by the author)
See Colour Plate Commentaries for further information.

Plate 16. Cleruchs of the phalanx, second century BCE
(Artwork by the author)
See Colour Plate Commentaries for further information.

Plate 17. Cleruchs of the phalanx, second century BCE
(Artwork by the author)
See Colour Plate Commentaries for further information.

Plate 18. Cleruchs of the phalanx, second century BCE
(Artwork by the author)
See Colour Plate Commentaries for further information.

Plate 19. Cleruchs of the phalanx, second century BCE
(Artwork by the author)
See Colour Plate Commentaries for further information.

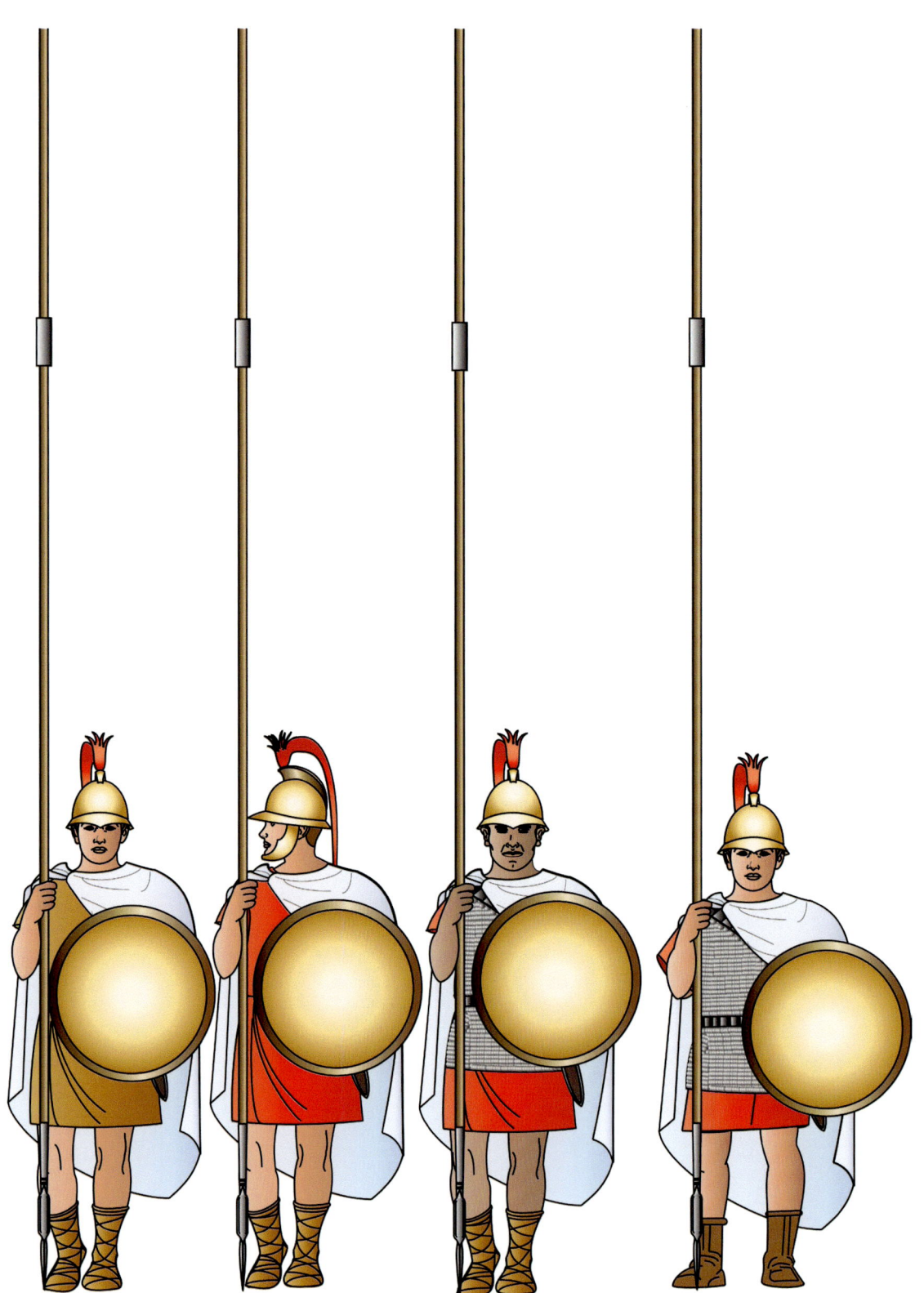

Plate 20. Cleruchs of the phalanx, second century BCE
(Artwork by the author)
See Colour Plate Commentaries for further information.

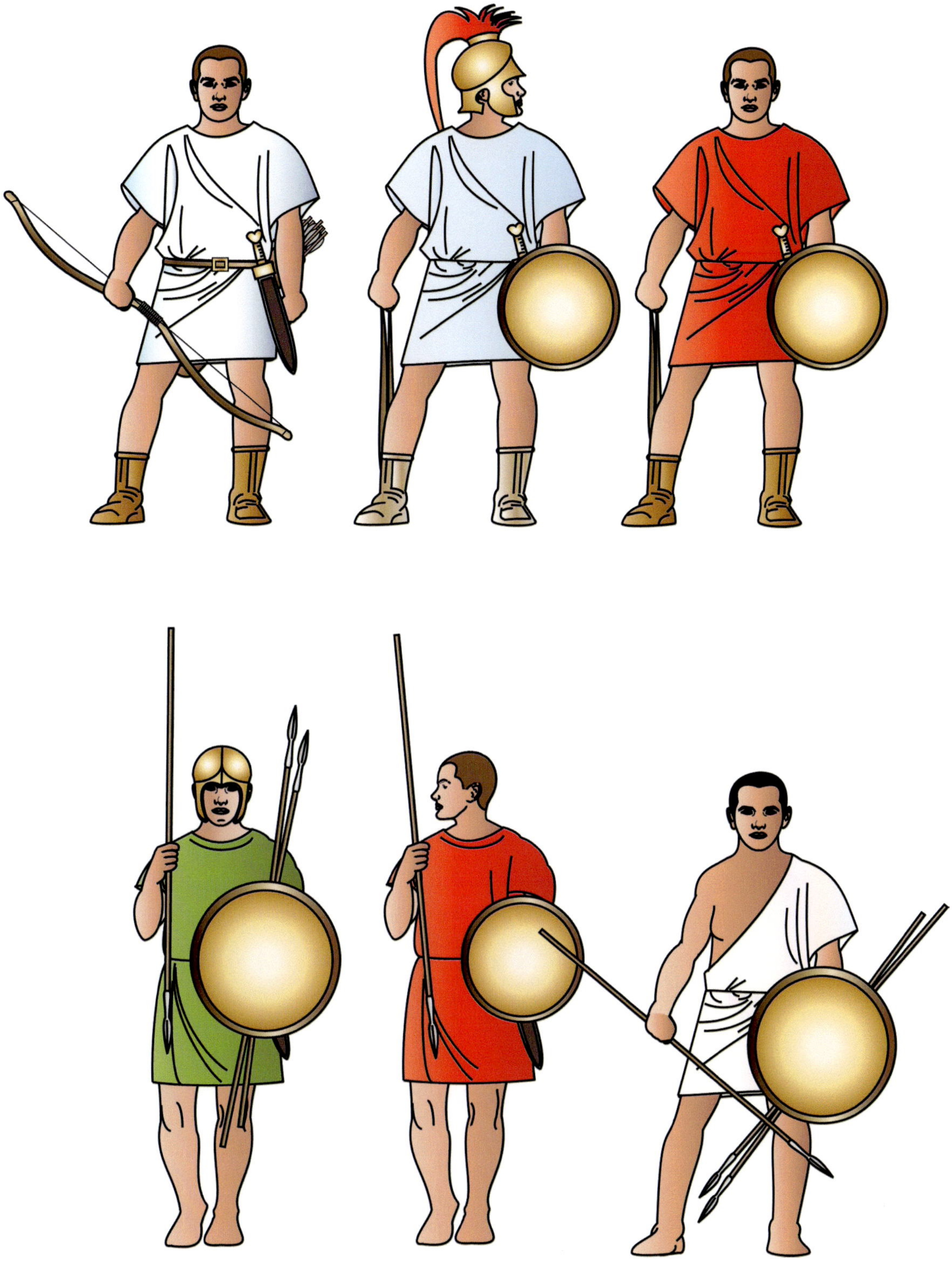

Plate 21. Ptolemaic light infantry, third century BCE
(Artwork by the author)
See Colour Plate Commentaries for further information.

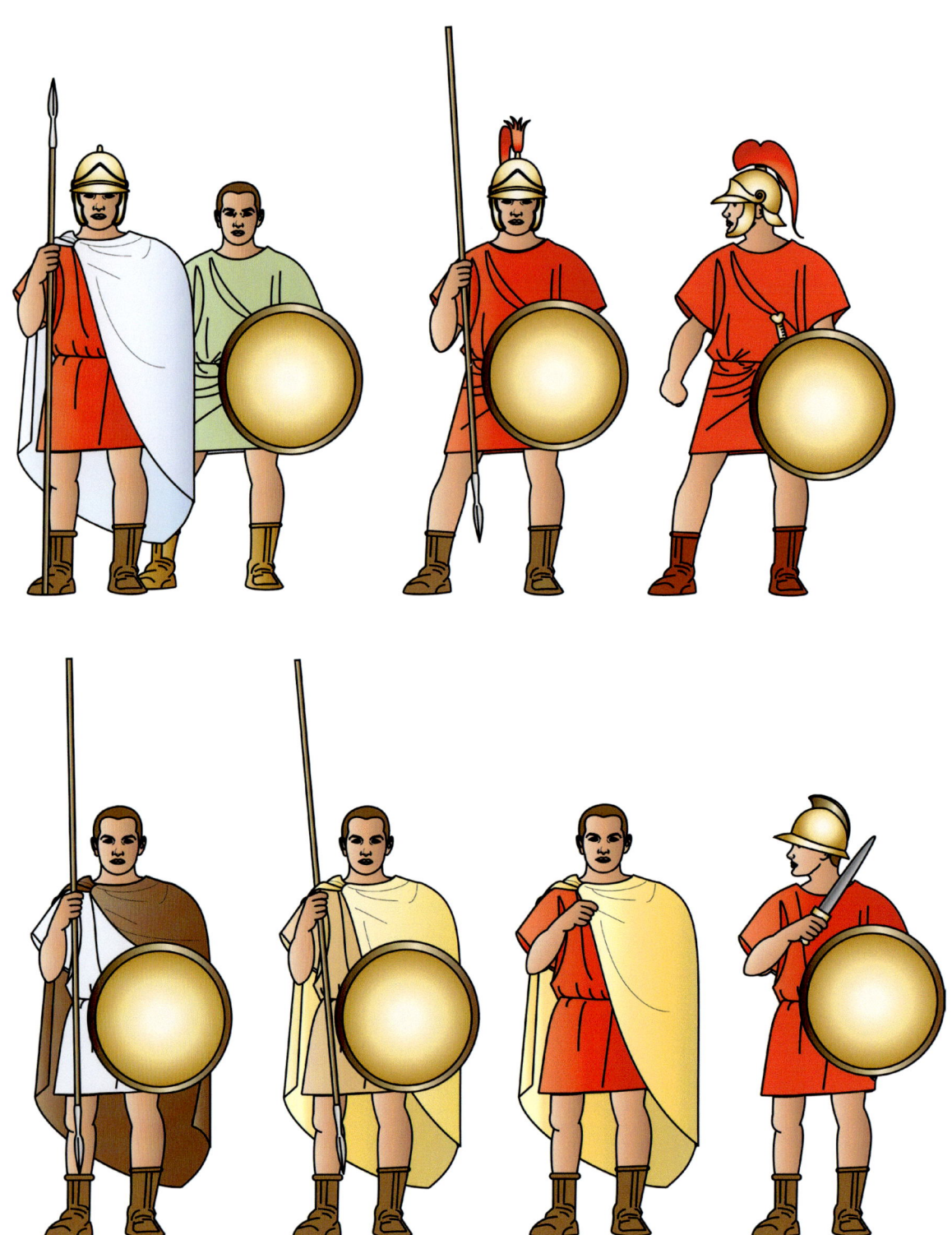

Plate 22. Ptolemaic light infantry, second century BCE
(Artwork by the author)
See Colour Plate Commentaries for further information.

Plate 23. Thracian mercenaries and cleruchs, third and second centuries BCE
(Artwork by the author)
See Colour Plate Commentaries for further information.

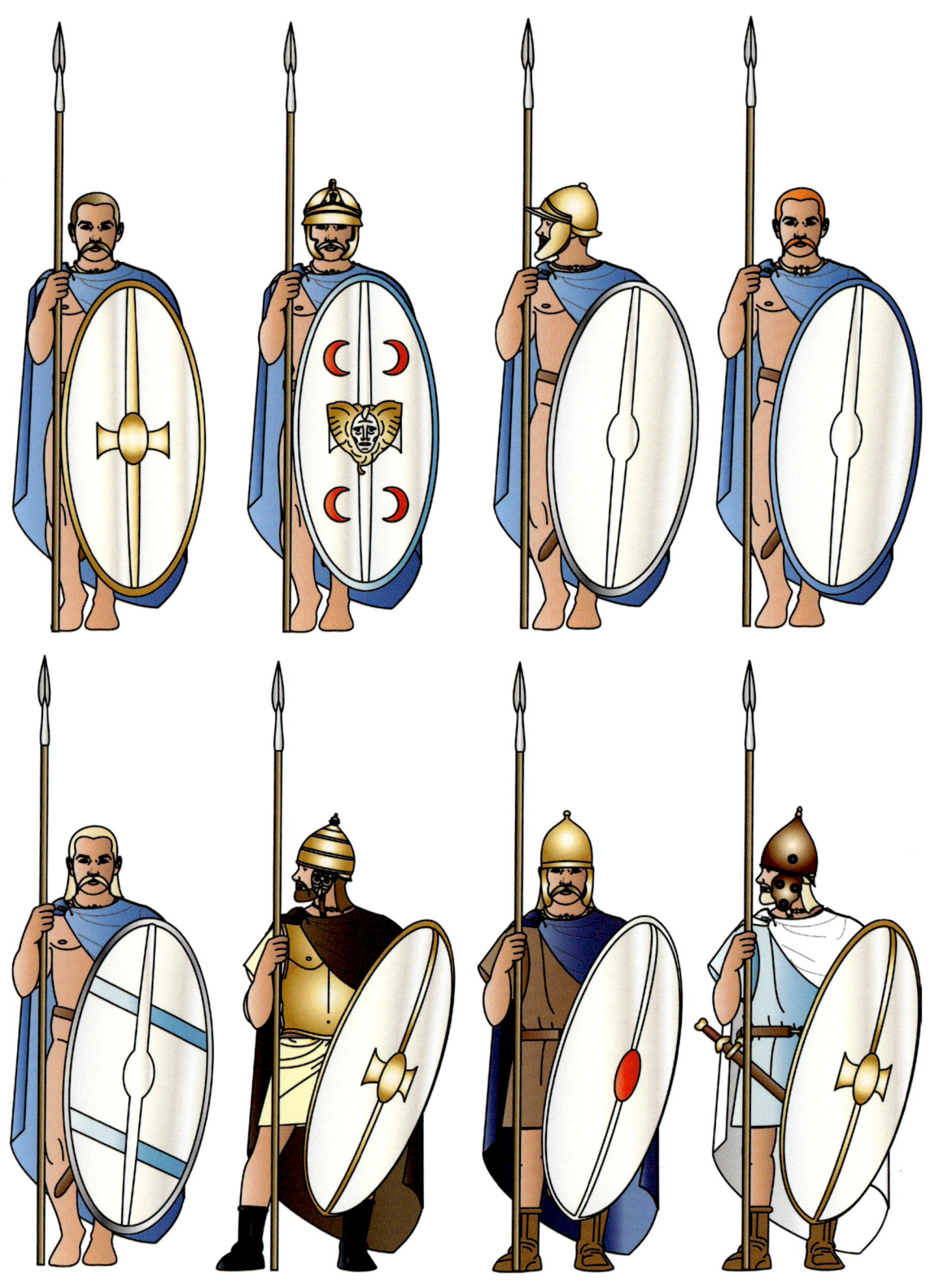

Plate 24. Galatian mercenaries and cleruchs, third and second centuries BCE
(Artwork by the author)
See Colour Plate Commentaries for further information.

Plate 25. *Thureophoroi* **mercenaries, second and first centuries BCE**
(Artwork by the author)
See Colour Plate Commentaries for further information.

Plate 26. *Thureophoroi* mercenaries and cleruchs, second and first centuries BCE
(Artwork by the author)
See Colour Plate Commentaries for further information.

Plate 27. *Thureophoroi* **mercenaries and cleruchs, first century BCE**
(Artwork by the author)
See Colour Plate Commentaries for further information.

Plate 28. Libyan and Nubian warriors, first century BCE
(Artwork by the author)
See Colour Plate Commentaries for further information.

**Plate 29. Soldiers' *chitons*, third to first century BCE;
Soldiers' *chlamydes*, third to first century BCE**
(Artwork by the author)
See Colour Plate Commentaries for further information.

Plate 30. Ptolemaic elephants, third century BCE
(Artwork by the author)
See Colour Plate Commentaries for further information.

Plate 31. Ptolemaic elephants, second century BCE
(Artwork by the author)
See Colour Plate Commentaries for further information.

Plate 32. Jewish soldiers, second to first century BCE
(Artwork by the author)
See Colour Plate Commentaries for further information.

4

The Ptolemaic Army in Battle: Gaza, Raphia, and Panion

Gaza (312)

At the Battle of Gaza in 312, Ptolemy Soter's army consisted of 22,000 Macedonians and mercenaries, plus a large number of Egyptians, some of whom were usable for combat: 'After gathering his troops from all sides, Ptolemy went from Alexandria to Pelusium with 18,000 infantry and 4,000 cavalry, both Macedonians and mercenaries, in addition to a large number of Egyptians, some of whom were tasked with transporting baggage and others armed for military purposes.'[1] Ptolemy and Seleucus concentrated their strength on the left wing, as Demetrius did on his side. However, Ptolemy, warned of his opponent's dispositions, reinforced his right wing at the last moment to better resist, placing iron chains on the front of his line to 'serve as defence against the elephants,'[2] as well as detachments of archers and javelinmen who were instructed to concentrate their projectiles on the animals and their handlers. The Indian elephants thus 'became stuck against the artificial barricade,'[3] and the beasts wounded by skirmishers caused disorder in their own ranks. The two wings of cavalry initially neutralised each other until Ptolemy and Seleucus managed to envelop the enemy's right wing. In the centre, all of Demetrius' elephants fell into the hands of the Ptolemies, leading to the flight of most of Demetrius' cavalry.

---

1 Diodorus Siculus, *Library of History*, book XIX, 80.
2 Diodorus Siculus, *Library of History*, book XIX, 83.
3 Diodorus Siculus, *Library of History*, book XIX, 84.

The First and Second Syrian Wars

The first Syrian War of 274 to 271 BCE opposed Ptolemy II Philadelphus to Antiochus. We know only that the armies manoeuvred without encountering each other. According to Pausanias:

> Magas, who had already married Apame, daughter of Antiochus, son of Seleucus, persuaded his father-in-law to violate the treaty that Seleucus had made with Ptolemy and to turn his arms against Egypt; but Ptolemy, having learned that Antiochus was setting out, sent troops into all the states of this prince, devastating the weakest peoples by incursions, restraining with armies those who were more powerful, thus occupying Antiochus to the extent that he no longer thought of attacking Egypt. This Ptolemy is, as I have already said, the one who, to aid Athens against Antigonus, King of Macedonia, sent a fleet that nevertheless was not very useful to the Athenians. Arsinoe, of whom he had children, was the daughter of Lysimachus; Arsinoe, sister and wife of Ptolemy, died before him without leaving children, and gave her name to one of the nomes of Egypt, the Arsinoïte.[4]

From the third Syrian War of 246–241 BCE, we only know from the Adulis stele that Euergetes:

> set out on an expedition to Asia with infantry and cavalry and a fleet plus Troglodyte and Ethiopian elephants that his father and he had been the first to hunt in these regions, which they had brought to Egypt and equipped for war. Having gained control of all the land this side of the Euphrates, and of Cilicia and Pamphylia and Ionia and the Hellespont and Thrace and all the Indian forces and elephants found in these regions, and having subjugated all the monarchs in the said places, he crossed the Euphrates River, and, having subdued Mesopotamia and Babylonia and Susiana and Persia and Media and all the rest as far as Bactria, and having sought out all the sacred objects taken from Egypt by the Persians and having brought them back to Egypt with all the other treasures from these places, he dispatched troops through the canals dug by human hands…[5]

---

4   Pausanias, *Description of Greece*, book I, 7, 2.
5   Cosmas, *The Christian Topography of Cosmas, an Egyptian monk* (London: McCrindle, 1897) book II, p.58–59.

THE PTOLEMAIC ARMY IN BATTLE: GAZA, RAPHIA, AND PANION

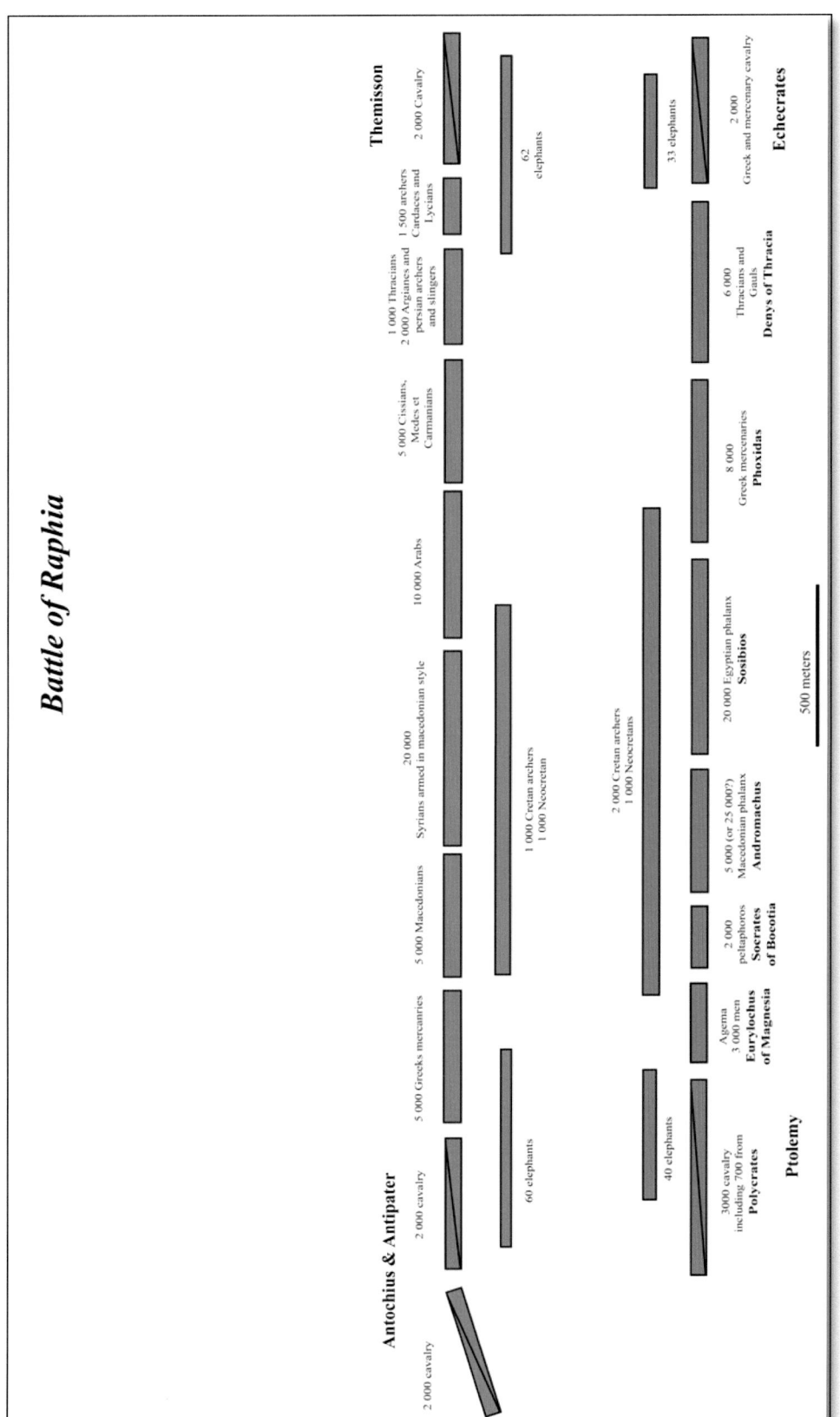

Battle of Raphia: the deployment of the two armies. (Map drawn by the author)

Raphia (217)

Of battles led by the Ptolemaic rulers, the Battle of Raphia in 217 is the best known. It took place during the Fourth Syrian War, 221–217 BCE. The detail provided by Polybius allows us to follow the assembly of the army by Agathocles and Sosibios, the two men who governed on behalf of Philopator:

> Eurylochus had under him the 3,000 men of the guard; Socrates commanded 2,000 peltasts; Phoxidas the Achaeans, Ptolemy son of Thrasaeas, and Andromachus led the phalanx and the Greek mercenaries. The latter two commanded the phalanx, which numbered 25,000 men, and Phoxidas led the Greeks, numbering 8,000. The 700 horsemen who formed the King's escort, the African cavalry, and that which had been raised in the country, totalling about 3,000 horsemen, were placed under the command of Polycrates. Echechrates, who had admirably trained the Greek cavalry, and all the mercenary cavalry, amounting together to 2,000 horsemen, were of great assistance in the battle. No one took more care in training the troops entrusted to him than Cnopias: he had about 3,000 Cretans, among whom were 1,000 Neocretans, whom he placed under the command of Philôn of Gnosus. Three thousand Africans had been armed in the Macedonian manner, and Ammonius commanded them. The Egyptian phalanx, consisting of 20,000 men, was led by Sosibios. In addition, there was a corps of 4,000 Thracians and Gauls, recently raised from among those who lived in the country, as well as from those who came from elsewhere to offer their services, and it was Denis of Thrace who led them. Such was the army of Ptolemy, and the different nations that composed it.[6]

In the spring of the year 217, Ptolemy left Alexandria for Pelusium with 50,000 infantry,[7] 5,000 cavalry, and 70 elephants. Antiochus then assembled his army, which numbered 62,000 infantry, 6,000 cavalry, and 102 elephants. It consisted of approximately 10,000 men armed in the Macedonian fashion, mostly *Argyraspides*, 20,000 men of the phalanx, 5,000 skirmishers from Dae, Carmania, and Cilicia commanded by Byttacus, 2,000 Agrianian and Persian archers and slingers, 1,000 Thracians, 5,000 Medes, Kissians, and

---

6   Polybius, *Histories*, book V, 2, 65.
7   There is some debate about the number of men in the phalanx: 45,000 or 25,000. There are in fact two ways of interpreting Polybius's text. Here we follow Griffith's argument, giving 25,000 men for the whole phalanx (i.e. 'Macedonian' and Egyptian). Griffith, *The Mercenaries of the Hellenistic world*, pp.122–123. If we do not correct Polybius's possible error, the total of the Ptolemaic infantry will be 70,000.

THE PTOLEMAIC ARMY IN BATTLE: GAZA, RAPHIA, AND PANION

Carmanians, 10,000 Arabs, about 5,000 Greek mercenaries, 1,500 Cretans, 1,000 Neocretans, 500 Lydian archers, and 1,000 Galatian Cardaces. The cavalry consisted of 6,000 horses, with 4,000 commanded by Antipater and 2,000 by Themison.

After camping at Pelusium, Ptolemy crossed Mount Casius and arrived at Gaza, where his army rested. After five days of marching, he arrived 50 stades (about 9km) from Raphia, in Coele-Syria, where he camped. At the same time, Antiochus passed Raphia and camped 10 stades (1.8km) from the Ptolemaic camp. But 'a few days later, wanting to secure the best positions and inspire confidence in his troops, he approached closer to Ptolemy, so that the two camps were only 5 stades apart. There were many skirmishes between foragers and those fetching water; there were also skirmishes between the two camps involving cavalry and infantry'.[8]

The Aetolian Theodotus, a Ptolemaic officer who had deserted to Antiochus, then managed to infiltrate the Egyptian camp in an attempt to assassinate Ptolemy, but without success. Then, after five days, the two Kings 'resolved to engage in a decisive battle'.[9] The two phalanxes and the *epilektoi*, that is, the permanent troops, were arranged 'in the Macedonian fashion'[10] facing each other.

On Ptolemy's side, Polycrates' cavalry formed the left wing. The Cretans, the *agema*, Socrates' peltasts, and the Libyans armed in the Macedonian fashion were placed in this order between Polycrates and the phalanx. Echechrates' cavalry was on the right wing. Between him and the phalanx, from right to left, the Galatians and Thracians were placed, then Phoxidas' Greek mercenaries and the Egyptian phalanx. The elephants were distributed on both wings, 40 on the left wing and 33 in front of the right wing. Ptolemy was on the left wing.

On Antiochus' side, 60 elephants covered the right wing, facing Ptolemy. Antipater's 4,000 cavalry were placed behind, arranged to form an angle. Then came the Cretans, followed by the Greek mercenaries, and Byttacus's 5,000 'lightly armed' men from Dae, Carmania, and Cilicia. They could have either been skirmishers or *thureophoroi*. Themison's 2,000 horsemen formed the left wing, then from left to right, the Galatian and Lydian archers, the 3,000 Agrianians, Persians, and Thracians, the Kissians, Medes, and Carmanians, and finally the Arabs were placed next to the phalanx. The remaining 42 elephants covered the left wing.

With the deployment completed, it was time to exhort the troops:

> With the armies thus arranged in battle, the two Kings, accompanied by their favourites and chiefs, went from body to body along the front of the line to encourage the troops; they focused especially on their phalanx, from which they hoped for the most. Ptolemy was

---

8   Polybius, *Histories*, book V, 2, 80.
9   Polybius, *Histories*, book V, 2, 82.
10 Polybius, *Histories*, book V, 2, 82.

accompanied by Arsinoe, his sister, Andromachus, and Sosibios; Antiochus, by Theodotus and Nicarchus: they were, on both sides, the leaders of the phalanxes.[11]

Ptolemy then takes his position on the left wing. Antiochus, having joined his cavalry on the right wing, is thus opposite him. Taking the initiative, Ptolemy sounds the charge. The elephants are the first to engage in combat. 'Some of those from Ptolemy's side came crashing down on those of Antiochus: there was fierce fighting, with towers, the soldiers battling closely and piercing each other with their pikes.'[12] The Ptolemaic elephants are not up to the task and eventually give way. They retreat onto the troops behind them: the *agema* is overturned, the peltasts waver. Antiochus takes advantage of the disorder: at the head of his cavalry, he bypasses his elephants and charges at Polycrates's cavalry. The Greek mercenary infantry, following the movement, break through the disorganised peltasts due to the elephants. 'Thus, the entire left wing of Ptolemy was defeated and fled.'[13]

Echecrates, who commanded Ptolemy's right wing, kept his cool. Seeing the cloud of dust that was about to envelop the Ptolemaic left wing, he asked Phoxidas to charge the infantry facing him with his Greek mercenaries, while he himself, bypassing the elephants of both camps on the right, 'at the same time marches his cavalry through the end of the wing and, avoiding by this means the elephants of the left wing of Antiochus, fell on the cavalry of the enemies and, attacking some in the rear and others in flank, he overthrows them all in a short time.'[14] For his part, Phoxidas succeeded in putting the Arabs and Medes to flight. Polybius does not mention the role of the Thracians and Gauls, or what happened to the elephants on either sides. But he does make it clear that the entire Seleucid left wing fled: 'Antiochus won on his right and was defeated on his left.'[15] All that remains are the two phalanxes, still intact, in the middle of the plain. While Antiochus, triumphant but 'young and inexperienced',[16] pursued the fugitives, Ptolemy took up position behind his phalanx before launching the attack: 'Andromachos and Sosibios marched with their pikes lowered against the enemy.'[17] The elite of the Syrians withstood the shock for some time, but the corps led by Nicarchus lost its footing first. When Antiochus returned, warned of the turn of events, he saw the extent of the disaster and withdrew to Raphia. Ptolemy, after the phalanx had decided the battle and the cavalry of the right wing, together with the mercenaries, returned from pursuing the fugitives, many of whom had been killed, withdrew to

---

11   Polybius, *Histories*, book V, 2, 83.
12   Polybius, *Histories*, book V, 2, 84.
13   Polybius, *Histories*, book V, 2, 84.
14   Polybius, *Histories*, book V, 2, 85.
15   Polybius, *Histories*, book V, 2, 85.
16   Polybius, *Histories*, book V, 2, 85.
17   Polybius, *Histories*, book V, 2, 85.

his camp for the night. The next day, Antiochus took the road to Gaza after asking Ptolemy for his dead. According to Polybius, the Seleucid losses amounted to 10,000 infantry, 300 cavalry and 5 elephants, to which must be added 4,000 men taken prisoner by Ptolemy. Ptolemy left 1,500 infantry, 700 horses and 16 elephants on the plain of Raphia.

Panion (200)

The last battle of this century would be that of Panion, fought in the year 200, during the Fifth Syrian War. According to Flavius Josephus, 'upon the death of Ptolemy Philopator, his son sent against the inhabitants of Coele-Syria a strong army commanded by Scopas, who seized several of their cities and obtained by force the submission of our people. Shortly after, Antiochus, encountering Scopas near the sources of the Jordan, defeated him and destroyed a large part of his army.'[18]

This battle is known to us through Polybius's critique of Zenon's account. However, we can deduct from his arguments that the Ptolemaic Army, commanded by Scopas, included an experienced phalanx flanked by two wings of cavalry. One of these two wings was composed of Aetolian horsemen commanded by Ptolemaios, son of Aeropos, and perhaps light infantry of the same nation. Scopas, himself an Aetolian, had been sent to Greece in 202 to raise mercenaries. According to Polybius, Agathocles, who was then the guardian of Ptolemy V along with Sosibios, wished to,

> use the newly hired men to wage war against Antiochus and send on the other hand the mercenaries in service for a long time to the places in the interior and in the colonies established throughout the country. With those who would arrive from Greece, he could also complete the King's military household, as well as his guard and the other units stationed in the city'[19]

Livy specifies that Scopas raised 6,000 infantry and a corps of mercenary cavalry in Aetolia, which he sent to Egypt.[20]

The Aetolian horsemen under Ptolemaios' command numbered 500. Out of the 6,000 infantry, a part was used to reinforce the *agema*. The Aetolians being renowned as light infantry, particularly as javelinmen, it is likely that some of these mercenaries were skirmishers employed in the front line, facing the phalanx and to confront the elephants. Another part was probably enrolled as pikemen, since according to Zenon, 'Antiochus's

---

18   Flavius Josephus, *Antiquities of the Jews*, book XII, 3, 3.
19   Polybius, *Histories*, book XV, III, 25a.
20   Titus Livius, *The History of Rome*, book XXXI, 63, 5.

THE ARMIES OF PTOLEMAIC EGYPT

phalanx, dealing with soldiers more experienced than themselves, were hard-pressed by the Aetolians and had to give ground.'[21]

From Polybius's text, we can deduce that at least one of the two cavalry wings was defeated by the Seleucid cataphracts and that the Ptolemaic phalanx, in the centre, found itself surrounded by elephants and cavalry.[22] Scopas would bring 10,000 survivors back to Sidon. Antiochus then seized the cities of Coele-Syria and Samaria abandoned by Scopas. The Jews sided with Antiochus and joined him to fight against the Ptolemaic garrison of Jerusalem.[23]

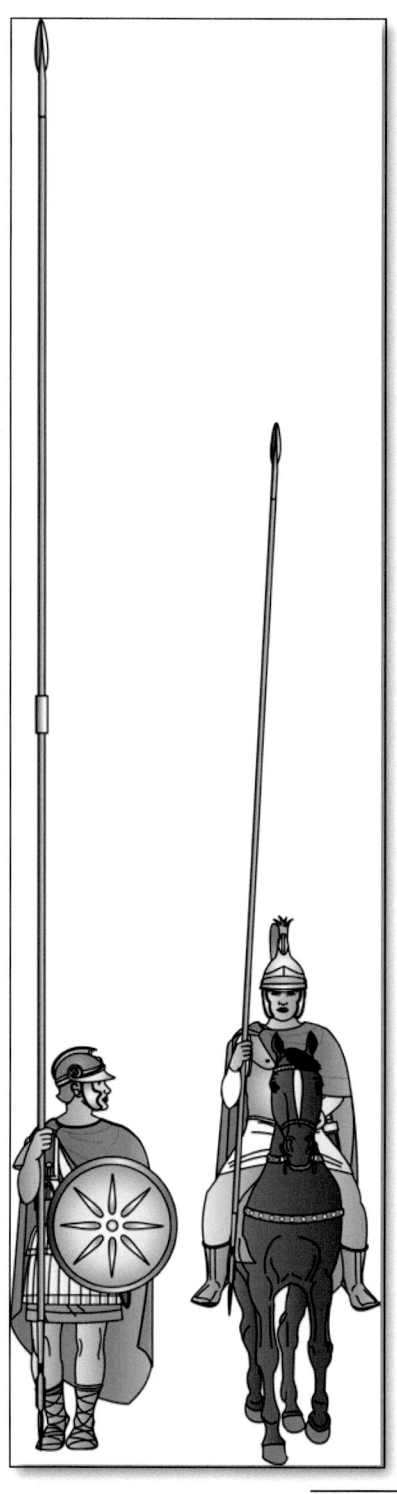

A Ptolemaic foot soldier from the phalanx beside a cavalryman from a numbered *hipparchia*. (Artwork by the author)

---

21 Polybius, *Histories*, book XVI, III, 19.
22 Polybius, *Histories*, book XVI, III, 19.
23 Polybius, *Histories*, book XVI, 8, 39; Flavius Josephus, *Antiquities of the Jews*, book XII, 3, 3.

5

The Transformation of the Ptolemaic Army in the Second Century BCE

In the second century, the size of the army seems to be as significant as in the previous century. Diodorus tells us that in 160 BCE, Ptolemy VI besieged his brother with a 'powerful army',[1] without giving us further indication. Then, in 146 BCE, this same Philometor defeated the army of Alexander Balas, described as 'considerable'.[2]

In 126–125 BCE, the Syrians asked Ptolemy Physcon to send them an heir of the family of Seleucus to replace Demetrius II Nikâtor, the Seleucid King. He sent them Alexander, nicknamed Zebinas, at the head of an army. Demetrius was defeated and killed.[3]

In 103 BCE, while the generals of Cleopatra seized Cyprus, Ptolemy IX Lathyros, at the head of an army of about 30,000 cavalry and infantry, fled the island and went to the aid of the inhabitants of Ptolemais, besieged by the Jews.[4] Joined by Zoilus and the Gazans, he defeated the Jewish Army of Alexander Jannaeus at Asophon on the banks of the Jordan. According to Flavius Josephus, Alexander's army numbered 50,000 men of the country, '80,000 men according to some historians'.[5] After this victory, Ptolemy increased his forces, which worried Cleopatra. The total forces of Egypt must therefore have exceeded 70,000 or 80,000 men by combining those of the two adversaries, Ptolemy IX and Cleopatra. The forces that Cleopatra

---

1   Diodorus Siculus, *Library of History*, book XX, 23.
2   Flavius Josephus, *Antiquities of the Jews*, book XIII, 4, 8. Later, referring to Herod's army, Flavius Josephus would write that the King had "considerable forces, about 30,000 men." This gives us an indication of Philometor's troop strength.
3   Flavius Josephus, *Antiquities of the Jews*, book XIII, 9, 3.
4   Flavius Josephus, *Antiquities of the Jews*, book XIII, 12, 3.
5   Flavius Josephus, *Antiquities of the Jews*, book XIII, 12, 4.

would then send against her son Ptolemy Soter are still described as 'considerable'.[6]

Composition of the Ptolemaic Army

At this time, the Ptolemaic and Syrian armies fighting in Coele-Syria were mainly composed of mercenaries recruited from Crete, Cilicia, Pisidia, Caria, or Lydia, and militia from the coastal cities. As for the regular Ptolemaic troops, not much is known, except that in 146 BCE, Philometor brought the regiment of the Mysians to Pelusium, then to Ptolemais in Coele-Syria.[7] He had elephants in his army since he would die that year from a fall from his horse, caused by the trumpeting of one of the beasts. But following his death, his son-in-law and ally Demetrius II, the Seleucid King of Syria, managed to get hold of all of the elephants of the Ptolemaic army.[8]

At the twilight of the previous century, many men from Greece came to take charge of the Ptolemaic army. Thessalians Echecrates and Eurylochus, Achaeans Phoxidas, Boeotian Socrates, Cretan Cnopias, Argive Polycrates, Pamphylian Andromachos at Raphia, or Aetolians Scopas and Ptolemaios at Panion all show that the Ptolemaic Army was essentially formed and organised by Greeks. The organisation of the Ptolemaic Army thus follows the development of its Greek and Macedonian counterparts. The unit of peltasts, which appeared in the Ptolemaic Army on the eve of Raphia, has a direct lineage to the Macedonian unit. This elite unit was very active, in the service of Antigonus Doson and then of Philip V, from 222 to 217 BCE.

Greek standard formations must necessarily have served as a model for the Ptolemaic leaders. At the same time, in Greece, units were composed of 100, 200, 300, or even 500 men. A treaty between the Rhodians and Hierapytnians dating to 201 or 200 BCE mentions a contingent of 200 armed men and officers commanding at least 50 men.[9] Another treaty between Rhodes and Olonte, dating from the same year, mentions contingents of at least 100 armed men and officers commanding at least 20 men.[10] During the War of the Allies from 222 to 217 BCE, Polybius testifies to Greek contingents of 200 or 300 men, citizens or mercenaries: such was the case of the contingent of 300 Achaeans and 200 mercenaries sent to garrison

---

6 Flavius Josephus, *Antiquities of the Jews*, book XIII, 12, 3.
7 Schubert, *Les papyrus de Genève*, Vol. 3, p.107.
8 Flavius Josephus, *Antiquities of the Jews*, book XIII, 4, 8–9.
9 Jean-Christophe Couvenhes, 'Quelques remarques sur le recrutement des soldats crétois outre-mer à travers les traités de symmachia' *Dialogues d'histoire ancienne,* supplément 16 (2016), pp.177–121; Launey M., *Recherches sur les armées hellénistiques*, Tome I, p.37.
10 Couvenhes, 'Quelques remarques sur le recrutement des soldats crétois outre-mer à travers les traités de symmachia, p.193.

Mantinea,[11] the 500 infantrymen and *thorakites* under Aratus at Caphyae,[12] or the 200 Achaeans, 100 Phocians, and 500 Polyrrhenians who reinforced the army of Philip of Macedon in 220 BCE.[13] A little later, 300 Achaean slingers and 500 Cretans would arrive as reinforcements.[14]

A New Organisation

If Ptolemaic prosopography is to be believed, the *taxis* (unit of 128 men), the *pentakosiarchia* (unit of 256 men) and the *syntagma* (unit of 512 men) seem to have disappeared by the end of the third century. Except for one example dating from the time of Ptolemy XI (80 BCE), referring to Sosipatros, *hêgemôn* and *chiliarchos*, the same seems to be true of the *chiliarchia* of 1024 men.[15]

A new unit appears in the papyri from 190 BCE onwards.[16] This is the *sêmeia*, *sêmea* or *sêmeion*, a term that Polybius uses to refer to the Roman maniple, but which originally means 'standard'. The *sêmeia* would replace the syntagma of 256 men within the Ptolemaic infantry from this date. A *sêmeia*, abbreviated as *stn* in Egyptian demotic inscriptions,[17] would comprise two *hekatontarchies*, with each *hekatontarchia* consisting of two *pentekontarchies*. However, the inscription *stn* is found several times applying to cavalry units as well, indicating that the abbreviation is not exclusive to infantry and the *sêmeia*. Examples of *sêmeia* can be founded in papyri of 190–189 BCE,[18] 171 BCE,[19] 169–163 BCE,[20] 165 BCE,[21] 163 BCE,[22] 158–156 BC[23] and 108 BCE.[24] An inscription dating from 170–164 BCE referring to a *sêmeia* says:[25]

---

11 Polybius, *Histories*, book II, 3, 58.
12 Polybius, *Histories*, book IV, 1, 12.
13 Polybius, *Histories*, book IV, 3, 55.
14 Polybius, *Histories*, book IV, 3, 61.
15 Peremans & Van 't Dack, *Prosopographia Ptolemaica*, pp.56–60; Lesquier J., *Les institutions militaires de l'Egypte sous les Lagides*, p.344–345.
16 Edmond Van 't Dack, *Ptolemaica Selecta*, (Louvain: Studia Hellenistica, 1988), pp.71–77.
17 Van 't Dack, *Ptolemaica Selecta*, pp.71–73.
18 Van 't Dack, *Ptolemaica Selecta*, p.71.
19 Van 't Dack, *Ptolemaica Selecta*, p.71.
20 Peremans & Van 't Dack, *Prosopographia Ptolemaica*, p.16.
21 *Notices et extraits des manuscrits de la bibliothèque impériale et autres bibliothèques publiés par l'institut impérial de France*, (Paris: Imprimerie Impériale, 1865), p.63 (Papyrus n°23).
22 Peremans & Van 't Dack, *Prosopographia Ptolemaica*, pp.27 & 212.
23 Van 't Dack, Van 't Dack, *Ptolemaica Selecta*, p.10.
24 Van 't Dack, *Ptolemaica Selecta*, p.72.
25 SB 1 :1436, https://epigraphy.packhum.org/text/220489

THE ARMIES OF PTOLEMAIC EGYPT

Ἱερωνύμου τοῦ ἀρχ[ισ]ωματοφύλακος καὶ στρατηγοῦ πρόσγραφο[ι] τρίτης σημέας, [meaning Ierônymos (Jerome) of the *archisômatophylakos* (guards) and soldier of the third *sêmeia*.]

And a second inscription referring to a *semeia*, from Memphis and dating from 156 BCE:[26]

ἀδικοῦμαι ὑπ' Ἀργείου ὑπηρέτου τῆς Δεξιλάου σημέας· [meaning 'I am avenged by the hypêretes of Dexilaos' *sêmeia*.']

Several documents use the term *hêgemônia*[27] *to refer* to the unit superior to the hekatontarchia, rather than the appellation of *sêmeia*. There may be up to six *sêmeiai* within a regiment possibly called a *syntaxis*. Three stelae from Hermoupolis Magna dated from the end of the second century BCE to the first half of the first century BCE[28] list eponymous units that appear to be made of four *pentekontarchies*, each unit probably together forming

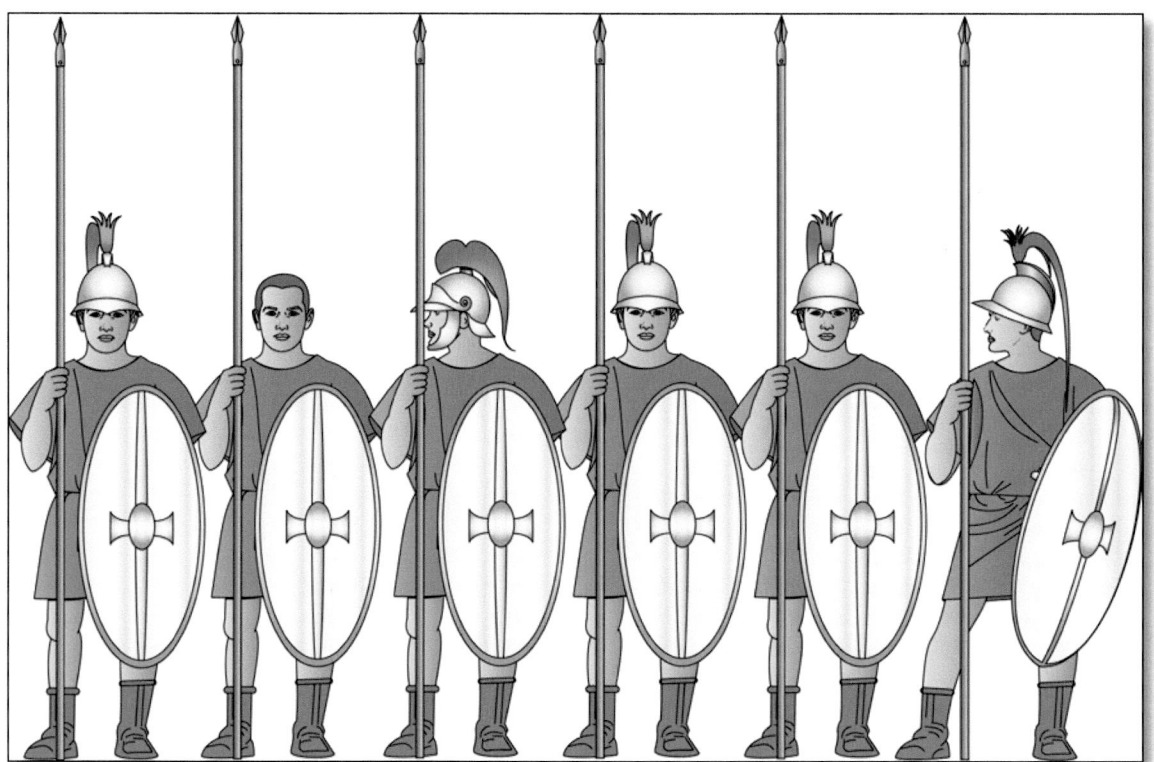

Types of soldiers making up a *sêmeia*. They are carrying the *thureos*-type shield, and have helmet, spear and a sword. (Artwork by the author)

---

26   UPZ 1.16, https://papyri.info/ddbdp/upz;1;16
27   For several examples, see Lesquier, *Les institutions militaires de l'Egypte sous les Lagides*, p.342.
28   Bernand, *Inscriptions grecques d'Hermoupolis Magna et de sa nécropole*, pp.21–72; Peter M. Frazer, 'The Ptolemaic Garrison of Hermoupolis Magna', *Proceedings of the British Academy,* 148 (2007), pp.69–85.

THE TRANSFORMATION OF THE PTOLEMAIC ARMY IN THE SECOND CENTURY BCE

a *sêmeia*. The 'Roeder' and probably the 'Jouguet' stelae from Hermoupolis Magna refer to a unit called 'The Apolloniate Mercenaries' composed of men from the Idumean city of Apollonia[29] and commanded by Herakleidês, son of Apollônios. It seems that both stelae list together six *sêmeiai*, the last one being preceded by the number six. Other inscriptions mention three *sêmeiai*, numbered from one to three. Therefore, the *sêmeiai* seem to be numbered, at least in the first century, only two, dubious, inscriptions give numbers higher than six.[30]

The first stele from Hermoupolis Magna dating from the late second century BCE, also called the 'Lefebvre' stele from the name of its publisher,[31] lists only five eponymous *sêmeiai*, within a unit whose commander's name is not known. These units are therefore not numbered but referred as those of Komanos, Attaniaphantos and Sthenelaos, Diados, Pasinos and Drytônos, Aglaomachos and Menophilos. However, two important pieces are missing from this stele, and therefore possibly an additional unit. The garrison also includes other units: a contingent of Cretans, another of Cyreneans, another of Egyptians from Thebaid. There is a staff or non-ranking staff (*exô taxeôn*)[32] with its commander, who is also a *phrourarchos*, meaning the chief of the garrison, and its officers. Finally, a small number of citizens (*politikoi*), and an equally short list of mercenaries who have received amnesty close the list.

The unit superior to the *sêmeia* would be the *syntaxis*, commanded by a *hêgemôn ep'andrôn*. Indeed, a *grammateus syntaxeôs*, meaning a secretary of the syntaxis, appears on line 48 in the 'Lefebvre' stele from Hermoupolis Magna. But the *syntaxis* can also refer to an army arrayed for battle or a military contingent. It is equally possible that the unit superior to the *sêmeia* has no designation: thus, in the papyri, we find a 'first *sêmeia* of Memphis'.[33]

The *syntaxis*, if it exists, would then have up to six *sêmeiai*, for a total of 1,200 to 1,500 men plus a small number of officers and soldiers outside of the ranks (*hoi exô taxeôn*).

We have seen that the *sêmeia* would consist of two *hekatontarchies*, 'units of 100'. The two *hekatontarchies* were numbered within the *sêmeia*. Papyri preserved in the Louvre, British Museum, and Vatican museum thus mention *sêmeiai* designated solely by the name of their commander, for example, Desilaos or Eumele. But members of these *sêmeiai* are named as belonging to 'the first' of Desilaos or Eumele's *sêmeia*. The term used is *proteron*, which means 'first of the two'.[34]

---

29   Bernand, *Inscriptions grecques d'Hermoupolis Magna et de sa nécropole*, p.61.
30   Van 't Dack, *Ptolemaica Selecta*, pp.82–83.
31   Bernand, *Inscriptions grecques d'Hermoupolis Magna et de sa nécropole*, p.21; Sekunda, *The Ptolemaic Army*, p.10.
32   Van 't Dack, *Ptolemaica Selecta*, p.68.
33   Van 't Dack, *Ptolemaica Selecta*, p.73.
34   Peremans & Van 't Dack, *Prosopographia Ptolemaica*, p.10.

THE ARMIES OF PTOLEMAIC EGYPT

An attempt to interpret *sêmeia* banners (technically *vexilla*) of the third and second century BCE. The eagle is inspired by Ptolemaic coins. The first, top left, is a conjectural *agema* banner. The next six display signs for numbers one to six, corresponding to each *sêmeia* of a *syntaxis* or to six cavalry *hipparchies*. The last five banners represent city contingents: Ptolemais, Hermoupolis Magna, Arsinoë, Gaza and Sidon. These types of inscriptions can be found on coins minted in these cities. (Artwork by the author).

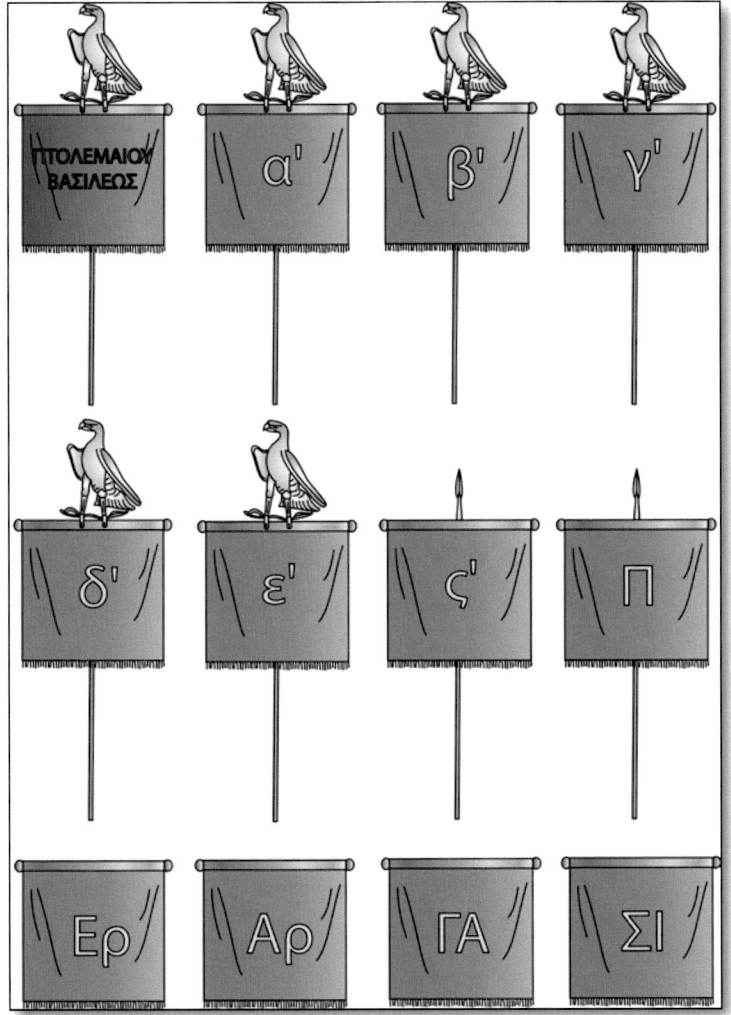

Each *hekatontarchia* is formed of two units of '50 men': the *pentekontarchia*. Thus, a *sêmeia* would count among its ranks approximately six to seven officers, around 200 soldiers (*stratiôtai*) and four additional men: the ensign (*sêmeiophoros*), a quartermaster or 'attendant' (*hypêretês*), a herald (*kêrux*) or flutist (*ieraulês*),[35] and an officer distinct from the *pentekontarchos*, the *ouragos*.[36] The *ouragos*, who appears at the end of the list within the *sêmeia*, unlike the ensign and herald, was originally a file closer within the file of 12 or 16 men. He would now seem to have become a lieutenant who stands behind the unit during its deployment, similar to the

---

35　Bernand, *Inscriptions Grecques d'Hermoupolis Magna et de sa Nécropole*, p.39 & pp.57–61.
36　Van 't Dack, *Ptolemaica Selecta*, p.77; Sekunda, *The Ptolemaic Army*, pp.10–12.

THE TRANSFORMATION OF THE PTOLEMAIC ARMY IN THE SECOND CENTURY BCE

Roman *optio*. The *hypêretês* appears in an inscription of 158–156 BCE where Argeios is *hypêretês* of the *sêmeia* of Dexelaos.[37]

As an example, the epitaph of the Koptos stele praises the courage of Ptolemaios, Officer of Macedonians:

> Passerby, beneath this tomb I lie, I, Ptolemaios, an officer, who met his end in the fury of the melee, along with my son, Menodoros, intrepid and bold ensign [*sêmeiophoros*] in battles, when I led fierce Ares against the enemies, with the Macedonian soldiers under my command. I was at the forefront, and we had slaughtered a multitude of enemies when cruel Ares took us both. We departed after rendering immense services to him for the homeland, within which I had previously served as a gymnasium superintendent, valiant on numerous occasions among the infantry, and when counsel was needed, my wisdom was rewarded with praise. So, hail to you, even among the dead, brave Ptolemaios. After bidding farewell to his son, traveller, continue your journey.[38]

It is possible that Ptolemaios, who is likely the leader of a *sêmeia* of 'Macedonians' and whose son is the ensign, met his end during an uprising in Thebaid around 164 BCE, or during the Sixth Syrian War in 169 or 168 BCE.

The *exô taxeôn*, according to ancient authors like Diodorus Siculus, are non-combatants. It seems that in the third and second centuries, they were commanders (*hêgemônes*) 'outside the *taxis*' (i.e. outside the unit) without active service.[39] In the case of the garrison of Hermoupolis Magna, the *sêmeia* therefore includes a certain number of soldiers out of rank with their own commander. Table 1 gives an overview of the Lefebvre stele, dated to the end of the second century BCE.

Terracotta from Egypt probably depicting the Goddess Athena. She wears a helmet reminiscent of the Sidon A type (Perdrizet, *Les terres cuites grecques d'Egypte de la collection Fouquet*, 1921, plate LX)

---

37 Peremans & Van 't Dack, Prosopographia Ptolemaica, p.70 (2437).
38 Etienne Bernand, *Inscriptions métriques de l'Egypte Gréco-Romaines, recherches sur la poésie épigrammatique des Grecs en Egypte* (Paris: Les Belles Lettres, 1969), pp.49–50.
39 Van 't Dack, *Ptolemaica Selecta*, p.67.

Table 3: Lefebvre Stele, Hermoupolis Magna[40]

Column 1	
(line 4)	Komanos and others
Kêrux (herald)	Menodoros, son of Menodoros
Sêmeiophoros (ensign)	Theodoros, son of Herakleitos
Hekatontarchos	Demetrios, son of Apollônios
(line 24)	Atthaniaphan and Sthenelaos
Sêmeiophoros	Andremôn, son of Balakros
Pentekontarchos	Dionysios son of Ptolemaios
(line 35)	Those who once came with Drytôn
Hêgemôn (officer)	Garrison commander (*phrourarkos*)
Exô taxeôn (non-ranking)	Timokles, son of Timokles
Exô taxeôn	Aristarchos, son of Diognetos
Exô taxeôn	Kritôn, son of Archas
Hêgemônon uioi (son of officer)	Dionysios, son of Dionysios
Hêgemônon uioi	Panteles, son of Dionysios
Hêgemônon uioi	Diogenes, son of Dionysios
Grammateus syntaxeos (secretary)	Eudoxos, son of Timokles
Column 2	
(line 86)	
Pentekontarchos	Hermippos, son of Leôn
(line 92)	
Pentekontarchos	Pytheas, son of Neoptolemos
(line 124)	
Pentekontarchos	Leônides, son of Apollônios
(line 133)	
Ouragos	Perigenes, son of Alexitimos
(line 135)	Diades and his sons
Kêrux (herald)	Diophantos, son of Iason
Column 3	
(line 148)	
Pentekontarchos	Neôn, son of Metrodôros
(line 155)	
Ouragos	Apollodôros, son of Aristomachos
(line 157)	Pasinos and Drytôn
Kêrux (herald)	Drakôn, son of Hegesias
Sêmeiophoros (ensign)	Mikkos, son of Ptolemaios
Hekatontarchos	Ptolemaios, son of Tryphôn
Pentekontarchos	Zoilos, son of Zoilos
(line 190)	
Pentekontarchos	Achilleus, son of Dionysios

---

[40] Bernand, *Inscriptions métriques de l'Egypte Gréco-Romaines, recherches sur la poésie épigrammatique des Grecs en Egypte*, pp.22–25.

THE TRANSFORMATION OF THE PTOLEMAIC ARMY IN THE SECOND CENTURY BCE

The file or *lochos*,[41] remains the smallest unit used. Some garrisons, in desert outposts called *phrourion*, had a strength not exceeding that of the file. Thus, Cillès, who is part of Neoptolemus' unit (perhaps an eponymous *sêmeia*), commands a garrison of 14 men in 255 BCE.[42]

If Asclepiodotus and Arrian use the terms *taxis* and *tetrarchia* instead of *hekatontarchia* and *pentekontarchia*, they do, however, use the latter two terms to describe equivalent units in light infantry.[43] It is therefore possible that the *hekatontarchia* of 100 men and the *pentekontarchia* of 50 men were used interchangeably for both heavy and light infantry within the Ptolemaic army or, more likely, that over time the units of *thureophoroi* took on the name of light infantry units to differentiate them from the phalanx of pikemen.

There is no trace of an organisation higher than the presumed *syntaxis*, but in 127 BCE, a certain Polianthes would have been in charge of a unit whose name, difficult to decipher, could be the phalanx or the *phalangarchia* of Asclepiodotus. Indeed, this officer is mentioned later in the papyrus as commanding a *hêgemôny*, a term meaning 'command'.[44] But as with the previous century, it is unlikely that a formation superior to the *syntaxis* existed in peacetime.

In his work *The Ptolemaic Army*, Nick Sekunda interprets the emergence of the *sêmeia* as a willingness to 'Romanise' the army. He attributes this reorganisation to a man named Kallikles, son of Kallikles of Alexandria, who

Representations of phalanx soldiers as they would have looked in the second century BCE. (Artwork by the author)

---

41 The *dekania* and his commander, the *dekanikos*, do not seem to be attested after 165 BCE: see Lesquier J., *Les institutions militaires de l'Egypte sous les Lagides*, p.347; and Sekunda, *The Ptolemaic Army*, p.5.
42 Launey M., *Recherches sur les armées hellénistiques*, Tome II, p.984; OGIS 38.
43 Arrian, *Ars Tactica*, 14.3; Asclepiodotus, Tactica, VI, 3.
44 Van 't Dack, *Ptolemaica Selecta*, p.55.

was an *ilarchês* in the royal cavalry and a 'tactics instructor to the King'.[45] He estimates the creation of this new unit to around 165–163 BCE.[46] Therefore, he sees the *sêmeia* as equivalent to the Roman *manipulus*. However, while the *manipulus* consists of two centuries of 60 men, the *sêmeia* would consist of two centuries (*hekatontarchies*) and theoretically comprising 100 or 128 men, although no stele lists more than 100 names for a *sêmeia*. The *syntaxis* would then be an intermediate unit, in terms of numbers, between the cohort and the legion.

Moreover, the *sêmeia* can have appeared a little before 165 BCE, between 169 and 164BC, a period corresponding to a known inscription referring to Ierônimos, an elite soldier of the third *sêmeia*.[47] If most inscriptions mentioning *sêmeia* or *stn*, or the officers and *epistatês* composing them, are found between 169–164 and 69 BCE, there is one dating potentially from 190–189 BCE.

Furthermore, the equipment of the Ptolemaic or Seleucid soldier, as described by Nick Sekunda, is that of the Hellenistic *thureophoros,* not necessarily that of the Roman legionary. As mentioned above, the *thureos*, inspired by the Gallic shield, indeed spread throughout the Hellenistic world from the second quarter of the third century BCE. The defensive equipment of the *thureophoros* differs from that of the Roman legionary by the size of the *thureos*, which is smaller than the Roman *scutum*, as well as the absence of a mail shirt. Certainly, *thorakitai*, or *thureophoroi* wearing a cuirass or mail shirt, are attested in Achaia and in the Seleucid army, but evidence regarding the Ptolemaic army remains scant. While the stele of Salmas of Adada does depict such a *thorakitai*, the city of Sidon, at that time, was more often under Seleucid control than Ptolemaic, as Coele-Syria had been lost by Ptolemy V Epiphanes in 199 BCE, after the Battle of Panion. Even though there was a new occupation of this region by Ptolemy VI in 147–146 BCE and Sidon's allegiance to Ptolemy IX Lathyros in 103 BCE, this representation does not assure us of the existence of such a unit in the service of the Ptolemies. It may also represent an officer rather than a soldier of a specific unit. Regarding offensive equipment, neither the depictions of *thureophoroi* nor the texts mention an equivalent weapon to the Roman *pilum*.

Nevertheless, the phenomenon of imitation is a common practice throughout history, and in all armies. The Ptolemaic soldiers could thus quickly imitate their Seleucid enemies, as well as their Roman or Achaean allies. Conversely, in 180 BCE, according to Polybius, Ptolemy V sent shields and 'a squadron of 10 fully equipped *penteconters*' to the Achaean League![48]

---

45 Sekunda, *The Ptolemaic Army*, p.6.
46 Sekunda, *The Ptolemaic Army*, pp.6–7.
47 Lesquier J., *Les institutions militaires de l'Egypte sous les Lagides*, p.363 and Van 't Dack, *Ptolemaica Selecta*, p.73; SB 1 :1436.
48 Polybius, *Histories*, book XXIV, 4, 6.

THE TRANSFORMATION OF THE PTOLEMAIC ARMY IN THE SECOND CENTURY BCE

The emergence of the *syntaxis* and the *sêmeia* likely follows the adoption of this new type of soldier known as the *thureophoros*. More versatile than the phalanx soldier, yet not to be equated with a light infantryman,[49] the *thureophoros* is better suited for the typical tasks of peacetime, such as guarding cities and defending borders. As early as the year 220 BCE, the Seleucids fielded units of *thureophoroi*. Therefore, it is in this latter half of the third century BCE that the need for a tactical unit less deep than the phalanx described by Asclepiodotus or Arrian must have been felt. As for the name of the unit, it is probably linked to the appearance of the sign carried by the *sêmeiophoros*.

We have seen that there are two elite units within the Guard, which will probably evolve towards police missions: the *logchophoroï* (spear carriers) and the *machairophoroï* (sword carriers). Through the second century, these two units were probably equipped in the same way, with a *thureos*-type shield and a sword. The *logchophoroï*, if not both units, were also armed with a spear. Finally, these two units probably wear helmets and a linen cuirass. Later in the century the cuirass may have evolved into mail.

Finally, we have seen that *machimoi* were grouped into several *laarchies* each commanded by a *laarchês*. For the second century BCE, we have some evidence: Chomênis at the end of the second century BCE,[50] and possibly Ôros with less certainty, the transcription being 'λ. ( )' and not directly *laarchês*.[51] *Laarchies* units seem to be composed of infantrymen and cavalrymen as Chomênis (see above) is also designated as a cavalryman of the *machimoï*.[52]

Representation of a Hellenistic soldier according to Froehner (W. Froehner, *Terres cuites d'Asie de la collection Julien Gréau*, 1886.)

Cavalry in the Second Century

The evolution of cavalry organisation is not as clear-cut as for the infantry. While the *hipparchia* remained a major unit used until the end of the first century BCE, we lose track of *ilarchês*, *lochagos*, *epilochagos* and *dekanikos* from the end of the third century: after Raphia for the *ilarchês* and the *epilarchês*, to the last years of the century for the *lochagos* and the *dekanikos*.[53] Nevertheless, without any evidence of new formations below

---

49   Arrian classifies it as heavy infantry: Arrian, *Ars Tactica*, 3,2.
50   Peremans & Van 't Dack, *Prosopographia Ptolemaica*, p.33 (2047); PSI XIII 1312; P. Tebt. 1.61a: https://papyri.info/ddbdp/p.tebt;1;61a
51   Peremans & Van 't Dack, *Prosopographia Ptolemaica*, p.34 (2049); BGU VI 1258: https://papyri.info/ddbdp/bgu;6;1258a.
52   Peremans & Van 't Dack, *Prosopographia Ptolemaica*, p.33 (2047); for an example, PSI 10 1098: https://papyri.info/ddbdp/psi;10;1098
53   Peremans & Van 't Dack, *Prosopographia Ptolemaica*, pp.52–55; Lesquier J., *Les*

the *hipparchia* level, we cannot conclude that these subdivisions have been abandoned.

On the other hand, we note the appearance, in the middle of the second century, of a new senior officer, the *epitagmatos*. This is not a completely new term, since Asclepiodotus uses it to designate the largest formation in the light infantry. Hence, the largest cavalry formation would now be the *epitagma*, commanded by this officer. According to Arrian,[54] this unit would consist of 4,096 horsemen, or eight *hipparchies*. This number is purely theoretical: the ideal army, according to tacticians, consists of 16,384 heavy infantry, 8,192 light infantry, and 4,096 cavalry.[55] The papyri have left us the names of two *epitagmatoi*. In the years 145–143 BCE, we find, at Philae, an Archean named Mnasis, son of Dionysos, who is appointed as *diadochos*, *epitagmatos*, and *hipparchês*.[56] At the same time, a son of Dionysos (presumably the same man, his name, illegible, ending in -is) is named in a record made in Thebes. He is *diadochos*, *epitagmatos*, *hipparchês*, and *epistatês* of Pathyris. In the years 129–126 BCE, a Cretan named Drytôn, son of Pamphylos, appears in the papyri, with the titles *diadochos*, *epitagmatos*, and *hipparchês* in Pathyris.[57] This formation would therefore have appeared after the battle of the river Oinoparas, perpetuating a formation, perhaps a complete wing of cavalry, comprising a variable number of *hipparchies*, eight if we are to believe Arrian.[58] At the Battle of Raphia, one wing of cavalry counted around four to six *hipparchies*. Inscriptions do not provide us with the name of any formation between the *epitagma* and the *hipparchia*, but Asclepiodotus and Arrian mention, between the two, the *ephipparchia*, which consists of two *hipparchies*, and the *telos*, which consists of two *ephipparchies*.[59]

Going back to the epigraphy, we already mention empirical evidence of horsemen of the first *hipparchia*. We also find two commanders of units which were part of the first *hipparchia* in 174–173 BCE: Dositheos and Diodoros.[60] Regarding the second *hipparchia*, the name of an *hipparchês*, Agathodôros, appears in 137 BCE, and of three sub-commanders, Theodoros in 182 BCE, Kineos in 173 BCE and Galestos in 154–153 BCE. A Dionysios is also a sub-unit commander of an *hipparchia* at the beginning of the second century BCE, whether the first or the second one, regarding his area of recruitment.

We have also seen that there were a few inscriptions mentioning the third, fourth and fifth *hipparchies* in the second century BCE. For instance,

---

institutions militaires de l'Egypte sous les Lagides, pp.343–344.
54 Arrian, *Ars Tactica*, 18,4.
55 Asclepiodotus, Tactica, II, 7; Arrian, *Ars Tactica*, 10,8, 14.2 and 18,1.
56 Van 't Dack, *Ptolemaica Selecta*, p.52.
57 Van 't Dack, *Ptolemaica Selecta*, p.52.
58 Arrian, *Ars Tactica*, 18,4.
59 Asclepiodotus, *Tactica*, VII, 11; Arrian, *Ars Tactica*, 18,4.
60 Launey, *Recherches sur les armées hellénistiques*, tome II, see Appendix for page references.

THE TRANSFORMATION OF THE PTOLEMAIC ARMY IN THE SECOND CENTURY BCE

a horseman of the unit of Hexakontos is recruited at Theadelphia in Arsinoïte, in 150–149 BCE, the probable recruitment area of the third *hipparchia*. Hekatontos is therefore probably a unit commander of the third *hipparchia* at this time. And Demetrios leads a sub-unit of the fourth *hipparchia* between the beginning of the second century and 140 BCE. Only one inscription designates the sixth *hipparchia*. Somewhere between 190 and 150 BCE, Prôtogemos is a sub-unit commander of this *hipparchia*. Finally, two uncertain inscriptions refer to an eighth *hipparchia*, the first around 158–156 BCE, the second around 114–80 BCE: Polykrates, 'of the Macedonians', seems to be a sub-commander within this *hipparchia* in 158–156 BCE.

From the mid-second century BCE, the names of *katoikoi* begin to appear, including seven *hipparcheis*. With regard to sub-commanders, four *katoikoi* belonged to the unit of Drytônos between 113 and 90 BCE, but we do not know their *hipparchia*'s number. These horsemen are from Akoris in Hermopolite. A fifth rider recruited in this same area is attached to the unit of Apollopharos in 110–109 BCE and, still in this recruitment area, a sixth is member of the mercenary *hegemonia* of Dokos. Five other *katoikoi* cavalrymen, whose area of recruitment is not known, are members of the unit of Ammônios and Nikostratos in the years 90–50 BCE, while another is member of the unit of Kononos at the same time. Finally, Kastôr Mithrodatos is a Macedonian *hipparchês* in 77 BCE. A Thessalian cleruch, Timasikratès, is member of the unit of Kainônos in 72–71 BCE.

These are significant formations adopted only in times of war. Missions in peacetime or for small-scale warfare did not require units larger than the *hipparchia*. This is the case in Greece, where the size of cavalry contingents does not exceed 500 men during the War of the Allies. Polybius gives us some typical figures for this period. He lists, for example, 300 Macedonian cavalry, 300 mercenary cavalry, 200 Boeotian cavalry, and 50 Epirote cavalry in Antigonus' army, which would face Cleomenes' army in 222 BCE.[61] Or 300 Achaean cavalry under Aratus,[62] followed by 500 Achaean cavalry a little later.[63] These few examples are not far from the rare figures known for the Ptolemaic sources: thus, shortly before Raphia, Hippolochos would change sides with his 400 Thessalian cavalry.[64] Later, in 163 BCE, the rebellious Cyrenians fielded 500 cavalry.[65]

61　Polybius, *Histories*, book II, 3, 65.
62　Polybius, *Histories*, book IV, 1, 10.
63　Polybius, *Histories*, book IV, 1, 14.
64　Polybius, *Histories*, book V, 2, 70.
65　Polybius, *Histories*, book XXXI, 18.

The Campaigns of the Second Century BCE

The second century was rich in military campaigns, although they are far less known than those of the previous century. The first one will be disastrous for the Ptolomies. In 169 BCE, the Seleucid Antiochus IV Epiphanes, 'seeing the affairs of his kingdom going smoothly, resolved to make an expedition against Egypt, of which he coveted possession.'[66] It is Flavius Josephus who gives us some details about this campaign. Ptolemy Epiphanes had just died, leaving two young sons:

> the elder of whom was nicknamed Philometor and the younger Physcon…. [Antiochus] disdaining the sons of Ptolemy, still too weak and incapable of governing such a kingdom, marched with considerable forces against Pelusium and, after deceiving Ptolemy Philometor by cunning, invaded Egypt; arriving near Memphis, he took the city and marched on Alexandria to besiege it, capture it, and seize Ptolemy who ruled there.[67]

In 168 BCE, the Romans having ordered him to leave the country, the Seleucid was ejected from all of Egypt.

Queen Cleopatra Thea Epiphanes, Cleopatra I, (204–176 BCE, r.193–180 BCE, Regent of Egypt 180–176 BCE) disliked her eldest son and could not tolerate him reigning. The years 168 to 150 BCE would therefore see mother and son clash. Cleopatra had convinced her husband to send their eldest son to Cyprus with the title of general. As he had become a formidable general, she hatched a plot to oust him. In October 164 BCE, Philometor managed to escape the Alexandrians, who placed the younger son, Alexander, now known as Ptolemy VIII Euergetes II, or Physcon, on the throne. According to Pausanias, 'Cleopatra was punished for her injustice to Ptolemy because Alexander, who owed her the crown, had her killed.'[68] Having discovered this crime, the people expelled Physcon and Philometor returned to the throne in the following year. According to Diodorus:

> Ptolemy the elder, with the help of a powerful army, laid siege to his brother and reduced him to the last extremity. However, he did not dare to kill him, as much because of his clemency and their kinship as because he feared the Romans. He therefore granted him his life and concluded a treaty under which his younger brother was to be content with possession of Cyrene and a certain quantity of wheat

---

66   Flavius Josephus, *Antiquities of the Jews*, book XII, 5, 2.
67   Flavius Josephus, *Antiquities of the Jews*, book XII, 5, 2.
68   Pausanias, *Description of Greece*, book I, IX, 3.

supplied annually. This was the unexpected and benevolent end to a bitter war between these two Kings.[69]

Physcon thus obtained Cyrenaica, but Polybius reported that in 163:

> …after the two Ptolemies had divided the kingdom, the younger of them went to Rome to request the annulment of this division…. [so] the Senate, seeing that the shares of the two Kings were quite unequal and considering it good policy to consecrate the division of the kingdom by itself proceeding to a new division, granted Physcon what he asked for, thinking only of the interest of Rome.[70]

Thus, the civil war resumed. The following year, Physcon raised a 'powerful body of mercenaries'[71] in Greece and secured the services of the Macedonian Damasippus. But the Roman Senate intervened, demanding that he disband his soldiers and abandon his expedition against Cyprus. Ptolemy the younger complied but began to raise a thousand soldiers in Crete. Philometor having 'succeeded in winning over the Roman commissioners' to his cause, Physcon 'does not know what to think anymore.'[72] He then returned to Africa to suppress a revolt of the Cyrenaeans.

The Cyrenaeans, reinforced by Libyans, had deployed their army on the slopes of the Great Catabathmos, between the Nile Delta and Cyrenaica. Ptolemy Physcon then embarked half of his troops 'and ordered them to bypass the rugged terrain, in order to emerge on the enemy's rear,' while he personally, 'with the other half of his army, advanced straight towards the heights to force the passage.'[73] The manoeuvre succeeds: 'Attacked from both sides at once, the Libyans became afraid and abandoned their positions.'[74] Consequently, Physcon resumed his march but the Cyrenaeans had withdrawn to a second position, with an army of 8,000 infantry and 500 cavalry. The exact numbers of Ptolemy's forces are not known, but they were probably of the same order. Ptolemy was defeated but managed to remain master of the country by negotiating concessions with the cities.

Around 147 BCE, Apollonius, general of Alexander Balas, King of Syria, suffered a defeat against the Jew, Jonathan. 'At the same time, King Ptolemy, nicknamed Philometor, arrived in Syria with a fleet and troops to assist Alexander, who was his son-in-law.'[75] But, unexpectedly, Ptolemy 'nearly perished as a victim of Alexander's ambushes, at the hands of Ammonius, a

---

69   Diodorus Siculus, *Library of History*, book XXI.
70   Polybius, *Histories*, book XXXI, 10.
71   Polybius, *Histories*, book XXXI, 17.
72   Polybius, *Histories*, book XXXI, 18.
73   Polybius, *Histories*, book XXXI, 18.
74   Polybius, *Histories*, book XXXI, 18.
75   Flavius Josephus, *Antiquities of the Jews*, book XIII, 4, 5.

friend of his.'[76] While Alexander, now his enemy, crossed from Cilicia into Syria 'with a considerable army'[77] and plundered the territory of Antioch, Ptolemy marched against him with his son-in-law Demetrius. In 146 BCE, Alexander was defeated and fled. But in the battle, 'Ptolemy's horse, startled by the trumpet of an elephant, reared and threw off the King; the enemies, noticing this, rushed upon him, inflicted many head wounds, and put him in mortal danger; snatched from their hands by his bodyguards, Ptolemy was in such a serious condition that for four days he neither regained consciousness nor speech.'[78] Zabelus, prince of the Arabs, sent Alexander's head to Ptolemy, who had recovered from his wounds. But Ptolemy died shortly after, 'full of joy to know that Alexander was dead.'[79]

Ptolemy Euergetes II was then recalled from Cyrene by his supporters. However, he had to marry Cleopatra II, widow of Philometor, to obtain power. From this time, we have a letter to the 'Armed Forces of Cyprus' from the new ruler of Egypt, probably dating from the year 144 BCE. This letter aims to thank the infantry, cavalry, and navy forces stationed in Cyprus who supported Euergetes II when he seized power, and he therefore grants them a lifelong pension.

According to Diodorus Siculus, in the years 143–140 BCE,

> Ptolemy had become odious due to his cruelty, his murders, his debauchery, and the ignoble corpulence of his body, which earned him the nickname Physcon. But the general Hierax, a man well versed in military art, very eloquent in popular assemblies, preserved Ptolemy's kingdom. This King lacked money, and the troops were about to defect to the party of Galaestes when Hierax paid them from his own coffers and quelled the rebellion. – The Egyptians completely despised Ptolemy when they saw him behaving like a child in assemblies, indulging in the most shameful debaucheries, and enfeebled by intemperance.[80]

In 128 BCE, according to Diodorus Siculus,

> Hegelochus, lieutenant of Ptolemy the Elder, was sent with an army against Marsyas, general of the Alexandrians. He captured him and nearly destroyed his entire army. Marsyas was brought before the King, and everyone expected him to be cruelly punished; but Ptolemy pardoned him: he was already beginning to repent of his

---

76 Flavius Josephus, *Antiquities of the Jews*, book XIII, 4, 6.
77 Flavius Josephus, *Antiquities of the Jews*, book XIII, 4, 8.
78 Flavius Josephus, *Antiquities of the Jews*, book XIII, 4, 8.
79 Flavius Josephus, *Antiquities of the Jews*, book XIII, 4, 8.
80 Diodorus Siculus, *Library of History*, book XXIII.

crimes and sought, by a benevolent conduct, to make the masses more favourable towards him.[81]

Diodorus probably refers to Physcon as Ptolemy the Elder, with the Alexandrians being in rebellion since 131 or 130 BCE.

The internal troubles were far from over, and the successor of Euergetes II, Ptolemy X Philometor Soter II, also known as Lathyros, who reigned from 116 to 81 BCE, would have to suppress a new revolt of the Thebans towards the end of his reign. Initially, a familiar scenario unfolds once again before the eyes of the Egyptians. Cleopatra, widow of Euergetes II, despised her eldest son, Ptolemy Lathyros, and forced him to divorce his wife, Cleopatra IV, who is also his sister. In 114 BCE, Cleopatra IV marries Antiochus IX Cyzicenus, one of the claimants to the kingdom of Syria, bringing with her as dowry the army of Cyprus. Having defeated his rival, Antiochus VIII Grypus, Antiochus IX seeks help from Ptolemy Lathyros against the Jews of Hyrcanus. Cleopatra III, who despises the Cyzicenus as much as her son, set up a scheme that incites the people against Lathyros. He fled to Cyprus in 108 BCE, and it would be 10 years before he regained the throne of Egypt.

The Battle of Asophon (103 BCE)

At that time, Alexander Jannaeus, or Jonathan, King of the Jews, is in the process of conquering Coele-Syria. In 104, the inhabitants of Ptolemais, besieged, appealed to Ptolemy Lathyros : 'The envoys made him hope that, if he went to Syria, he would find as allies, along with the people of Ptolemais, those of Gaza and Zoilus; the Sidonians and many others would join him.'[82] Lathyros manages to assemble an army of 30,000 men. During the crossing, he learned that the people of Ptolemais had changed their minds. Nevertheless, he continued the crossing, landed at Sycaminos and led his army to the walls of Ptolemais. Zoilus and the people of Gaza then come to him against Alexander Jannaeus, who was ravaging their territory. He raises 50,000 men from the country and goes to meet Ptolemy. The battle takes place at Asophon, on the banks of the Jordan, in 103 BC: 'Alexander went to meet him on the banks of the Jordan, in a place called Asophon, not far from the river, and pitched his camp near the enemy. He had as front-line fighters 8,000 men, whom he called 'champions of a hundred men,' armed with bronze-covered shields.'[83] According to Flavius Josephus, 'the front-line soldiers of Ptolemy also had similar shields; but inferior in all other respects, Ptolemy's soldiers approached the danger more timidly.'[84]

---

81   Diodorus Siculus, *Library of History*, book XXIV-XXXV (parts).
82   Flavius Josephus, *Antiquities of the Jews*, book XIII,.12, 2.
83   Flavius Josephus, *Antiquities of the Jews*, book XIII,.12, 5.
84   Flavius Josephus, *Antiquities of the Jews*, book XIII,.12, 5.

THE ARMIES OF PTOLEMAIC EGYPT

Representation of a typical Ptolemaic soldier in the second and first centuries BCE (Artwork by the author)

It is difficult to interpret this assertion. According to the 'Dead Sea Scrolls', the Hasmonean Jews carried shields of the *thureos*-type and pikes of 3.15 metres or even 3.60 metres for elite troops.[85] In what way were the Ptolomies inferior? If, like the Jews, the front-line Egyptian soldiers carried the *thureos*, it is probably because they are no longer equipped with *sarissas*. Otherwise, since the Ptolemaic *sarissa* was longer than the Hasmonean pike, the Jewish historian would have written that their shields were inferior and the rest of their equipment superior.

The 'tactician' Philostephanos commands Ptolemy's army. After 'inspiring great confidence'[86] in his troops, he leads them to cross the Jordan, without Alexander attempting to oppose him. The latter thinks that if the enemies have the river at their back, their retreat will be cut off and they will be more easily crushed. The battle at first seemed balanced: 'When they came to blows, at the beginning, same exploits on both sides, same ardour; both armies suffered great losses.'[87] But Alexander's soldiers eventually gain the upper hand. It was then that Philostephanos, 'cleverly dividing his troops, came to reinforce the ranks that were weakening.'[88] Since Alexander Jannaeus had not taken such precautions, the Jewish troops, shaken, 'ended up fleeing, without finding any help in the neighbouring troops, which he instead dragged into his rout.'[89] The Ptolemaic soldiers then pursued the Jews whom they cut to pieces: 'having routed the entire army, they chased and massacred them until their swords were blunt and their hands tired of killing.'[90] The Jewish losses were said to be 30,000 men according to Flavius Josephus, or 50,000 according to Timagenes.

After the battle, Ptolemy Lathyros ravages Judea, take Ptolemais and Gaza. Cleopatra, his mother, reacts and without delay, she assembles both military and naval forces and leads 'an expedition against him, of which she gave overall

---

85 Michael Wise, Martin Abegg Jr, Edward Cook, *Les manuscrits de la mer Morte* (Paris: Perrin, 2003), 8, pp.182–181.
86 Flavius Josephus, *Antiquities of the Jews*, book XIII,.12, 5.
87 Flavius Josephus, *Antiquities of the Jews*, book XIII,.12, 5.
88 Flavius Josephus, *Antiquities of the Jews*, book XIII,.12, 5.
89 Flavius Josephus, *Antiquities of the Jews*, book XIII,.12, 5.
90 Flavius Josephus, *Antiquities of the Jews*, book XIII,.12, 5.

command to the Jews Chelkias and Ananias.'[91] Then, 'after ordering her son Alexander to sail to Phoenicia with a considerable fleet, she herself came at the head of all her forces to Ptolemais, and, the inhabitants having refused to receive her, besieged the city.'[92] The cunning Ptolemy, thinking to find Egypt ungarrisoned, directs his army there to seize it by surprise. But Cleopatra reacts quickly, sending troops to Pelusium, and Chelkias pursues him before meeting his death in Coele-Syria. Ptolemy retraces his steps and spends the winter at Gaza while Cleopatra take Ptolemais, after a siege in due form.

---

[91] Flavius Josephus, *Antiquities of the Jews*, book XIII,.13, 1.
[92] Flavius Josephus, *Antiquities of the Jews*, book XIII,.13, 1.

6

The Fall: the First Century BCE

In 89 BCE, an uprising of the Alexandrians forces the ruler, Ptolemy Alexander, to flee. He will recruit a mercenary army in Syria to retake the city, but he dies the following year, and Ptolemy X Soter II is restored. The Thebans take advantage of this to revolt once again. It will take three years for Ptolemy, from 87 to 85 BCE, to suppress these revolts, but the size and composition of his army are not known. An inscription tells us that Soter II, 'headed towards Memphis while Hierax, with numerous troops, advanced to subdue Thebes.'[1] Pausanias wrote that he, 'left no trace of their former opulence, once superior to that of the richest cities of Greece, even that of the temple of Delphi, and of Orchomenos in Boeotia.'[2]

'The power of Rome, which Italy could no longer contain, was beginning to spread towards the East,' wrote Justin.[3] Ptolemy Lathyros had wisely stayed out of the conflict between Rome and Mithridates of Pontus. But in 80 BCE, Sulla, now dictator, imposed Ptolemy Alexander II on the throne of Egypt. Accused of the murder of his stepmother, he is quickly assassinated by the Alexandrians, and this crime marks the end of the Ptolemaic dynasty. To escape the annexation of their country by the Romans, the Alexandrians place on the throne an illegitimate child of Ptolemy Lathyros: Ptolemy XIII Philopator Philadelphus, also called Neos Dionysos and Auletes. Tolerated by Rome, this makeshift King ruled from 80, fled in 58, then was restored to the throne of Egypt in 55 BCE with the help of Gabinius. Before leaving for Syria, this Roman consul left cohorts of Gallic and Germanic legionaries in Alexandria. Ptolemy Auletes dies in 51 BCE. Cleopatra VII Philopator, aged 17, then marries her brother Ptolemy XIV, who is only 10. In 49 BCE, Pompey comes to requisition the Egyptian fleet. Cleopatra complies with his request and entrusts him with a squadron of 50 to 60 ships carrying 500 men from Gabinius. The defeat of Pharsalus brings Pompey back to Egypt,

---

1.   Pierre Jouguet, 'Documents ptolémaïques', *Bulletin de Correspondance Helléniques*, 21 (1897), pp.141–147.
2.   Pausanias, *Description of Greece*, book I, IX.
3.   Justin, *History of the world*, book XXXIX, 5.

where he is assassinated. Caesar, following in the footsteps of his rival, arrives in Alexandria a few days later, at the head of two legions numbering only 4,000 men, including 800 cavalry. Pompey's head is handed over to him by the regent Theodotus, but the people of Alexandria do not accept Caesar's presence.

To fight against Caesar, the Alexandrians make levies throughout the kingdom and beyond the borders. 'The Alexandrians, on their part, did not delay or procrastinate in their preparations. Indeed, they had sent delegates and commissioners throughout Egypt and to all the borders of the kingdom, tasked with hastening the levies, and already they had amassed a considerable stock of weapons and machines, and attracted an immense crowd of men.'[4]

Achillas 'commanded the veteran troops,'[5] writes Caesar, specifying, 'The troops commanded by Achillas were not to be underestimated, either because of their number or because of their courage and experience. He had under arms 20,000 men.'[6] These troops were partly composed of former legionaries of Gabinius, partly of mercenaries from Syria and Cilicia, and finally of condemned criminals, exiles, and runaway slaves. Caesar adds that there were, 'also 2,000 cavalrymen seasoned in the wars of Alexandria: these were the ones who had restored Ptolemy, killed the two sons of Bibulus, and fought against the Egyptians. They had therefore enough experience in warfare.'[7] The Ptolemaic infantry was thus made up of three distinct groups: 'Gabinius's troops are gathered into a unit organised in the Roman manner, commanded by the tribune L. Septimius.' Julius Caesar considers these men to have lost some of their quality after experiencing the pleasures of Alexandria: 'They were Gabinius's soldiers: accustomed then to the life and customs of Alexandria, they had lost the memory of the Roman people and its discipline; they had married, and most of them had children.'[8] These veteran cohorts were placed in the most important posts of the city.

The mercenaries, who constitute the largest part of the 20,000 men, were recruited in Asia: 'To them was joined a rabble of thieves and brigands, from Syria, Cilicia, and neighbouring countries.'[9] Caesar does not say where these units of mercenaries are placed: they probably form part of what Caesar describes as the veteran troops.

Finally, the last part of Achillas's troops consists of the condemned criminals, et cetera. Caesar mentions 'a crowd of people condemned to death and banished,'[10] and adds:

---

4 Julius Caesar, *Commentaries on The Alexandrian War*, 2,1.
5 Julius Caesar, *Commentaries on The Alexandrian War*, 4,1.
6 Julius Caesar, *Commentaries on the Civil War*, III, 110, 1–2.
7 Julius Caesar, *Commentaries on the Civil War*, III, 110, 1, 5–6.
8 Julius Caesar, *Commentaries on the Civil War*, III, 110, 2.
9 Julius Caesar, *Commentaries on the Civil War*, III, 110, 3.
10 Julius Caesar, *Commentaries on the Civil War*, III, 110, 3.

THE ARMIES OF PTOLEMAIC EGYPT

Our runaway slaves found in Alexandria a safe refuge and a certain existence, as soon as they registered themselves among the soldiers. If any one of them was arrested by his master, all ran to the rescue and snatched him from his hands, because being equally guilty, they defended their own cause. According to an ancient custom of the army of Alexandria, they could demand the death of the favourites who displeased them, enrich themselves by looting the rich, besiege the palaces of their Kings, take and give the crown.[11]

He then specifies, in *The Alexandrian War*, that, 'all slaves of serving age had been armed, and those whose masters were wealthy were given daily pay and rations.'[12] This 'multitude, well distributed,'[13] is tasked with defending the fortifications of the most remote quarters.

Terracotta from Fayoum probably depicting an Egyptian *machimos* of the late period. This type of rectangular shield appeared in the first century BCE. It is also depicted in the Nile mosaic at Preneste (Perdrizet, *Les terres cuites grecques d'Egypte de la collection Fouquet*, 1921, plate XXXII)

Missing from this enumeration are the new recruits raised, 'throughout Egypt and at the kingdom's borders,' contributing to form the 'countless multitude.'[14] These troops were likely used outside Alexandria, at Pelusium for example. Against Mithridates of Pergamon, Ptolemy sent troops that probably included *katoikoi* and *machimoi*, remnants of ancient institutions. Indeed, inscriptions reveal, between 55 and 30 BCE, several names of *hipparcheis* of *katoikoi* cavalry or 'Macedonians.'[15] The first *hipparchia* seems to still exist. The inscriptions also reveal names of *laarchia*, which are units formed of indigenous troops.

Van 't Dack noted the emergence at this time of a new term referring to a military unit: the *speira*,[16] a term often translated as 'cohort' or 'band' in other contexts. This is probably a new unit inspired by the Roman cohort. This term appears

---

11   Julius Caesar, *Commentaries on the Civil War*, III, 110, 4.
12   Julius Caesar, *Commentaries on The Alexandrian War*, 2,2.
13   Julius Caesar, *Commentaries on The Alexandrian War*, 2,3.
14   Julius Caesar, *Commentaries on The Alexandrian War*, 2,1.
15   Launey M., *Recherches sur les armées hellénistiques*, Tome I, p.328.
16   Van 't Dack, *Ptolemaica Selecta*, p.222.

THE FALL: THE FIRST CENTURY BCE

in a papyrus dating from 51–50 BCE, mentioning the *speira* of Diphilos,[17] and another one from 49 BCE mentioning the *speira* of Sadaleios and the *laarchês* Alexandros.[18]

The officer ranks systematically appearing on the stelae are the *hekatontarchos*, the *pentekontarchos*, the *ouragos*, the *sêmeiophoros*, and the *ieraulês*, suggesting that the entire army is now organised into *sêmeia* of soldiers of the *thureophoros* type. The garrisons seem to be now primarily composed of mercenaries.

A detail of the Nile mosaic of Palestrina, depicting Ptolemaic soldiers as well as Ethiopians hunting. This mosaic dates from *c.* 100 BCE. (Public Domain)

---

17 Van 't Dack, *Ptolemaica Selecta*, p.222; BGU 8 1806.
18 Van 't Dack, *Ptolemaica Selecta*, p.222; BGU 8 1763.

As mentioned in the previous chapter, three stelae from Hermoupolis Magna dated from the end of the second century for the first one (Lefebvre stele), 80–79 BCE for the second one (Jouguet stele) and 78 BCE for the third one (Roeder stele) provide additional views of the composition of what seems to be the *sêmeia*, which appeared in the previous century. These stelae list the names of six of these units, with missing lines where the numbers of the first and third units should be. The Jouguet stele also lacks the first 15 lines, which may have contained the names of the overall staff. Each of the six units has a commander (*hêgemôn*), a lieutenant (*ouragos*), an ensign (*sêmeiophoros*), and four *pentekontarchoi* designated by the letter N (meaning 50). The second *sêmeia* also includes a flute player (*ieraulês*) among its ranks, and the sixth includes an *hypêretês* (quartermaster or 'attendant'). The *ouragos* now appears in second position in the list, probably making him a lieutenant. The presence of a flautist is also new. Finally, the commander of the fifth unit is also designated as a *phrourarchos*, meaning garrison commander.[19] Tables 4 and 5, below, give an overview of Jouguet and Roeder stelae.

Table 4: Jouguet Stele, Hermoupolis Magna (80 or 79 BCE)[20]

Column 2	
(line 105)	
Number 2 *Hêgemôn*	Aphrodisios, son of Serapiôn
Ouragos:	Pyrrhos, son of Pyrrhos
Sêmeiophoros	Aristomenes, son of Dalaïlos
N (*pentekontarchos*)	Diophantos, son of Apollodotos
N (*pentekontarchos*)	Demas, son of Hermias
N (*pentekontarchos*)	Dionys, son of Thedôros
N (*pentekontarchos*)	Nikaios, son of Argatos
(line 166)	
Ieraulês	Nikôn

---

19 Bernand, *Inscriptions grecques d'Hermoupolis Magna et de sa nécropole*, pp.21–72.
20 Bernand, *Inscriptions Grecques d'Hermoupolis Magna et de sa Nécropole*, pp.37–40.

THE FALL: THE FIRST CENTURY BCE

Table 5: Roeder Stele, Hermoupolis Magna (78 BCE)[21]

Column 1	
(Line 5) Number 4	
Hege(mon)	Zôpuros, son of Protarchos,
Oura(gos)	Kleidès, son of Zabdos,
Sême(iophoros)	…, son of Sôtiôn,
N'(*pentekontarchos*)	…, son of Zenon,
N'(*pentekontarchos*)	…, son of Lysas,
N'(*pentekontarchos*)	…, son of S…
N'(*pentekontarchos*)	(No)umenios, son of Akamas,
(line 39)	
Ierophaltes	Appolodotos,
(line 76)	
Kêrux	Hermola(os), son of Apollô(nios)
Column 2	
(line 76) Number 5	
(*Hêgemôn*) *kai p(hrourarkos)*	Herakleidês, son of Apollônios,
Oura(gos)	Apollônios, son of Kleôn,
Sême(iophoros)	Apollônios, son of Nikias,
N (*pentekontarchos*)	Maisaizabas, son of Menandros,
N (*pentekontarchos*)	Herakleôn, son of Ptolemaios,
N (*pentekontarchos*)	Kosakabos, son of Apollodotos,
N (*pentekontarchos*)	Apollôs, son of Apollônios,
Column 3	
(line 147)	
Number 6 *Hêgemôn*	Telauges, son of Nikomachos
Oura(gos)	Thradikas, son of Rabelos,
Sême(iophoros)	Isidoros, son of Alexandros,
N (*pentekontarchos*)	Demetrios, son of Apollônios,
N (*pentekontarchos*)	Theophilos, son of Apollônios,
N (*pentekontarchos*)	Isidotos, son of Gaios,
N (*pentekontarchos*)	Zôsimos, son of Zôsimos,
Hypê(retês)	Alexandros, son of Alexandros,

Note on tables 4 and 5: N or *nu* is the letter used in Greek to represent the number 50 and thus the *pentekontarchia*.

---

21   Bernand, *Inscriptions Grecques d'Hermoupolis Magna et de sa Nécropole*, pp.58–61.

THE ARMIES OF PTOLEMAIC EGYPT

Terracotta from Egypt representing the head of a man wearing a *pilos*-type cap. Achillas' rabble probably wore this type of cap (Perdrizet, *Les terres cuites grecques d'Egypte de la collection Fouquet*, 1921, plate LXIII)

In addition to the officers, these units contain 96 names of soldiers for the first, 55 for the second, 68 for the third, 64 for the fourth, 62 for the fifth, and 61 names for the sixth. The Jouguet stele adds a list of 17 'Elite Royal Sword Carriers' (*Eglelokismenoi machairphoroi Basilikoi*).[22] If these units are up to strength, it means that the strength of a garrison *sêmeia* in peacetime is now only about 100 men. But these two stelae are dedications related to a religious foundation made by the officers and soldiers of the garrison. There is no reason to believe that the entire unit contributed, even for religious beliefs. Therefore, these figures do not predict the theoretical strength in wartime, which can be, as in the previous century, 200 men excluding officers, in four *pentekontarchies* of 50 men, or 256 men, in four *pentekontarchies* of 64 men.

These hypotheses would be confirmed by the average size of units in the Hellenistic world, as noted in the previous chapter: Polybius often cites examples of units numbering 200 to 300 men.

Aside from the *semeia*, and from 51–50 BCE the *speira*, *machimoi* are still formed in *laarchies*. For the first century, we have some possible names of *laarchês*: Isidotos[23] and possibly Chomênis, already discussed in the previous section.

---

22 Bernand, *Inscriptions Grecques d'Hermoupolis Magna et de sa Nécropole,* p.40.
23 Peremans & Van 't Dack, *Prosopographia Ptolemaica*, p.32 (2045).

7

Military and Civilian Dress

If Ptolemaic soldiers sometimes received a clothing allowance from the state, the *imastismos*,[1] there is nothing to suggest that in some elite units the soldiers were distinguished by a uniform. In the case of the elite cavalry, there are solid indications that the cloak could be uniform. Diodorus tells us that Alexander the Great gave his companions clothes trimmed with purple.[2] And according to Plutarch, Eumenes of Cardia provided purple *chlamydes* to his Macedonians.[3] But even for these elite units, we lack evidence concerning the Ptolemaic army.

The *chlamys*, a type of cloak, and the *crepides*, which are boots, make up the typical attire of the Ptolemaic soldier. Theocritus, in his *15th Idyll* entitled 'The Syracusans or Adonis Festival,' has Gorgo exclaiming as she tries to make her way through the many warriors in Ptolemy Philadelphus's Alexandria: 'Everywhere you look, there are only wearers of *crepides* and *chlamydes*!'[4] Menander, in his play *The Sicyonian*, also distinguishes the soldier by his attire: 'My dear Stratophanes, you only have a simple *chlamys*, and just one boy. It seems that nothing invites contempt more than the appearance of a soldier, especially a mercenary soldier.'[5] *Chlamydes* can be plain, striped or trimmed and were fastened at the shoulder. Numerous funerary stelae show these items of clothing.

Underneath the *chlamys*, the soldier generally wears the *chiton*, a short-sleeved tunic. Ruben Post conducted a study on the colours of the cloaks. Out of 46 tunics whose colour could be identified, 40 percent were red, 18 percent white, 12 percent blue and the same

Stylised copies of a Greek statue showing a warrior wearing a *chlamys*, (Author's Artwork, based on Froehner, *Terres cuites d'Asie de la collection Julien Gréau*, Paris, 1886)

---

1   Launey M., *Recherches sur les armées hellénistiques*, Tome II, pp.727–728 & 734.
2   Diodorus Siculus, *Library of History*, book XVII, 77.
3   Plutarch, The Parallel Lives, *Life of Eumenes*, XVI.
4   Theocritus, Idyll XV, *The Festival of Adonis*.
5   Menander, *The Sicyonians*.

THE ARMIES OF PTOLEMAIC EGYPT

Stylised copies of two Greek statues showing men in *chiton*. (Author's Artwork)

Representation of light troops in *chiton*. (Author's Artwork)

MILITARY AND CIVILIAN DRESS

proportion yellow. The remaining colours included brown, pink, green, grey and purple.[6]

More than the uniform, it was the helmets and shields that contributed to a certain uniformity within the Ptolemaic army. As far as shields are concerned, the AllardPierson Museum, in Amsterdam, has a Ptolemaic round shield mould, in limestone, which has the inscription '*Ptolemaioy*' (i.e. 'Ptolemy') in the centre. This mould was found near Mit-Rahineh, the site of ancient Memphis, in Cairo. This limestone can have been used for the industrial production of bronze shields of the Ptolemaic phalanx, at least the *agema*, all with the same design. A further indication of uniformity is given by the colours of the *thureos* shields, which are often white. The illustrations in this book bear witness to this.

Regarding helmets, the AllardPierson Museum holds a mould of a Boeotian type helmet, also found in Memphis. This mould was, again, carved in limestone. Further evidence of the uniformity of the helmets can be found in the engravings and paintings. The stelae of Sidon, for instance, reveal only two different types of helmets for this part of the second century BCE. Nick Sekunda refers to them as 'Sidon type A' and 'Sidon type B'.[7] Some of these helmets can also be found depicted on terracotta figurines found Asia Minor.[8] Other types of helmets may have been worn in the third century BCE, such as shown on the model found near Ascalon.[9]

In the end, even though most Ptolemaic troops did not wear uniforms, a deployed army probably displayed a certain homogeneity, provided by the equipment and the type or colour of shields.

Terracotta from Egypt representing a man wearing a cloth headdress. (Perdrizet, *Les terres cuites grecques d'Egypte de la collection Fouquet*, 1921, plate CXVI)

Civilians and Servants

Armies have always been followed by their retinue of servants, tradesmen, soldiers' wives and children, and the Ptolemaic army is no exception to the rule. By the Hellenistic period, civilians were no longer dressed in the traditional Egyptian loincloth.

The tomb of Petosiris, discovered in 1919 and described by Gustave Lefebvre, contains frescoes that reveal civilians at the time of Alexander the

---

6   Ruben Post, 'Bright colours and uniformity, Hellenistic military costume', *Ancient Warfare*, 6:4 (2010), pp.14–19.
7   Sekunda, *The Ptolemaic Army*, pp.21–33.
8   Sekunda, *The Ptolemaic Army*, p.74.
9   G. Radan, 'Helmet found near Ascalon', *Israel Exploration Society*, 8:3 (1958), pp.185–188.

THE ARMIES OF PTOLEMAIC EGYPT

Great and Ptolemy I Soter. These include ploughmen wearing shirts slightly longer than the Greek *chiton* or *exomis*. Some of these peasants wear conical caps made of straw or papyrus.

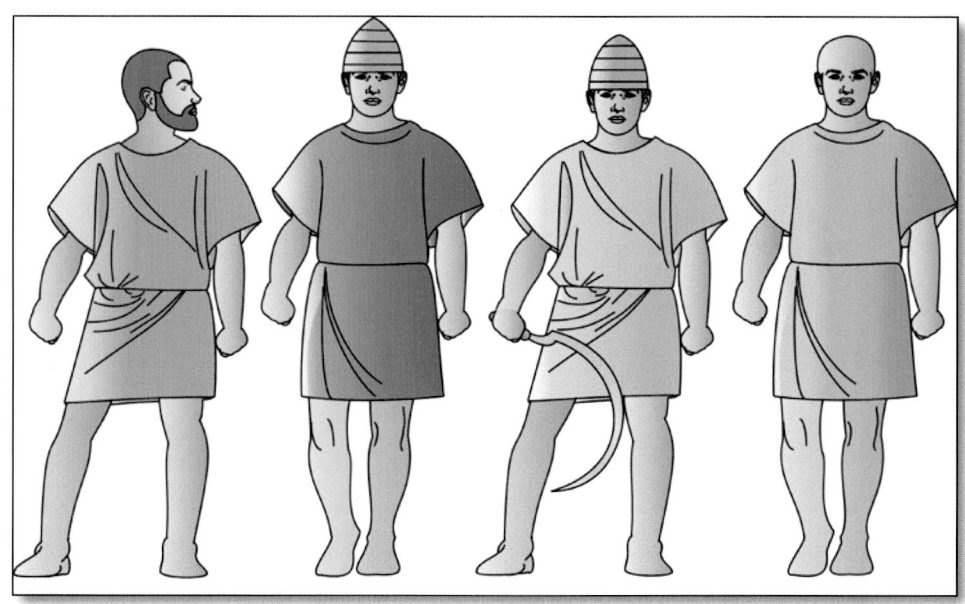

Egyptian peasants from the Petosiris frescoes (Author's Artwork)

Egyptian peasant from the Petosiris frescoes (Author's Artwork)

A set of terracotta from Egypt depicting different types of fabric caps. (Perdrizet, *Les terres cuites grecques d'Egypte de la collection Fouquet*, 1921, plate LXXII)

8

An Opponent of Ptolemaic Dynasty: The Jewish Army of the Second and First Centuries BCE

At the end of the second and during the first century BCE, the Semites constituted one of the main sources of recruitment for mercenaries for the Ptolemaic rulers. However, the Jews also became enemies of the dynasty during the second half of the second century BCE. The Battle of Asophon in 103 BCE, which pitted Ptolemy Lathyros against Alexander Jannaeus, better known as Jonathan, was the culmination of this conflict.

It is likely that the Maccabean Jews, from 168 to 104 BCE, and the Hasmoneans, from 103 to 63 BCE, inspired or were inspired by the Ptolemaic rulers in terms of organisation from the second century onwards. Therefore, it is interesting to dedicate a chapter to them. The main sources regarding the Jewish Army of this period are the *Books of the Maccabees*, the *Rule of War* (or 'War Scroll' as part of the 'Dead Sea Scrolls'), dating from the first century BCE, and the *Antiquities of the Jews* by Flavius Josephus.

Organisation of the Jewish Armies

According to the 'War Scroll', the Jewish Army is divided into myriads (a term which could denote 10,000 men or a multitude), thousands, centuries, fifties, and tens,[1] an organisation reminiscent of the Ptolemaic or Seleucid phalanx, *chiliarchia, hekatontarchia, pentekontarchia,* and *dekania*. The *First Book of Maccabees* confirms this: 'Judas appointed leaders of the people, leaders of thousands, of hundreds, of fifties, and of tens.'[2] Flavius Josephus uses the terms *chiliarchos* and *taxiarchos* to refer to the officers of the

---

1 Wise, Abegg & Cook, *Les manuscrits de la mer Morte*, pp.179–181.
2 *First Book of Maccabees*, 3, 55.

Maccabean Army that face those of Ptolemy, Nicanor and Gorgias, sent against him by Lysias, the guardian of the young Antiochus: 'Following the old national custom, he placed them under the command of *chiliarchoi* and *taxiarchoi* and sent away those who had recently married.'[3] The *chiliarchos* thus commanded the *chiliarchia*, while the *taxiarchos* likely commanded a *taxis*, with this rank being akin to the centurion in Polybius' works.

Each of these units are supposed to have its own banner, each bearing phrases associated with their rank. Thus, the banner of the tens should display 'a song of praise to God on the ten-stringed harp,'[4] along with the name of the leader and the nine men under him.

According to the 'War Scroll', the 12 Jewish tribes are required to provide 28,000 infantry and 6,000 cavalry.[5] However, interpreting this document poses several difficulties. Some scholars believe that the document was written by two authors at different times, and this view helps explain the inconsistencies in the text.

The 28,000 foot soldiers are to be divided into four divisions of 7,000 men, including a vanguard division. Indeed, the first section that discusses formation, following descriptions of trumpets, banners, and the commander's shield, deals with 'the deployment of divisions in battle when the army is fully assembled to form an advanced battle line.'[6] This 7,000-strong division would be arranged in seven ranks of 1,000 men each, as would the other three. Further along, it is written that this unit would fight in three groups: the first group composed of the first two lines, the second group composed of the next three lines, and the last group comprising the final two lines. The first group would consist of skirmishers, the second line of slingers, but the text does not specify the composition of the first line, likely archers or slingers. The soldiers of the next three lines, who would intervene after the first group had made seven shots, were supposed to be equipped with seven javelins each. Once the skirmishers returned to the line, this second group would hurl their javelins. Finally, the last two lines, forming the final group, were supposed to be equipped with melee weapons: spear and shield for the sixth line, sword and shield for the seventh and final line. The remaining 21,000 men would probably form three support divisions, one after the other.

To face Ptolemy IX on the banks of the Jordan in 103 BCE, Alexander Jannaeus assembled an army of 50,000 to 80,000 men. Flavius Josephus states that there were, '8,000 front-line fighters, whom he called 'hundred men champions,' armed with shields covered in bronze.'[7] If each file had seven rows, with 8,000 files, then the total would be 56,000 men. And if

---

3   Flavius Josephus, *Antiquities of the Jews*, book XIII,.12, 7, 3.
4   Wise, Abegg & Cook, *Les manuscrits de la mer Morte*, p.181.
5   Wise, Abegg & Cook, *Les manuscrits de la mer Morte*, p.181–183.
6   Wise, Abegg & Cook, *Les manuscrits de la mer Morte*, p.182.
7   Flavius Josephus, *Antiquities of the Jews*, book XIII,.12, 5.

each file had 10 men, then the total would be 80,000 men. The 'hundred men champions' were likely file leaders rather than actual champions.

A second regulation, called the 'regulation concerning the manoeuvres of battle divisions,'[8] mentions another, heavier formation. But the gaps in the document force us to formulate new hypotheses about it. This regulation, much of which is missing, describes formations consisting of 'slingers and towers' and 'bows and towers.' This formation consisted of four 'towers', each with 300 heavy infantrymen, armed with large shields and pikes. Each 'tower' consists of a 100-man unit at the front, flanked by two 100-man units in column on each flank. The appearance of this unit is reminiscent of a three-sided tower open at the rear, with the men's pikes measuring around 3.60 metres. It is in fact a square formation, the Romans also used the word *turris* to designate an equivalent formation.

Each of these four towers is identified by its name, inscribed on each shield (Michael, Gabriel, Sariel, and Raphael), and has two 'gates.' These were probably openings to allow other units, i.e. slingers and archers, to leave or enter to protect themselves, because these four 300-man towers, making a total of 1,200 for the whole line, seem to be preceded or accompanied by one or two lines of skirmishers, made up of slingers and archers. However, it is difficult to explain the sentence, placed between the description of the shields and the description of the composition of a tower: 'And the towers shall go out from the line,' or 'the towers shall go out from the line with 100 shields per side.' Is the battle line composed of units of archers and slingers between which the four towers are inserted? Or are the four towers, each preceded by their units of skirmishers who will then take refuge within them, intended to be inserted into, or between, the formations in seven lines described above? Nothing in the text allows us to answer this question precisely. However, the most likely hypothesis would be that, once the skirmishers are collected, the flanks of 100 men can come into line with the front, to form a continuous line of 1,200 men.

If the reason for the existence of these towers is the need to protect archers and slingers, where does this idea or representation come from? The relevant 'Dead Sea Scrolls' were probably written between 150 and 100 BCE. In 190 BCE, perhaps at the instigation of Antiochus III the Great, the Seleucids inaugurated a new way of deploying the army: the phalanx was divided into 10 formations of 1,600 men, in bodies of 50 men abreast and 32 deep. These blocks of pikemen flanked two elephants escorted by light troops.[9] Appian wrote, 'the phalanx looked like a rampart and the elephants like towers.'[10] Later, the phalanx opened its ranks to allow through the light infantry that was skirmishing ahead.[11] The Hasmonean Jews were familiar

---

8 Wise, Abegg & Cook, *Les manuscrits de la mer Morte*, pp.185–186.
9 Titus Livy, *The History of Rome*, book XXXVII, 40; Appian, *The Syrian Wars*, 32, 161–162.
10 Appian, *The Syrian Wars*, 32, 162.
11 Appian, *The Syrian Wars*, 32, 178.

with this provision since they had to face this beautiful order when they confronted Antiochos V Eupator at the Battle of Beth Zachariah in 162 BC:

> And they divided the beasts into the phalanxes, and they arrayed either side of each elephant 1,000 men in mail armour, and on the heads of them were helmets of brass, and 500 horses set apart for each of the beasts.... And there was on each elephant a wooden tower, a stronghold of wood arranged on the beast. And for each of them 2 and 30 men that fought with them, and their mahout.[12]

The word 'tower' is used in both cases to describe elephants. Nevertheless, the bodies of pikemen, probably 32 men abreast by 32 men deep at Beth Zachariah, must also have represented formidable towers behind which the skirmishers could take refuge.

Of the 6,000 horsemen, 1,400 are to be officers or elite riders attached to each of the lines. The passage concerning them can probably be translated as: '1400 mounts for officers of the lines, 50 for each line.'[13] These 1,400 elite cavalry must thus be distributed at a rate of 50 for each of the 28 lines (four waves of seven lines totalling 28 lines). The remaining 4,600 make up the rest of the cavalry armed with javelins and bows.

The cavalry regulation also specifies that they should be organised into formations of 700 men, arranged in seven lines, one of these formations on each wing of the infantry divisions. Thus, a division of 7,000 infantry will be flanked by two regiments of 700 cavalry, for a total of 1,400 men. As discussed above, each line of cavalry must also include 50 elite men, 25 on each wing, or one man in four. Finally, since there are four waves of seven lines, 28 lines in total, there should be 5,600 cavalrymen positioned on the flanks, with 2,800 on each wing. This leaves 400 men in reserve, perhaps assigned to the general's guard.

The organisation described by this regulation is original, although it is inspired by the Roman model. Each of the four successive divisions, each with seven lines, recalls the four lines of the Roman cohort, formed by maniples of *velites*, *hastati*, *principes*, and *triarii*, each arranged in six ranks, except for the latter. The overall depth of this formation would thus be about 18 to 24 ranks, whereas the four Jewish divisions would have a depth of 28 ranks. However, there seems to be a conceptual difference between these two systems: each Jewish division includes three specialised groups, as we have seen, namely two ranks of skirmishers, three of men with javelins, and two of spearmen and swordsmen, while each of the four Roman maniples is specialised: *velites* armed with javelins, *hastati* and *principes* armed with the *pilum*, and *triarii* armed with spears.

12　*First Book of Maccabees*, 6, 34–37.
13　Wise, Abegg & Cook, *Les manuscrits de la mer Morte*, p.183.

AN OPPONENT OF PTOLEMAIC DYNASTY

The organisation of the Jewish Army is therefore closer to the Roman model than to the Hellenistic model, the latter typically consisting of a phalanx usually formed in 16 ranks, preceded by a screen of skirmishers in eight ranks. It also seems to have been designed specifically to combat the phalanx. The first line of archers or slingers will unleash seven shots, then the first line of men seven javelins, and so on until the fifth line. Finally, the sixth line of spearmen and the seventh of swordsmen, reinforced by the first five lines which will have reformed behind them, will attempt to push back the weakened phalanx. And if these seven initial waves fail to break through, it will be the turn of the seven lines of the second division, placed in support, and so on.

Of course, care must be taken when using this as the primary source. We must bear in mind that the 'Dead Sea Scrolls' form a religious corpus, in which reality gives way to the theological dimension. Indeed, the number 'seven' is supposed to bring good luck because it is a sacred number in many religions. In the Bible, God created the world in seven days.

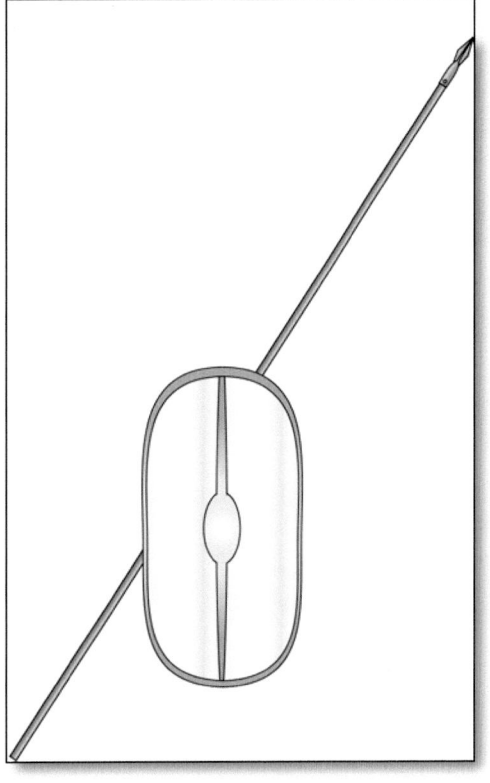

An interpretation of Maccabean Jewish military equipment: spear and shield. (Author's Artwork)

Troop Strength of the Maccabean and Hasmonean Armies

Against Nikanor, Judas Maccabee assembled 6,000 men,[14] whom he divided into four cohorts. He later had 10,000 men when facing Lysias.[15] Then Judas came with 8,000 men to Gilead while Simon came with 3,000 'elite' men to Galilee,[16] and Joseph led the rest of the forces.

At the Battle of Elasa in 160 BCE, where Judas Maccabee met his death against Judah Bacchides, the Jewish Army reportedly assembled only 3,000 men.[17] Later, Jonathan assembled 10,000 men,[18] who were joined by reinforcements brought by Simon prior to the Battle of Azotus in 148 BCE. Then, to confront Demetrius II, Jonathan managed to gather an army of 40,000 men in 142 BCE.[19] When Jean, the son of Simon, defeated Kendebae, he arranged his army with the cavalry, though small in number, in the

---

14 Second Book of Maccabees, 5, 8.
15 Flavius Josephus, *Antiquities of the Jews*, book XII, 7, 5.
16 Flavius Josephus, *Antiquities of the Jews*, book XII, 8, 2; First Book of Maccabees, 5, 20.
17 Flavius Josephus, *Antiquities of the Jews*, book XII, 11, 1.
18 Flavius Josephus, *Antiquities of the Jews*, book XIII, 4, 4.
19 First Book of Maccabees, 12, 41.

midst of 20,000 infantry.[20] In 103 BCE, Alexander Jannaeus assembled an army of 50,000 to 80,000 men to fight Ptolemy IX Lathyros on the banks of the Jordan.[21] Later, against Demetrius, Alexander deployed around 20,000 Jews and 10,200 mercenaries from Pisidia and Cilicia.[22]

Equipment of the Maccabean and Hasmonean Soldiers

According to the 'War Scroll', all infantrymen are to be equipped with a bronze shield, polished like a mirror, edged with a braid of interweaving of gold, silver, and bronze, adorned with gemstones and with a multi-coloured decorative device.[23] The 8,000 elite men that Alexander Jannaeus placed in the front line in 103 BCE carried 'shields covered with brass.'[24] Their dimensions were to be two and a half cubits high by one and a half wide (approximately 112.5 by 67.5cm). The text further describes 'tower soldiers', whose shields are to be larger, measuring 3 cubits high (about 135cm).[25] This is the size of the Roman *scutum*, which according to Polybius, measured 4 feet and a palm by 2.5 feet (or 136cm by 80cm). Flavius Josephus reported that, at the Battle of Elasa, Jonathan,

> …ordered his men to take cover under their armour and receive the shots fired by the enemy horsemen. The soldiers carried out this order; the enemy fired their shots at them, every last one of them, without harming them in any way, because the shots did not reach the men, who were protected by their shields, which, thanks to this thick carapace, were easily able to stop the projectiles, which fell harmlessly.[26]

The infantrymen were also to be armed with a sword one and a half cubits long (67.5cm) and a long spear of 7 cubits (3.11m), with the blade and socket measuring half a cubit (22.2cm).[27] The 'tower soldiers' are to have a pike of 8 cubits, or 3.55m.[28] The size of the pike is reminiscent of the peltast spear of Iphicrates, which, according to Diodorus, was one and a half times longer than the hoplite spear, which measured between 2.2m and 2.5m.[29]

---

20 First Book of Maccabees, 16, 4.
21 Flavius Josephus, *Antiquities of the Jews*, book XIII, 12, 4.
22 Flavius Josephus, *Antiquities of the Jews*, book XIII, 14, 1.
23 Wise, Abegg & Cook, *Les manuscrits de la mer Morte*, p.182.
24 Wise, Abegg & Cook, *Les manuscrits de la mer Morte*, p.182.
25 Wise, Abegg & Cook, *Les manuscrits de la mer Morte*, pp.185–186.
26 Flavius Josephus, *Antiquities of the Jews*, book XIII, 4, 4.
27 Wise, Abegg & Cook, *Les manuscrits de la mer Morte*, p.182.
28 Wise, Abegg & Cook, *Les manuscrits de la mer Morte*, pp.185–186.
29 Diodorus Siculus, *Library of History*, vol.1, book XV, 64.

The soldiers of the three middle lines of each division are to be armed with seven javelins, the same as the Roman *velites*. Finally, slingers are mentioned briefly as part of the second line and perhaps the first. As we have seen, the first lines of the four corps may be partly composed of archers.

The elite officers or riders, numbering 1,400, seasoned men aged 40 to 50, are to be protected by a round shield, a breastplate, a helmet, and greaves. They are armed with a long spear of 8 cubits (3.55m). The other riders, aged 30 to 40, are armed with javelins and bows.[30] The *Book of Maccabees* confirms that the Jews, following their early victories, quickly become well-equipped: Judas and Simon recovered some equipment.[31]

Finally, the 'Dead Sea Scrolls' distinguish two classes of soldiers within the army: the elite officers who must be between 40 and 50 years old, and the rank-and-file soldiers aged 30 to 40. The younger men, aged 25 to 30, are tasked with stripping the dead, gathering loot, preparing supplies, and guarding weapons. Those aged 50 to 60 serve as stewards. Seven priests – dressed in tunics and linen breeches, with a linen sash adorned with a purple, scarlet, and crimson motif, and a decorated turban – are to be placed at the forefront of the battle line to encourage the troops. Six of them will have trumpets to sound the various orders.[32]

---

30 Wise, Abegg & Cook, *Les manuscrits de la mer Morte*, p.183.
31 First Book of Maccabees, 5, 22; 5, 28.
32 Wise, Abegg & Cook, *Les manuscrits de la mer Morte*, pp.183–184.

Conclusion

The Ptolemaic Kingdom offers a fascinating example of the evolution of a military force over nearly three centuries. Originating as the powerful instrument of conquest established by Philip of Macedon and wielded by his son, the Ptolemaic Army was compelled to adapt to new adversaries and challenges. Initially facing the Seleucid neighbour – essentially an army of similar composition – the Kings of Egypt subsequently resized their military during intervals of peace, only to confront new types of opponents: Ethiopians, Jews, and internal rebels at first, before the ultimate confrontation with Rome.

The Ptolemaic Army thus transitioned from a characteristically Hellenistic force, with a central heavy phalanx flanked by cavalry wings and fronted by elephants and skirmishers, into a more flexible entity composed of mobile and, therefore, more versatile infantry units.

This study shows that while Asclepiodotus's treatise, later adapted by Arrian and Aelian, does not fully represent reality, it does provide an accurate theoretical outline of this army's organisation and composition. However, empirical sources, especially papyri and stelae, reveal that this military organisation had to adjust to peacetime and to the evolving political-strategic landscape of the Middle East. Large phalanxes of pikemen gradually gave way to smaller units, the *sêmeia*, and later the *speira*, consisting of soldiers armed with spears and *thureos*-type shields. The cavalry, in contrast, appears to have been less impacted by these changes. No region bears greater witness to this development than Egypt, with its remarkable corpus of inscriptions preserved by papyrus and the dry climate.

Ultimately, despite being one of the leading powers at the beginning of the third century BCE, the Ptolemaic Kingdom could not withstand a gradual decline from the second to the first century BCE. It was internal instability and conflict, rather than its institutions, that ultimately led to the downfall of the Ptolemaic dynasty.

Of course, this study has some limitations. To begin with, ancient historians are often subjective or largely base their accounts on previous works. The fact that we can rely on a reliable historian such as Polybius does not fully compensate for this weakness. Secondly, the primary written sources, whether stelae or papyri, are often damaged or incomplete. The stelae of Hermoupolis Magna, for example, while clearly identifying the

CONCLUSION

pentakosiarchia as a military unit, do not mention the superior unit, which we have assumed to be the *sêmeia*. And we may have doubts about missing letters, as in the case of *larchia* or *ilarchia* in the OGIS 731 inscription. Finally, the missing data, hitherto unknown, may skew our analysis. This is what is known as survivor bias, which consists of overvaluing or extrapolating known data to the detriment of missing data that would be more representative. In our research, for example, the data concerning the *hipparchies* is largely dominant compared to that concerning infantry units. The fact that the cavalrymen who are members of the *hipparchies* are cleruchs explains this predominance: as owners of land granted by the authorities, they are subject to numerous administrative acts. However, at Raphia, the cavalry numbers less than 5,000 cleruchs riders, while the infantry has more than 12,000 cleruchs. Even if the size of the properties of the infantry cleruchs is smaller, this difference in representativeness in the data raises questions. It would therefore be useful for future studies to focus on this issue.

Interpretation of the Alexandria lighthouse (Author's Artwork)

Colour Plate Commentaries

Plate 1. Cavalrymen of the Guard, third century BCE. (Artwork by the author)

Cavalry of the *Aulên*. Alexander the Great equipped his companions (*hetairoi*) with purple-edged clothing, according to Diodorus of Sicily. Two horsemen depicted on Alexander's sarcophagus from Sidon necropolis (now in the İstanbul Arkeoloji Müzeleri) wear chlamydes of this colour. The colours of the *chiton* (tunic) and *chlamys* (cloak) of the Macedonian horseman on the right are inspired by the Nikanor stele held by the Alexandria Museum.

Plate 2. The Macedonian cavalry: Macedonian cavalrymen of the numbered *hipparchies*, third century BCE. (Artwork by the author)

Three cavalrymen of the numbered *hipparchies*. They are all armed with the *xyston*. The colours of the *chiton* and *chlamys* of the rider on the left are inspired by the stele of (-)xenos, Macedonian, held by the Alexandria National Museum. The colour of the *chlamys* of the horseman in the centre is inspired by the tomb of Mustapha Pacha in the Alexandria National Museum and by a stele held by the Musée du Louvre. The colours of the *chiton* and *chlamys* of the horseman on the right are inspired by a stele held by the Alexandria National Museum.

Plate 3. Greek mercenary cavalry, Ethiopian campaign, *c.* 275 BCE. (Artwork by the author)

Conjectural reconstruction, particularly with regard to the shape and material of the horse armour. As for the weaponry, it more likely consisted of the spear, like the horsemen on the left, than the *xyston*. 'He clothed them and their horses in tightly woven woollen blankets, known in the country as *kasas*, so that the body was entirely covered, with the exception of the eyes' (Agatharchides of Cnidus).

Plate 4. Cavalrymen of the Thessalian *hipparchy*, third century BCE. (Artwork by the author)

Cavalryman on the left: the colours of the chiton come from the Thessalian Pelopides stele held by the Alexandria National Museum. He is wearing a Boeotian helmet. Cavalryman in the centre: the colours of the chiton and chlamydia are inspired by the Thessalian horseman represented on the sarcophagus of Alexander the Great. Cavalryman on the right: the colours of the chiton and chlamydia are based on the stele of Polyoktos, a Thessalian, in the collection of the Alexandria National Museum. He is wearing a particular variation of Boeotian helmet, developed in the third or second century BCE.

Plate 5. Cavalrymen of the Thracian *hipparchy*, third century BCE (Artwork by the author)

Thracian cavalry. The colours are inspired by the frescoes in the tombs of Kazanluk (late fourth or early third century BCE) and Alexandrovo (first half of fourth century BCE). The rider in the centre is wearing the Thracian helmet found at Pletena, dating from the first half of the fourth century BCE. The rider on the left is wearing a Chalcidian helmet and the rider on the right is wearing a Phrygian helmet. Shields, of the *thureos* or *pelte* type, were part of Thracian cavalrymen's equipment from the fourth century BCE onwards.

Plate 6. Cavalrymen of the Mysian *hipparchy*, third century BCE (Artwork by the author)

Mysian cavalry: conjectural representation. Nothing is known about this type of cavalry in the third century BCE. It was probably made up of light horsemen, equipped in the manner of the Tarentines. They are shown here armed with javelins, protected by either a large or small round shield and wearing various types of helmets that were widely used in the Hellenistic world: Chalcidian, Antigonid and Attic.

Plate 7. Cavalrymen of the Guard, second century BCE (Artwork by the author)

Cavalry of the *Aulên*, second century BCE: possible representation of cavalry of the Guard. Apart from the type of helmet, we have suggested that the weaponry is close to those of the previous century. Purple was chosen for the *chlamydes* and some of the tunics, but this all remains hypothetical.

Plate 8. Cavalrymen of the cleruch *hipparchies*, second century BCE (Artwork by the author)

Cleruch cavalrymen, second century BCE: possible representation of heavy cleruchs cavalrymen. In the choice of colours, we have maintained the dominant colours of the previous century. Although we are not certain, they are shown here armed with *xyston*.

Plate 9. Light cavalrymen, second century BCE (Artwork by the author)

Light cavalrymen: left and middle: conjectural reconstructions of two light horsemen. Right: Eurostides, son of Nicanor, a Perrhabaean (Thessalian), from a painted stele from Sidon.

Plate 10. Cleruch pikemen of the Agema, third century BCE (Artwork by the author)

Cleruch pikemen of the agema. Top right: Lykinos, son of Lykon, Thessalian, from a stele in the Alexandria Museum. Bottom: possible representation of soldiers of the *agema*.

Plate 11. Socrates' Peltasts, end of third century BCE (Artwork by the author)

The peltasts: possible reconstructions of peltasts around 218–217 BC, with different sizes of pikes possible: 7 cubits (3 metres 15), 8 cubits (3 metres 60) and 10 cubits (4 metres 50). According to Asclepiodotus, 'the best shield in use in the phalanx is the Macedonian, made of bronze with eight palms and not too concave'. Top left: phalangite shield (60–65cm) and supposed peltast shield (around 55 centimetres in diameter). The helmet is of the Melos or Antigonid type.

Plate 12. Cleruchs of the phalanx, third century BCE (Artwork by the author)

The phalanx of the third century BCE: cleruchs of the phalanx wearing the Melos-type helmet and carrying *sarissa* and Macedonian shield. The colours of the *chiton*, *chlamys* and cuirass of the characters from above are based on stelae in the Alexandria Museum.

Plate 13. Cleruchs of the phalanx, third century BCE (Artwork by the author)

The phalanx of the third century BCE. These soldiers wear the same equipment as for plate 12. Only the colours, hypothetical but based on representative colour schemes, have been changed.

Plate 14. Cleruchs of the Agema, second century BCE (Artwork by the author)

The agema, second century BCE: possible representation of soldiers of the agema in the second century BCE. It is possible that this unit adopted the *thureos* in the years 165 to 145 BCE, as represented on the figure on the right. The helmets are of the so-called Ascalon model. The only known example, was found in Romania, but many coins found in Ascalon in Coele-Syria show this type of helmet. It is also depicted on painted stelae from Sidon. A fresco in Alexandria shows soldiers wearing stylised helmets, but the shape is close to this one. The soldier on the left is wearing the old Melos-type helmet. The shield has been reproduced from a mould found in Alexandria and now in the collection of the AllardPierson Museum in Amsterdam. The colours of the helmets, breastplates and chitons are conjectural.

Plate 15. Cleruchs of the phalanx, second century BCE (Artwork by the author)

The phalanx of the second century BCE. There are no representations of phalanx soldiers from this period. This type of infantryman probably disappeared between 165 and 145 BC. The only distinctive feature of this illustration is the type of helmet. The soldier on the right is wearing an Ascalon-type helmet, while the other three are wearing Sidon type helmets. The name of this second helmet comes from the painted stelae of this city in Coele-Syria, depicting soldiers wearing this type of helmet. It is also depicted on terracotta figurines from Asia Minor.

Plate 16. Cleruchs of the phalanx, second century BC (Artwork by the author)

The phalanx of the second century BCE. Another conjectural representation of soldiers from the Ptolemaic phalanx, with a shield device representative of the Hellenistic armies. This device is inspired by Antigonid Macedonian shields.

Plate 17. Cleruchs of the phalanx, second century BCE (Artwork by the author)

The phalanx of the third century BCE. Essentially the same as plate 16, except that the shield is of the type held by the AllardPierson Museum in Amsterdam.

Plate 18. Cleruchs of the phalanx, second century BCE (Artwork by the author)

The phalanx of the second century BCE. Another hypothetical representation of soldiers from the Ptolemaic phalanx. The pink colour of the cuirass shoulder-guard is inspired by a fresco from Alexandria, owned by Dr Lilian Malcove. (Sekunda, *The Ptolemaic Army*, p.74)

Plate 19. Cleruchs of the phalanx, second century BCE (Artwork by the author)

The phalanx of the second century BCE. Another possible interpretation is that soldiers no longer wore linen cuirasses. The two figures on the left, without cuirass, are possible rear rank soldiers. It is also possible that mail was adopted shortly before the disappearance of the phalanx, in the first half of the second century. The model shown here is of the type worn by Salmas of Adada, a mercenary depicted on a stele from Sidon.

Plate 20. Cleruchs of the phalanx, second century BCE (Artwork by the author)

The phalanx of the second century BCE. Same representation as CP019, but these soldiers wear a white *chlamys* and have no specific design on their shields. These shields are inspired by those depicted on many terracotta figurines of the Fouquet collection (see, for example, the figurines representing the God Bes). The white colour of the cloak is from a fresco from Alexandria, owned by Dr Lilian Malcove. (Sekunda, *The Ptolemaic Army*, p.74)

Plate 21. Ptolemaic light infantry, third century BCE (Artwork by the author)

The light infantry of the third century BC. Depictions of light infantrymen show them wearing the *chiton* (tunic) and sometimes *crepides* (boots). The javelinist at the bottom right wears the *exomis*, which leaves the right arm free. The colours of the *chiton* are based on those most commonly seen on Hellenistic representations of soldiers.

Plate 22. Ptolemaic light infantry, second century BCE (Artwork by the author)

The light infantry of the second century BCE. Cretans and Pisidians were among the mercenaries most frequently used by Ptolemaic rulers in the second century BCE. This plate illustrates the soldiers depicted on the Sidon stelae, dated to the middle of the second century BCE, and on some of the stelae held by the Alexandria and Louvre museums. The colours of the *chitons* and *chlamydes* are those identified on the stelae cited. The two figures at the top are inspired by Diodote, son of Patron, a Cretan from Hyrtakyna, and his servant, as depicted on a stele from Sidon. The figure in the middle, above, is inspired by the Sidon stele depicting (Hermolaos), son of Demetrios. The figure at the top right is inspired by the Sidon stele representing Saëttas, a Pisidian from Thermessos. The figure on the lower left is inspired by a stele in the Alexandria Museum. The second figure from the bottom left is inspired by a stele in the Musée du Louvre. The third figure at the bottom was inspired by a stele in Alexandria. The last figure on the bottom right is inspired by a terracotta figurine dating from the third or second century BCE, found in Asia Minor and in the collection of the Musée du Louvre. (Sekunda, *The Ptolemaic Army*, p.74)

Plate 23. Thracian mercenaries and cleruchs, third and second centuries BCE (Artwork by the author)

Thracian mercenaries and cleruchs, third and second century BC. The colours are inspired by the frescoes in the Kazanluk and Alexandrovo tombs. The soldier at the bottom left is wearing a Thracian helmet from the fourth century BCE, discovered at Bryastovets (Bulgaria). The two soldiers at the top are armed with a blade known as a romphaia. It is unlikely that the mercenaries in the service of the Ptolemies were equipped with them. The soldier at the top right is depicted wearing the equipment of

THE ARMIES OF PTOLEMAIC EGYPT

the mercenaries of King Perseus of Macedonia in 171 BCE. They carried the romphaia, and white *thureos* and wore a black tunic. (Plutarch, *Parallel Lives, Life of Aemilius Paullus*, XXX)

Plate 24. Galatian mercenaries and cleruchs, third and second centuries BCE (Artwork by the author)

Galatians mercenaries and cleruchs, third and second century BCE. These illustrations are based on stelae described by M. Launey and V. Kraus (see Bibliography), the colours of which have been reconstructed. The warriors pictured are, from left to right, Bitos, son of Lostoielcos, (-)attos and Isidoros, whose stelae come from Alexandria and are in the collection of the Metropolitan Museum of Art, New York. The warrior at top right is inspired by the Arêstodymokamestas stele from Alexandria, in the collection of the Musée du Louvre. The warrior at bottom left is inspired by a terracotta statuette in the Fouquet collection. The second warrior below represents Ketositos, whose stele, held by the Musée du Louvre, comes from Alexandria. The third warrior is inspired by the Aidéaratos stele, from Alexandria, held by the Musée de Saint-Germain en Laye. Finally, the fourth warrior, bottom left, was inspired by the Sisono stele from Alexandria in the collection of the Metropolitan Museum of Art, New York.

Plate 25. *Thureophoroi* mercenaries, second and first centuries BCE (Artwork by the author)

Thureophoroi mercenaries from the second and first centuries BC. All these figures are inspired by the painted stelae of Sidon. The figure at the top left is Salmas d'Adada, a Pisidian. The second figure is Kartadis, the Lycian. The third figure is Hekataios from Theateria, a Lydian. Finally, the fourth figure on the top right is Dioskourides from Balboura, a Pisidian. The four figures at the lower left are anonymous figures from the Sidon stelae. The last figure, bottom right, is Zenon, a Lycian from Rhodiapolis.

Plate 26. *Thureophoroi* mercenaries and cleruchs, second and first centuries BCE (Artwork by the author)

Mercenaries or cleruchs *thureophoroi* from the second and first centuries BCE. The figure at top right is Dionysus, son of Bithys, a Bythinian. He was inspired by a stele from Alexandria. The second illustration at the top left is inspired by a figure on the Nile mosaic at Preneste. The two illustrations at the top right and the four at the bottom are inspired by two figures in a fresco from Alexandria, a Roman copy of an original from the Hellenistic period (mid-second century BCE). This fresco is owned by Dr Lillian Malcove (Sekunda, *The Ptolemaic Army*, p.74)

Plate 27. *Thureophoroi* mercenaries and cleruchs, first century BCE (Artwork by the author)

Mercenaries or cleruchs *thureophoroi* from the first century BCE. These eight figures are all inspired by Ptolemaic soldiers depicted on the Nile mosaic of Preneste (the ancient name of Palestrina), probably dating from the first century BCE. The figure at bottom left is an officer. The Preneste Nile mosaic is a late Hellenistic pavement mosaic depicting the course of the Nile from Ethiopia to the Mediterranean Sea. It was found in a classical grotto-sanctuary in Palestrina, Italy. It is thought to date from 100 BCE. These kinds of Nilotic scenes are supposed to have been introduced to Rome by Demetrios the Topographer, a Greek artist from Ptolemaic Egypt who practised his art around 165 BCE. The mosaic is interesting because it gives us an idea of what soldiers looked like at the time.

Plate 28. Libyan and Nubian warriors, first century BCE (Artwork by the author)

Libyan and Nubian warriors, first century BCE. The illustration at the top left shows a Libyan based on a Fayum terracotta statuette, probably an officer. The two illustrations top centre and right show Libyans from the Nile mosaic at Preneste (ancient Palestrina). The three lower illustrations show Nubian warriors inspired by the Nile mosaic from Preneste.

Plate 29.
Soldiers' *chitons*, third to first century BCE (Artwork by the author)

Chitons. Illustrations based on the results of Ruben Post's study of frescoes, stelae and painted figurines. (*Ancient Warfare* magazine IV.6). The *chitons* here show the most popular colours, with their frequency of appearance.

Soldiers' *chlamydes*, third to first century BCE (Artwork by the author)

Chlamydes. Illustration based on the results of Ruben Post's study of frescoes, stelae and painted figurines (*Ancient Warfare* magazine IV.6). The different colours of *chlamydes* are represented.

THE ARMIES OF PTOLEMAIC EGYPT

Plate 30. Ptolemaic elephants, third century BCE (Artwork by the author)

Ptolemaic elephants, third century BCE. Representation of two Ptolemaic African elephants from the third century BCE, based on a terracotta from the Fouquet collection. Each is carrying a tower and two fighters. Only the largest specimens were fitted with a tower.

Plate 31. Ptolemaic elephants, second century BCE (Artwork by the author)

Ptolemaic elephants, second century BCE. Hypothetical representation of African-type Ptolemaic elephants in the second century BCE. Only the largest specimens were fitted with a tower.

Plate 32. Jewish soldiers, second to first century BCE (Artwork by the author)

The Jewish Army, second and first century BC. Jewish Maccabean or Hasmonean soldiers, from the 'War Scroll' of the 'Dead Sea Scrolls'. The illustration shows a soldier of the line on the left, a soldier of the towers in the centre and an elite horseman on the right. The helmets, not mentioned in the manuscript for the infantry, were looted from enemy bodies. The same is probably true of the cuirass. The dimensions of the weapons and shields have been represented according to the data in the manuscript. The shape of the shield on the left is inspired by the *thureos* and that of the middle shield by the Roman *scutum*. The spear on the left measures 3 metres 15, the other two 3 metres 60.

Appendix

Numbered and ethnic evidence of hipparchies, compiled from the work of Launey,[1] Lesquier,[2] and Van't Dack.[3]

---

[1] Launey M., *Recherches sur les armées hellénistiques*.
[2] Lesquier J., *Les institutions militaires de l'Egypte sous les Lagides*.
[3] Van't Dack, *Ptolemaica Selecta*.

THE ARMIES OF PTOLEMAIC EGYPT

Name	Origin	Garrison	Date	Rank	Unit	Aroures	Officer	Reference
Eudêmos or Euthydêmos	Unidentified	Bousiris ?	245	Hipparchês	Agêma		tôn archaiou agêmatos hipparchês	Pros. Ptol. 2209 p. 49
Aristodenos	Arcadia	Théogonis (Arsin.)	236-235	Cavalier	Hipparchia ?	100		Launey p. 1122; P. Petrie I 11 & 35
Néandros	Oita	Topsa (Arsin.)	219-218	Cavalier	Hipparchia ?	100		Launey p. 1133
Térêpês	Thrace	Pito (Memph.)	273	Cavalryman	Hipparchia ?	40	tôn Lykophronos	Launey p. 1200; PSI 321; SB 6707
Dionisios	Thrace	Pito (Memph.)	273	Cavalryman	Hipparchia ?	60	tôn Lykophronos	Launey p. 1194
???	Macedonia	Hermopolis	141	Cavalryman	Hipparchia ?	80	tês hipparchia?	Launey p. 1187
Aristomakos	Macedonia	Samareia (Arsin.)	221	Cavalryman	Hipparchia ?	80	tôn Eteôneos	Launey p. 1173
Polindikos	Macedonia	Krokodilopolis (Arsin.)	226-225	Cavalryman	Hipparchia ?	80		Launey p. 1183; P. Petrie I 20
Ptolemaîos	Persia	Philadelphia (Arsin.)	195-150	Cavalryman	Hipparchia ?	80	tôn Dionysiou xai tôn niôn	Launey p. 1249
Leônidés Ptolemaiou	Thrace	Théadelphia (Arsin.)	150-149	Cavalryman	Hipparchia ?	80	tôn Hexakontos	Launey p. 1197, SB 6157-6158
Philôtas	Thrace	Arsinoïte	220	Cavalryman	Hipparchia ?	80		Launey p. 1201; P. Petrie III 112
Poseidônios	Thrace	Pito (Memph.)	273	Cavalryman	Hipparchia ?	80	tôn Lykophronos	Launey p. 1198; SB 6707
Parménôn	Macedonia	Arsinoïte	228-221	Cavalryman	Hipparchia ?	100	kpo hipparkên	Launey p. 1182
Lysanias	Tarento	Arsinoïte	247	Cavalryman	Hipparchia ?	100		Launey p. 1261
??? Ptolemaiou	Thrace	Arsinoïte	220-219	Cavalryman	Hipparchia ?	100		Launey p.1202; P. Petrie III 112
?unês	Thrace	Krokodilopolis (Arsin.)	238	Cavalryman	Hipparchia ?	100		Launey p. 1201; P. Petrie III 5
Demês	Thrace	Arsinoïte	220	Cavalryman	Hipparchia ?	100	tês hipparchia	Launey p. 1193; P. Petrie III 112
Démétrios	Thrace	Arsinoïte	219-218	Cavalryman	Hipparchia ?	100	tôn Ptolemaiou tou Et(eôneôs)	Launey p. 1193
Maraîos Ptolemaiou	Tuppênoi (Italie)	Arsinoïte	300-200	Cavalryman	Hipparchia ?	100		Launey p. 1263; P. Petrie III 57
Bithes	Thrace	Pito (Memph.)	273	Cavalryman	Hipparchia ?	100	tôn Lykophronos	Launey p. 1193; PSI 321; SB 6707
Polémôn Stratônos	Macedonia	Birta (Ammanitide)	259	Cavalryman	Hipparchia ?	Cleruch	tôn Toubiou ippeôn	Launey p. 1183; SB 6709
?os Ananiou	Persia	Birta (Ammanitide)	259-258	Cavalryman	Hipparchia ?	Cleruch	tôn Toubiou ippeôn	Launey p. 1250; SB 6709
Timasikratès	Thessaly	Hérakléopolite	72-71	Cavalryman	Hipparchia ?	Cleruch	tôn Kainônos	Launey p. 1142
Dio????	Unidentified	Arsinoïte	220-219	Cavalryman	Hipparchia ?	Cleruch	tôn Eteôneos	P. Petrie III 112
Eryodatés Agriophanous	Unidentified	Arsinoïte	220-219	Cavalryman	Hipparchia ?	Cleruch	tôn Eteôneos	P. Petrie III 112

NUMBERED AND ETHNIC EVIDENCE OF HIPPARCHIES

Apollônios Satyrou	Eolide	Akôris (Hermop.)	113	Cavalryman	Hipparchia ?	Katoikos	tôn Drytônos	Launey p. 1207
Diôn Démêtriou	Eolide	Hérakléopolis	90-10	Cavalryman	Hipparchia ?	Katoikos	tôn Démêtriou	Launey p. 1206
Karinos Lysikratou	Eolide	Akôris (Hermop.)	113	Cavalryman	Hipparchia ?	Katoikos	tôn Drytônos	Launey p. 1207
Aléxandros Ptolémaiou	Macedonia	Egypt	90-50	Cavalryman	Hipparchia ?	Katoikos	tôn Ammôniou xai Nikostratou katoikôn hippeôn	Launey p. 1171
Ammônios Démêtriou	Macedonia	Akôris (Hermop.)	90-50	Cavalryman	Hipparchia ?	Katoikos	tôn Drytônos kai Drytônos	Launey p. 1172
Asclépiadès Asclépiadou	Macedonia	Egypt	90-50	Cavalryman	Hipparchia ?	Katoikos	tôn Kononos	Launey p. 1174
Dionysios Dionysiou	Macedonia	Herakleopolite	100-50	Cavalryman	Hipparchia ?	Katoikos		Launey p. 1175
Herakleides Herakleidou	Macedonia	Herakleopolite	51-0	Cavalryman	Hipparchia ?	Katoikos		Launey p. 1177
Herakleios Herakleiou	Macedonia	Herakleopolite	78-77	Cavalryman	Hipparchia ?	Katoikos		Launey p. 1177; SB 7422
Herakles Akousillaou	Macedonia	Arsinoïte	30-0	Cavalryman	Hipparchia ?	Katoikos		Launey p. 1177
Theophantos Anthagorou	Peparêthios	Egypt	90-50	Cavalryman	Hipparchia ?	Katoikos	tôn Ammôniou xai Nikostratou katoikôn hippeôn	Launey p. 1149
Dyonysios Asklêpiadou	Persia	Akôris (Hermop.)	110-109	Cavalryman	Hipparchia ?	Katoikos	tôn Apollopharou xai hexakontos katoikôn ippéôn	Launey p. 1246
Eyphrôn Eyphronos	Persia	Akôris (Hermop.)	113	Cavalryman	Hipparchia ?	Katoikos	tôn Drytônos ka drytonos katoikôn ippéôn	Launey p. 1247
Dolêdelmis Ablouzélmios	Thrace	Egypt	90-50	Cavalryman	Hipparchia ?	Katoikos	tôn Ammôniou xai Nikostratou katoikôn hippeôn	Launey p. 1194
Hérodotos Kard?	Thrace	Egypt	90-50	Cavalryman	Hipparchia ?	Katoikos	tôn Ammôniou xai Nikostratou katoikôn hippeôn	Launey p. 1195
Kallippos Philôtou	Thrace	Egypt	90-50	Cavalryman	Hipparchia ?	Katoikos	tôn Ammôniou xai Nikostratou katoikôn hippeôn	Launey p. 1196
Theodôros Leontos	Thrace	Berenikis Thesmophorou (Arsin.)	137-136	Cavalryman	Hipparchia ?	Katoikos		Launey p. 1195; PSI 1311

THE ARMIES OF PTOLEMAIC EGYPT

Name	Origin	Location	Date	Rank	Hipparchia	Unit	Reference
Heypolis	Athens	Thôlthis (Oxyrh.)	230-229	Cavalryman	Hipparchia ?	tôn Zôïlou	Launey p. 1125; SB 6278
Nikobios	Euboea	Phébichis (Hérakl.)	259-258	Cavalryman	Hipparchia ?	tôn Zôïlou	Launey p. 1130; P. Hibeh p. 56
Pyrros	Euboea	Oxyrhynchite	230-229	Cavalryman	Hipparchia ?	tôn Zôïlou	Launey p. 1130; SB 6278
Zénophilos	Herakleia	Oxyrhynchite	230-229	Cavalryman	Hipparchia ?	tôn Zôïlou	Launey p. 1265; SB 6278
?!kiag? Dôsithéou	Libya	Oxyrhynchite	230-229	Cavalryman	Hipparchia ?	tôn Zôïlou	Launey p. 1259
Praxias	Macedonia	Arsinoïte	222-220	Cavalryman	Hipparchia ?		Launey p. 1183; P. Petrie III 112
Menônidês	Persia	Oxyrhynchite	250-245	Cavalryman	Hipparchia ?	tôn Zôïlou	Launey p. 1247
Dizapopis	Thrace	Kerkesoucha	220	Cavalryman	Hipparchia ?		Launey p. 1193
Dzsapês	Thrace	Arsinoïte	220	Cavalryman	Hipparchia ?		Launey p. 1193
Métrodôros	Thrace	Oxyrhynchite	230-229	Cavalryman	Hipparchia ?	tôn Zôïlou	Launey p. 1197; SB 6278
Seuthês	Thrace	Ammonias (Arsin.)	221	Cavalryman	Hipparchia ?		Launey p. 1199
Menônidês	Persia	Thôlthis (Oxyrh.)	214-213	Cavalryman	Hipparchia ?	tôn Philônos	Launey p. 1247
Ermias	Persia		109	Cavalryman	Hipparchia ?	tôn Pheromenôn en Kleopatraï ippeôn misthophorôn	Launey p. 1246
Aristiôn	Cyrenaica	Arsinoïte	228-221	Dekanikos	Hipparchia ?	tôn Me(?)	Launey p. 1254
Philônadês	Cyrenaica	Takona (Oxyrh.)	203-202	Dekanikos	Hipparchia ?	tôn Philônos	Launey p. 1257
Ptolemaïos	Herakleia	Arsinoïte	228-221	Dekanikos	Hipparchia ?		Launey p. 1266
Diodôros	Macedonia	Thôlthis (Oxyrh.)	222-221	Dekanikos	Hipparchia ?	tôn Philônos	Launey p. 1175
Ebryzelmis Ziokorou	Thrace	Hiéra Nèsos (Arsin.)	238	Dekanikos	Hipparchia ?	tôn Lika	Launey p. 1194; P. Hibeh p. 81
Alexandros Andronikou	Palestine	Phébichis (Hérakl.)	259	Dekanikos?	Hipparchia ?	tôn Zôïlou?	Launey p. 1232; P. Hibeh p. 96
Polémaïos	Macedonia	Hiéra Nèsos (Arsin.)	222	Epïlarchês	Hipparchia ?	tôn Pythaggélou kai Ptolemaiou	Pros. Ptol. 2264 p. 54; Launey p. 1182
Herakleidês		Krokodilopolis (Arsin.)	235-234	Epïlarchês	Hipparchia ?	Cleruch	Pros. Ptol. 2261 p. 54; P. Petrie I 17
Kephalôn	Macedonia	Krokodilopolis (Arsin.)	235-234	Epïlarchês	Hipparchia ?	Cleruch	Pros. Ptol. 2263 p. 54; P. petrie I 17
Ammônios Androumakou	Andromache ?		236-235	Epïlarchês mercenary cav.	Hipparchia ?	Cleruch	tôn Eteôneos	Pros. Ptol. 2258 p. 53; P. Petrie III 54

NUMBERED AND ETHNIC EVIDENCE OF HIPPARCHIES

Name	Ethnic	Location	Date	Title	Hipparchia?	Cleruch	Description	Reference
Ergodatēs			221-220	Epilarchēs mercenary cav.			tōn Eteōneos	Pros. Ptol. 2260 p. 54; P. Petrie III 112
Theodōros Phanokléous	Greek of Thracia	Pharbaitha (Arsin.)	243	Epilarchēs mercenary cav.			tōn Eteōneos	Pros. Ptol. 2262 p. 54; Launey p. 1191
Melagkomēs Philodamon	Aetolia	Kition	145-120	Hegemon				Launey p. 1136; OGIS 134
Andromachos	Unidentified	Herakleopolite	59-58	Hipparchēs	Hipparchia ?	Katoikos	hipparchēs ep andrōn en tōi katoikōn ippeōn	Pros. Ptol. 2190 p. 47
Antiphilos	Greek	Hermoupolis Magna	55	Hipparchēs	Hipparchia ?	Katoikos	tōn katoikōn ep andrōn	Pros. Ptol. 2193 p. 47
Dēmētrios	Unidentified	Aphroditopolis	57-56	Hipparchēs	Hipparchia ?	Katoikos	hipparchēs ep andrōn katoikōn ippeōn	Pros. Ptol. 2200 p. 48; SB 7746
Komanos	Unidentified	Herakleopolite	59-58	Hipparchēs	Hipparchia ?	Katoikos	hipparchēs katoikōn ippeōn	Pros. Ptol. 2220 p. 50
Lysikratēs	Unidentified	Hermoupolite	142	Hipparchēs	Hipparchia ?	Katoikos	hipparchēs tou autou v(o) mou katoikōn	Pros. Ptol. 2221 p. 51
Opl(...)	Unidentified	Theogonis	86	Hipparchēs	Hipparchia ?	Katoikos	hipparchēs ep andrōn katoikōn ippeōn	Pros. Ptol. 2229 p. 51
Ptolemaios	Unidentified	Perithebes? Pathyris?	114-108	Hipparchēs	Hipparchia ?	Katoikos	(katoi)kois ipparchōn	Pros. Ptol. 2236 p. 51
Drytōn Pamphilou	Crete	Pathyris	190-110	Hipparchēs	Hipparchia ?		tōn Diodotou hippeōn	Launey p. 1160
Antipatros	Macedonia	Theadelphia or Philadelphia	200-150	Hipparchēs	Hipparchia ?		hhipparchēs tōn ex tou Arsinoïtou	Launey p. 1172; Pros. Ptol. 2191 p. 47
Kastōr Mithrodatou	Macedonia	Arsinoïte	77	Hipparchēs	Hipparchia ?		hipparkēs ep' andrōn	Launey p. 1179
Agathis	Unidentified		241-0	Hipparchēs	Hipparchia ?		stratēgōi kai hipparchēs	Pros. Ptol. 2184 p. 47; P. Petrie III 31
Di(...)	Unidentified	Perithebes	127-126	Hipparchēs	Hipparchia ?		hipparchēs ep andrōn kai archiphylakitēs tou Peri Thēbas	Pros. Ptol. 2205 p. 48
Drytōn	Crete	Pathyris	135-126	Hipparchēs	Hipparchia ?		tōn diadochōn kai (tōn) tou epitagmatos hhipparchēs	Pros. Ptol. 2206 p. 49
Eirēnaios	Unidentified	Diospolis Magna	119	Hipparchēs	Hipparchia ?		tōn philōn kai hipparchēs ep andrōn	Pros. Ptol. 2208 p. 49

THE ARMIES OF PTOLEMAIC EGYPT

Name	Origin	Location	Date	Title				Reference
Iasibis	Unidentified	Diospolis Magna	158	Hipparchês	Hipparchia ?		epistatês hipparchias	Pros. Ptol. 2214 p. 50
Mikros	Unidentified	Ombos	141-16	Hipparchês	Hipparchia ?		hipparchês ep andrôn	Pros. Ptol. 2226 p. 51
Paniskos	Berenike	Ptolemaïs Hermiou	138-137	Hipparchês	Hipparchia ?		hipparchês ep andrôn	Pros. Ptol. 2230 p. 51; SEG 6184
Ptolemaios	Unidentified	Hermoupolis Magna?	143-142?	Hipparchês	Hipparchia ?		ip(parchês) ep a(ndrôn)	Pros. Ptol. 2233 p. 51
Ptolemaios	Unidentified	Diospolis Magna	119	Hipparchês	Hipparchia ?		tôn philôn kai hipparchês ep andrôn	Pros. Ptol. 2235 p. 51
Philôtas	Unidentified	Alexandria	239	Hipparchês	Hipparchia ?		hipparchês tôn di' Antandrou tou par' Ainêsidêmou	Pros. Ptol. 2240 p. 52
Dorymémos	Aetolia		219-218	Hipparkês of Nokolaos	Hipparchia ?			Launey p. 1135; Polybius, V, 61, 9
Menippos	Ainianes	Krokodilopolis (Arsin.)	238-236	Ilarchês	Hipparchia ?	Cleruch	tôn Eteôneos	Pros. Pol. 2253; p. 53; Launey p. 1134; P. Petrie I 16
?ntougelis	Thrace	Arsinoïte	220-219	Ilarchês	Hipparchia ?	Cleruch	tôn Eteôneos	Launey p. 1201; P. Petrie III 112
Theukles	Pisidia	Arsinoïte	228-221	Ilarchês	Hipparchia ?			Pros. Ptol. 2250 p. 53; Launey p. 1224
Dêmoklês	Unidentified		237-236	Ilarchês	Hipparchia ?			Pros. Ptol. 2247 p. 52; P. Petrie III 4
Erkamis	Unidentified	Phebichis?	228-227	Ilarchês	Hipparchia ?		tôn Zôilou	Pros. Ptol. 2248 p. 52; P. Hib. 105
Euklês	Unidentified		248-247	Ilarchês	Hipparchia ?			Pros. Ptol. 2249 p. 53; P. Petrie III 54
Menedêmos	Chalcidia		243-240	Ilarchês	Hipparchia ?			Pros. Ptol. 2251 p. 53; P. Petrie II 35
Menekratês		Phebichis?	231-230	Ilarchês	Hipparchia ?			Pros. Ptol. 2252 p. 53; P. Hibeh 143
Polemôn	Peonia		243-240	Ilarchês	Hipparchia ?			Pros. Ptol. 2255 p. 53; P. Petrie 35
Nomos		Herakleopolite	282-281	Ilarchês	Hipparchia ?			Pros. Ptol. 2254 p.53
Sôsandros	Aetolia	Arsinoïte	250-150	Ilarchês	Hipparchia ?			Launey p. 1136
? Hêrakléidou	Agriana	Krokodilopolis (Arsin.)	235	ilarchês?	Hipparchia ?	100	tôn oupô upo' hipparkên	Launey p. 1203; P. Petrie III 10
Theotimos	Thrace	Philadelphia (Arsin.)	200	Ilarchês?	Hipparchia ?		tôn oupô upo' hipparkên	Launey p. 1195; P. Petrie II 46 & III 57

NUMBERED AND ETHNIC EVIDENCE OF HIPPARCHIES

???	Cyrenaica	Arsinoïte	237	Lochagos	Hipparchia ?		tôn Damônos	Launey p. 1258; P. Petrie I 13
Sitaklês	Thrace	Boubastos (Arsin.)	?-238	Lochagos	Hipparchia ?			Launey p. 1199; P. Hibeh p.81
Zipuros Bithyos	Thrace	Pito (Memph.)	273	Zygklêros	Hipparchia ?		tôn Lykophronos	Launey p. 1195; PSI 321
Kallias Apollodôrou	Macedonia	Philadelphia (Arsin.)	190-150	Cavalryman	Hipparchia 1	80		Launey p. 1178
Nikanor Iasonos	Palestine	Trikômia (Arsin.)	174	Cavalryman	Hipparchia 1	80	tôn dia Dôsithéou	Launey p. 1234
Théodôros Theodôrou	Palestine	Trikômia (Arsin.)	174	Cavalryman	Hipparchia 1	80	tôn dia Dôsithéou	Launey p. 1233
Diogenês	Cyrenaica	Krokodilopolis (Arsin.)	173	Cavalryman	Hipparchia 1	100	tôn Diodôrou	Launey p. 1254
Philisxos	Cyrenaica	Arsinoë (Arsin.)	240	Cavalryman	Hipparchia 1	100		Launey p. 1138; P. Petrie III 35
Appolônios ?	Macedonia	Philadelphia (Arsin.)	190-110	Cavalryman	Hipparchia 1	100	tôn Kritônos	Launey p. 1173
Aristokratês	Thrace	Autodiké (Arsin.)	218-227	Cavalryman	Hipparchia 1	100		Launey p. 1192
Polemôn	Persia	Krokodilopolis (Arsin.)	246-222	Cavalryman	Hipparchia 1	100		Launey p. 1248; P. Petrie II 35
Aristaîos	Laconia	Arsinoïte	240	Cavalryman	Hipparchia 1			Launey p. 1119, P. Petrie, II 35
Aristoclês	Olynthe	Arsinoïte	245-235	Cavalryman	Hipparchia 1			Launey p. 1170; P. Petrie II 35
Térês	Thrace	Arsinoïte	245-235	Cavalryman	Hipparchia 1			Launey p. 1200; P. Petrie II 35
Appolonios	Dolopes	Arsinoïte	245-235	Cavalryman	Hipparchia 1			Launey p. 1138; P. Petrie III 35
Dôsitheos	Palestine	Arsinoïte	174	Eponymous Officer	Hipparchia 1			Launey p. 1233
Kastôr	Unidentified	Kerkeêsis	100-0	Hipparchês	Hipparchia 1	80	hipparchês ep andrôn tês a ipparcheias	Pros. Ptol. 2218 p. 50
Timodênos	Cyrenaica	Arsinoïte	245-235	Lochagos	Hipparchia 1			Launey p. 1257; P. Petrie II 35
Démétrios Sinôpeys	Paphlagonia	Krokodilopolis (Arsin.)	176-165	Cavalryman	Hipparchia 2	70		Launey p. 1227
Sôpatros	Persia	Philadelphia (Arsin.)	154-153	Cavalryman	Hipparchia 2	80	tôn Galestou	Launey p. 1249; SB 7188
Nikandros	Syracuse		182	Cavalryman	Hipparchia 2	80	tôn Theodôrou	Launey p. 1261
?nês	Achaïa	Krokodilopolis (Arsin.)	222	Cavalryman	Hipparchia 2	100		Launey p. 1124; IG II 1957
Antaîos	Athens	Krokodilopolis (Arsin.)	173	Cavalryman	Hipparchia 2	100		Launey p. 1125
Ptolemaios	Ionia	Hiéra Nêsos (Arsin.)	222	Cavalryman	Hipparchia 2	100	tôn Ptolemaiou tou Eteônéôs	Launey p. 1210
Appolônios	Macedonia	Krokodilopolis (Arsin.)	173	Cavalryman	Hipparchia 2	100	tôn Kinéou	Launey p. 1173

THE ARMIES OF PTOLEMAIC EGYPT

Name	Origin	Location	Date	Rank	Hipparchia	Size	Notes	Reference
Dionysios	Macedonia	Krokodilopolis (Arsin.)	173	Cavalryman	Hipparchia 2	100		Launey p. 1176
Philios	Macedonia	Krokodilopolis (Arsin.)	173	Cavalryman	Hipparchia 2	100		Launey p. 1185
Ermôn	Persia	Hiéra Nèsos (Arsin.)	222	Cavalryman	Hipparchia 2	100	tôn Ptolemaiou tou Eteônéôs	Launey p. 1246
Sôstratos	Thrace	Krokodilopolis (Arsin.)	222	Cavalryman	Hipparchia 2	100	tôn Hippokratous	Launey p. 1200
Dèmokratidès	Thessaly	Krokodilopolis (Arsin.)	173	Cavalryman	Hipparchia 2	100	tôn Kinéou	Launey p. 1140
Nikanor	Non identifié		226-225	Cavalryman	Hipparchia 2	100		Lesquier P. 292; P. Petrie I 20
Appolonios	Ainianes	Krokodilopolis (Arsin.)	208	Cavalryman	Hipparchia 2	Cleruch	tôn Hippokratous	Launey p. 1133; P. Petrie II 47
Apollônios	Herakleia	Krokodilopolis (Arsin.)	208	Cavalryman	Hipparchia 2	100	tôn Hippokratous	Launey p. 1265; P. Petrie II 47
???	Macedonia	Krokodilopolis (Arsin.)	226-225	Cavalryman	Hipparchia 2		tôn Hippokratous tès deutépas hipparchias	Launey p. 1187; Lesquier p. 291; P. Petrie I 20
Diodôros Diodôrou	Persia	Arsinoïte	154-145	Cavalryman	Hipparchia 2			Launey p. 1246
???	Thrace	Philadelphia (Arsin.)	179-178	Cavalryman	Hipparchia 2			Launey p.1202
Ptolemaios	Thrace	Héphaistias (Arsin.)	173	Cavalryman	Hipparchia 2			Launey p. 1198
Agathodôros	Unidentified	Theadelphia (Arsin.)	137	Hipparchès	Hipparchia 2		hipparchês ep andrôn katoikôn ippeôn	Pros. Ptol. 2185 p. 47; SB 6253
Prôtarkos	Athens	Arsinoë (Arsin.)	228-221	Cavalryman	Hipparchia 2 ?	100	tôn Ptolemaiou tou Eteônéôs	Launey p. 1125
? Kallix?ratous	Pamphylia	Arsinoïte	268	Cavalryman	Hipparchia 2 ?			Launey p. 1222; P. Petrie I 24
???	Macedonia	Arsinoïte	190-110	Cavalryman	Hipparchia 3	80	tritès hipparchia	Launey p. 1187
Pyladès	Macedonia	Oxhyrhyncha (Arsin.)	171	Cavalryman	Hipparchia 3	80		Launey p. 1184
Ermas Aetou	Egypt	Arsinoïte	220-219	Cavalryman	Hipparchia 3	100		Lesquier p. 292; P. Petrie III 112
???	Euboea	Arsinoïte	220-219	Cavalryman	Hipparchia 3	100		Lesquier p. 292; P. Petrie III 112
Hérakleidès	Larissa	Arsinoïte	221-220	Cavalryman	Hipparchia 3	100		Launey p. 1267
???	Thrace	Arsinoïte	220-219	Cavalryman	Hipparchia 3	100		Launey p.1202; P. Petrie III 112
?s	Thrace	Arsinoïte	220-219	Cavalryman	Hipparchia 3	100		Launey p. 1201; P. Petrie III 112
???ypérètes	Unidentified	Arsinoïte	220-219	Cavalryman	Hipparchia 3	100		Launey p. 1201; P. Petrie III 112
??ton	Macedonia	Arsinoïte	222-220	Cavalryman	Hipparchia 3	100	tetartes hipparchias	Launey p. 1187; P. Petrie III 112

NUMBERED AND ETHNIC EVIDENCE OF HIPPARCHIES

Name	Origin	Location	Date	Role	Hipparchia		Description	Reference
?tos	Cilicia	Arsinoïte	228-221	Cavalryman	Hipparchia 3		tōn Ptolemaiou tou Nauta	Launey p. 1225
(...) Limnaiou?	Cyrenaica	Héracléopolite	200-0	Hipparchès	Hipparchia 3		(hipparchēs ep) andrōn tēs y ipp(archias)	Launey p. 1258; Pros. Ptol. 2243 p. 52
???		Philadelphia	226-225	Cavalryman	Hipparchia 3	100	tōn Hippokratous	Lesquier p. 291; P. Petrie I 19
???	Macedonia	Arsinoïte	235	Cavalryman	Hipparchia 3?		tēs hipparchia	Launey p. 1187; P. Petrie I 18
Jason	Achaïa	Krokodilopolis (Arsin.)	226-225	Cavalryman	Hipparchia 4	100		Launey p. 1124; P. Petrie I 19
Trokinidès	Boeotia	Arsinoïte	228-221	Cavalryman	Hipparchia 4			Launey p. 1128
Aristoklès	Cyrenaica	Arsinoïte	228-221	Cavalryman	Hipparchia 4	100	tōn Andriskou	Launey p. 1254
Philisxos	Cyrenaica	Arsinoïte	228-221	Cavalryman	Hipparchia 4	100		Launey p. 1257
???	Macedonia	Arsinoïte	220-219	Cavalryman	Hipparchia 4	100		Launey p. 1187; P. Petrie III 112
Théotimos Philéou	Mysia	Théadelphia (Arsin.)	104-103	Cavalryman	Hipparchia 4	100		Launey p. 1213; P. Petrie III 112
Kallikratès Apollôniou	Persia	Arsinoïte	228-221	Cavalryman	Hipparchia 4	100		Launey p. 1247
Stratippos Herakleidou	Syracuse	Arsinoïte	220	Cavalryman	Hipparchia 4	100		Launey p. 1261; P. Petrie III 112
???	Thrace	Arsinoïte	220-219	Cavalryman	Hipparchia 4			Launey p.1202; P. Petrie III 112
??kata	Unidentified	Egypt	233-232	Cavalryman	Hipparchia 4	100	tōn Lysanorou	Lesquier p. 292; P. Petrie II 2
Eutykos	Acarnania	Arsinoïte	139	Cavalryman	Hipparchia 4	100	tōn Démétriou	Launey p. 1137
KI? ?théos	Samios	Arsinoïte	228-221	Cavalryman	Hipparchia 4	100	tōn Menelaou prôtôn	Launey p. 1150
Nikandros	Thessaly	Arsinoïte	228-221	Cavalryman	Hipparchia 4	100		Launey p. 1142
And?r??nos?	Thrace	Arsinoïte (Hermopolite?)	228-221	Cavalryman	Hipparchia 4		tōn Menelaou prôtôn	Launey p. 1192
Ebryzelmis	Thrace	Pito (Memph.)	273	Cavalryman	Hipparchia 4		tōn Lykophronos	Launey p. 1194; P. Petrie III 14
???	Cyrenaica	Arsinoïte	228-221	Cavalryman	Hipparchia 4 ?			Launey p. 1258
Didymarkos Appoloniou	Macedonia	Kerkéosiris (Arsin.)	116-115	Cavalryman	Hipparchia 5	100		Launey p. 1175
?	Thessaly	Krokodilopolis (Arsin.)	227-226	Cavalryman	Hipparchia 5	100	tōn Andriskou	Launey p. 1143; Lesquier p. 292; P. Petrie III 21
?utos	Thessaly	Krokodilopolis (Arsin.)	227-226	Cavalryman	Hipparchia 5	100	tōn Andriskou	Launey p. 1143; Lesquier p. 292; P. Petrie III 21
Dōsitheos	Thrace	Lysimachis (Arsin.)	242-240	Cavalryman	Hipparchia 5	100		Launey p. 1194; P. Petrie III 14

THE ARMIES OF PTOLEMAIC EGYPT

Name	Origin	Location	Date	Role	Hipparchia	Number	Description	Reference
Hésiodos	Thrace	Arsinoïte	183	Cavalryman	Hipparchia 5	100		Launey p. 1195
N??os	Thrace	Krokodilopolis (Arsin.)	227–226	Cavalryman	Hipparchia 5	100	tôn Andriskou	Launey p. 1198; Lesquier p. 292; P. Petrie III 21
Sôsos Kôios	Kôios	Krokodilopolis (Arsin.)	290–210	Cavalryman	Hipparchia 5			Launey p. 1147; P.Petrie II 21
???	Macedonia	Oxyrhyncha (Arsin.)	171	Cavalryman	Hipparchia 5		tês pemtres hipparchia	Launey p. 1187
?mnaïos Ergeytos	Macedonia	Oxyrhynchite	171	Cavalryman	Hipparchia 5			Launey p. 1186
Asclépiadès Ptolémaiou	Macedonia	Arsinoïte	145	Cavalryman	Hipparchia 5			Launey p. 1174
Petrôn Theônos	Persia	Kerkeosiris (Arsin.)	119–115	Cavalryman	Hipparchia 5			Launey p. 1248
Menélaos	Chios	Krokodilopolis (Arsin.)	235	Cavalryman	Hipparchia 5 ?	100	tôn Andriskou	Launey p. 1151; Lesquier p. 294; P. Petrie III 10
Philothêros Sôpatrou	Achaïa	Arsinoïte	236–235	Cavalryman	Hipparchia 5 ?	100	tôn Andriskou	Launey p. 1124; Lesquier p. 294; P. Petrie II 36
Ptolemaïos	Cyrenaica	Arsinoïte	236–235	Cavalryman	Hipparchia 5 ?	100	tôn Andriskou	Launey p. 1257; Lesquier p. 294; P. Petrie III 10
Démokratès	Macedonia	Krokodilopolis (Arsin.)	236–235	Cavalryman	Hipparchia 5 ?	100	tôn Andriskou tôn Ptolemaiou tou Nauta	Launey p. 1175; Lesquier p. 294; P. Petrie III 10
Artemidôros	Thrace	Krokodilopolis (Arsin.)	236–235	Cavalryman	Hipparchia 5 ?	100	tôn Andriskou tou Nauta	Launey p. 1192; Lesquier p. 294; P. Petrie III 10
Menoitios	Macedonia	Oxhyrhyncha (Arsin.)	171	Cavalryman	Hipparchia 5 ?	100		Launey p. 1179
Ermôn Theokritou	Macedonia	Philadelphia (Arsin.)	190–150	Cavalryman	Hipparchia 7	80	tôn Prôtogémou kai Prôtogémou tou niu	Launey p. 1176
Meléagros	Macedonia	Tebtynis	158–156	Cavalryman	Hipparchia 8 ?	100	tôn Polykratou, tôn Makedonikou	Launey p. 1179; SB 4318
D?	Macedonia	Oxyrhynchite	114–80		Hipparchia 8 Sêmeia 8 ?			Launey p. 1176
Kephalôn Theodôrou	Macedonia	Egypt	228–227	Cavalryman	Hipparchia 9	50		Launey p. 1179; SB 7631
Akilléos Paniskou	Macedonia	Akôris (Hermop.)	113	Cavalryman	Mercenary unit		tês Dokou hegemonias hippeôn misthophoron	Launey p. 1174
???tès	Mysia	Arsinoïte	220–219	Cavalryman	Mysian Hipparchia	70		Launey p. 1215; P. Petrie III 112

NUMBERED AND ETHNIC EVIDENCE OF HIPPARCHIES

Hērakleitos Hērakleitou	Mysia	Arsinoïte	220-219	Cavalryman	Mysian Hipparchia	70		Launey p. 1213; P. Petrie III 112
Prōtarkos Iasonos	Mysia	Samareia (Arsin.)	220-219	Cavalryman	Mysian Hipparchia	70		Launey p. 1214; P. Petrie III 112
Ptolemaios Hermogénous	Persia	Arsinoïte	220-219	Cavalryman	Persian Hipparchia	70		Launey p. 1249; P. Petrie III 112
???tēs	Persia	Arsinoïte	220-219	Cavalryman	Persian Hipparchia	70		Launey p. 1250; P. Petrie III 112
Dionysios Kephala	"Macedonian"	Akōris (Hermop.)	105	Cavalryman	Persian Hipparchia ?			Launey pp. 1175-76
Hipponikos	Arcadia	Arsinoïte	219-218	Cavalryman	Thessalian Hipparchia	70		Launey p. 1122
???	Thrace	Philadelphia (Arsin.)	179-178	Cavalryman	Thessalian Hipparchia	70	tēs tōn Thessalōn kai tōn allōn Hellēnōn hipparchias	Launey p. 1202; SB 6822
??? Aristōnos	Unidentified	Arsinoïte	220-219	Cavalryman	Thessalian Hipparchia	70	Hērakleitou	Lesquier p. 296; P. Petrie III 112
?thraix	Thessaly	Arsinoïte	179-178	Cavalryman	Thessalian Hipparchia	70	tēs tōn Thessalōn xai tōn allōn Hellēnōn ipparchias	Launey p. 1143; SB 6822
Hipponikos Arkas	Thessaly	Arsinoïte	218	Cavalryman	Thessalian Hipparchia	70	tōn allōn Hellēnōn ipparchias	Launey p. 1141
Ptolémarkos	Macedonia	Philadelphia (Arsin.)	174-173	Cavalryman	Thessalian Hipparchia		tēs tōn Thessalōn xai tōn allōn Hellēnōn ipparchias	Launey p. 1184
Aristōn	Herakleia	Arsinoïte	222-220	Cavalryman	Thessalian Hipparchia		tōn thessalōn hipparchias	Launey p. 1265; P. Petrie III 112
?tēs	Thessaly	Arsinoïte	179-178	Cavalryman	Thessalian Hipparchia		tēs tōn Thessalōn xai tōn allōn Hellēnōn ipparchias	Launey p. 1142
Ariston Heracletès	Thessaly	Arsinoïte	220	Cavalryman	Thessalian Hipparchia		tēs tōn Thessalōn xai tōn allōn Hellēnōn ipparchias	Launey p. 1140
Ptolémarkos Makedon	Thessaly	Arsinoïte	174-173	Cavalryman	Thessalian Hipparchia		tēs tōn Thessalōn xai tōn allōn Hellēnōn ipparchias	Launey p. 1142

THE ARMIES OF PTOLEMAIC EGYPT

Kairéas Kairéou	Thrace	Arsinoïte	220-219	Cavalryman	Thracian Hipparchia	70		Launey p. 1201; P. Petrie III 112
Ptolemaios Nik??reys	Unidentified	Arsinoïte	220-219	Cavalryman	Thracian Hipparchia	70		Launey p. 1267
Ptolémaios Nik??reys	Thrace	Arsinoïte	220-219	Cavalryman	Thracian Hipparchia			Launey p. 1198; P. Petrie II 38

Bibliography

Ancient Authors

Anon., *First Book of Maccabees*
Anon., *Second Book of Maccabees*
Anon., *Third Book of Maccabees*
Appian, *The Syrian Wars*
Arrian, *Ars Tactica*
Arrian, *History of the Diadochi or Events after Alexander*
Arrian, *The Anabasis of Alexander*
Asclepiodotus, *Tactica*
Athenaeus, *Callixenes*
Caesar, Julius, *Commentaries on The Alexandrian War*
Caesar, Julius, *Commentaries on the Civil War*
Josephus, Flavius, *Antiquities of the Jews*
Justin, *History of the world*
Livius, Titus, *The History of Rome*
Menander, *The Sicyonians*
Nepos, Cornelius, *Lives of the Great Captains, Iphicrates*
Pausanias, *Description of Greece*
Pliny the Elder, *Natural History*
Polybius, *Histories*
Porphyry of Tyre, FGrH 260 F42
Plutarch, *The Parallel Lives, Life of Lycurgus*
Plutarch, *The Parallel Lives, Life of Philopoemen*
Siculus, Diodorus, *Library of History*
Strabo, *Geographika*
Jérôme of Stridon, Commentary on Daniel
Theocritus, *Idyll XV, The Festival of Adonis*
Xenophon, *Anabasis*
Xenophon, *Hellenica*

Prosopography

OGIS: Wilhelm Dittenberg, Orientis Graeci Inscriptiones Selectae, Supplementum Sylloges Inscriptionum Graecarum (Lepzig: Hirzel, 1903), vol. 1

PSI: Papyrus de la Societa Italiana

Books and Articles

Arrien, *L'Art Tactique & Histoire de la succession d'Alexandre*, texts introduced, translated and commented by Pierre-Olivier Leroy (Paris: Les Belles Lettres, 2017)

Armandi, Pier D., *Histoire militaire des éléphants* (Paris: D'Amyot, 1843)

Asclépiodote, *Traité de Tactique*, text compiled and translated by Lucien Poznanski (Paris: Les Belles Lettres, 1992)

Bernand, Etienne, *Inscriptions grecques d'Hermoupolis Magna et de sa nécropole* (Le Caire: Institut français d'Archéologie Orientale, 1999)

Bernand, Etienne, *Inscriptions métriques de l'Egypte gréco-romaines, recherches sur la poésie épigrammatique des grecs en Egypte* (Paris: Les Belles Lettres, 1969)

Bouché-Leclercq, Auguste, *Histoire des Lagides* (Paris: Ernest Leroux Editeur, 1907)

Cosmas, *The Christian Topography of Cosmas, an Egyptian Monk* (London: McCrindle, 1897)

Couvenhes, Jean-Christophe, 'Quelques remarques sur le recrutement des soldats crétois outre-mer à travers les traités de symmachia', *Dialogues d'histoire ancienne*, suppl. 16 (2016), pp.177–211

Ducrey, Pierre,' Nouvelles remarques sur deux traités attalides avec des cités crétoises', *Bulletin de Correspondance Hellénique*, 94 :2 (1970), pp.637–659

Charles, Michael B., 'Elephant Size in Antiquity: DNA Evidence and the Battle of Raphia', *Historia: Zeitschrift für Alte Geschichte*, 65:1 (2016), pp.53–65

Charles, Michael B., 'Elephants at Raphia: Reinterpreting Polybius 5.84–5', *The Classical Quarterly*, 57:1 (2007), pp.306–311

Feyel, Michel, 'Un nouveau fragment du règlement militaire trouvé à Amphipolis', *Revue Archéologique*, 16 (1935) pp.29–206

Feyel, Michel, *Polybe et l'histoire de la Béotie au IIIe siècle avant notre ère* (Paris: De Boccard, 1942).

Froehner, W., *Terres cuites d'Asie de la collection Julien Gréau* (Paris: Hoffman, 1886).

Grenfell, Bernard P. & Hunt, Arthur S., *The Hibeh Papyri Part I* (London: Egypt Exploration Fund, Kegan Paul, and Bernard Quaritch, 1906)

Griffith, Guy T., *The Mercenaries of the Hellenistic world* (Chicago: Ares Publisher, 1935)

Hatzopoulos, Miltiade, B., *L'organisation de l'armée macédoniennes sous les Antigonides: Problèmes anciens et documents nouveaux* (Athènes: Centre de recherche de l'antiquité grecque et romaine, Fondation Nationale de la Recherche Scientifique, 2001), 30.

Jouguet, Pierre, 'Documents ptolémaïques', *Bulletin de Correspondance Helléniques*, 21 (1897), pp.184–208

Kalliontzis, Yannis & Müller, Christel, 'Nouveaux catalogues militaires de Chorsiai en Béotie', *Bulletin de Correspondance Hellénique*, 144 :1 (2020) https://doi.org/10.4000/bch.1064

Kraus, Virginie, *Recherches sur les productions figurées faites pour les personnes privées vivant en Egypte à l'époque ptolémaïque* (Metz: Université de Lorraine, 2018)

Launey, Marcel, *Recherches sur les armées hellénistiques* (Paris: De Boccard, 1987)

Lefebvre, Gustave, *Le tombeau de Petosiris, première partie: description* (Le Caire: Service des Antiquités de l'Egypte, 1924)

Lesquier, Jean, *Les institutions militaires de l'Egypte sous les Lagides* (Paris: Ernest Leroux Editeur, 1911)

Lumbroso, Giacomo, *Recherches sur l'économie politique de l'Egypte sous les Lagides* (Turin: Bocca Frères, 1870)

Mahaffy, John P., *The Flinders Petrie Papyri with Transcriptions and Commentaries,* Part I (Dublin: The Academy House, 1891)

Mahaffy, John P., *The Flinders Petrie Papyri with Transcriptions and Commentaries,* Part II (Dublin: The Academy House, 1893)

Mahaffy, John P. & Smyly, J. Gilbart, *On the Flinders Petrie Papyri* (Dublin: Royal Irish Academy, 1905)

Micunco S., 'La géographie dans la Bibliothèque de Photios: Le cas d'Agatharchide', *Reims / San Marino: Ecole Doctorale de Sciences de l'Homme et de la Société / Scuola Superiore di Studi Storici*, Thesis (2008)

Mommsen, Theodor, *Polybii Historiae* (Berlin: F. Hultsch, 1897)

Perdrizet, Paul, 'Inscriptions d'Acraephiae', *Bulletin de Correspondance Hellénique*, 23 (1899) pp.193–205

Perdrizet, Paul, *Les terres cuites grecques d'Egypte de la collection Fouquet* (Nancy-Paris-Strasbourg: Berger-Levrault, 1921)

Peremans, W. & Van 't Dack, E., *Prosopographia Ptolemaica* (Louvain: Studia Hellenistica, 1952)

Post, Ruben, 'Bright Colours and Uniformity, Hellenistic Military Costume', *Ancient Warfare*, 4:6 (2010), pp.14–19

Radan, G., 'Helmet found near Ascalon', *Israel Exploration Society*, 8:3 (1958), pp.185–188

Roesch, Paul & Etienne, Roland, 'Convention militaire entre les cavaliers d'Orchomène et ceux de Chéronée', *Bulletin de Correspondance Hellénique*, 102 :1 (1978), pp.359–374

Schmitt, Hatto H., *Die Staatsverträge des Albertums* (Munich: Verlag C.H. Beck, 1969).

Schubert, Paul, *Les papyrus de Genève* (Genève: Bibliothèque Publique et Universitaire, 1996)

Sekunda, Nick, *Seleucid and Ptolemaic Reformed Armies 168–145 BCE, volume 1: The Seleucid Army* (Dewsbury: Montvert Publications, 1994)

Sekunda, Nick, *Seleucid and Ptolemaic Reformed Armies 168–145 BCE, volume 2: The Ptolemaic Army* (Dewsbury: Montvert Publications, 1995)

Van 't Dack, Edmond, *Ptolemaica Selecta, Etudes sur l'armée et l'administration lagide*, vol. 29 (Leuven: Studia Hellenistica, 1988)

Wise, Michael, Abegg, Martin & Cook, Edward Jr, *Les manuscrits de la mer Morte* (Paris: Perrin, 2003)